THE 7 PREREQUISITES TO SUCCESS

Pathways To Paramount Performance

SHAAN RAIS

FOREWORD BY
Eric D. Thomas, Ph.D. "ET,"
The Hip Hop Preacher.

Omni Solutions Publishing House
1925 Seagirt Blvd. Ste. 15B Queens, NY 11691
(833) XL-COACH
Omni Solutions Consultation LLC

ISBN: 978-1-5355-6682-7 (sc)
ISBN: 978-0-6920-4474-2 (e)

Publishing Services rev. date: 08/16/2018

CONTENTS

GUEST FOREWORD

BY ERIC D. THOMAS, PH.D.
"ET," THE HIP HOP PREACHER.
FOUNDER & CEO, ETA, LLC.

Everyone wants to be successful but, few actually plan and prepare for it. Believe it or not, there is a process that leads to success. There are prerequisites to follow that will increase your odds of becoming successful in your chosen field. I've found the most important thing you can do to prepare to be successful is to change your mindset by expanding your base of knowledge. In my travels, I've been privileged to sit at the feet of giants who all have one common pastime. They all read. That's right. Some of the wealthiest and most successful businessmen and women in the world are voracious readers. That says to me, reading will forever be the great equalizer. Shawn's *Seven Prerequisites of Success, Hard times, failure, acceptance, paradigm-shifting, belief, faith,* and tenacity are guideposts along the pathway to success in both business and in life. Every successful person I know will tell you that they followed a path that led to their success. It may look different for each person but, the road remains the same with, success dependent on how closely they followed the signs and, stayed on the path. I can attest to the power and truth of these seven points as my personal path to success has led me to every one of these points. Sometimes, more than once. It's my pleasure to recommend Shawn's book to you. If you're already on the path or just starting out, Shawn's *Seven Prerequisites of Success* can help to light the way ahead.

Eric D. Thomas, Ph.D.
"ET," The Hip Hop Preacher.
Founder & CEO, ETA, LLC.

ACKNOWLEDGEMENTS

'd like to take this time to acknowledge some of the most important people in the production of this work. First my **Lord & Savior**
without whom, nothing is possible, ever. My father, **Eugene**, and my
mother, **Sandra**, without whom I would not be here to have learned
the ways of the world they facilitated my arrival into. I do this with
my children in mind and heart, so it is to them that I express the most
gratitude following my parents. Thank you!

Those are some of my inspirational acknowledgements, now on to
the facilitation phase. I have to thank my cousin **Damien**, who sacrificed his laptop, which he did his beloved music upon, so that I could
attend college online, in the pursuit of success, and thereby changing
my life. Before this I had never typed in my life, and I am so thankful
to you for your selflessness. I also, owe the very utmost to my beautiful
wife **Kariema**, who has been the source of my strength and inspiration
in so many ways it goes beyond mention.

All that I am, and all that He has allowed me to become, has been
through you. You truly are my *salvation,* I recognized it when I met
you, and through all that we have been through, I have never doubted
it for one second. I thank you for being so generous and supportive, a
woman clearly made for me. I remember when I could not type a lick,
and you would come home from work and be on the phone with me
miles apart, supporting me through the wee hours when I was ready to
give up. You've never left my side, and it is with your strength that I have
been able to persevere. I could never, ever, ever, ever, thank you enough.

I need and want to thank every **Coach, counselor, supporter, helper, teacher, professor,** and every **motivational speaker** that I have ever encountered in my life, and there have been too many to list by name. **Gregory Haas, Eric Thomas, Les Brown, Tony Robbins, Dr. Joy Degruy, Mrs. Lee, Mr. Tucker, Mrs. Nelson** (*you are a most dear friend*), **Mrs. Evans, Mrs. Mian, Mrs. Tinker** (*thank you for affording me my first speaking engagement*), both **Donnas, Lila Boyer, Ph.D. Brown, Connie Pacheco** (*thank you for my allowing me my first class presentation*), **Rafael Rosado, Mrs. Burroughs, Mrs. Turpin, Mr. Canteen,** and **Mrs. Mendez** for all of the opportunity afforded me.

Nelson Muhammad, I cannot adequately speak to all that I owe you. You are so much more than my friend, but just that would be more than enough. I owe you so much, and will never be able to fully repay you, but you have my word, that I will try. **James Gunn, Rob** (you know why), and **Khayyan** – you began my journey, **Joe Wayne, Mr. Cruz,** and **Mr. Roper. CJ Calvert, Wayne, Rakim, Ricky, Eric, and Prince** – I owe you so much as well, and I thank you for giving me the proper direction that has made this, and so much more possible. I thank you for the introduction. **Minister Courtney, Greg** – your support knows no limits, thank you for everything, family.

My family **Ann, Babe,** all of my uncles, and my vast assortment of cousins, and those nieces and nephews, this is for you. You are an **Edmontson,** and there is nothing that you cannot do. I hope this helps you to believe, and have faith, that all is possible because it truly is. You can change your life (take it from a retired underachiever), no matter what you do wrong, you always have the chance to start over and make something of yourself, that you and others can be proud of. Take this torch and carry on our legacy. The blood that flows through your veins does not know surrender nor defeat. Grow up and show up. I love each and every one of you.

I want to give a special acknowledgement to my sons and my

daughter. **Face,** I have done this for you to erase some of the hurt you have had to experience. I hope this will be one of the things that you can count in my favor, and one of the motivational factors for yourself, whenever things get rough. **Muukis,** I am so proud of you, and everyone tells me how much you are like me every day. I hope this can be one of the reasons that comment makes you proud. **Mann,** I love you so much, and you are becoming so much more like your grandfather every day. You are strong beyond compare and you are destined for the greatest of things in life.

Bread, I love you tremendously, and I need you to be very careful because of your beautiful heart. I need you to use the intelligence you have to navigate this world, and I have no doubts that you will do it and do it well. You are named after the $$$! **Blade,** you are the youngest, and you might just be the bravest, and the greatest. We'll just have to see. This is so you can have something to show my great-great-grandchildren when they ask you who I was, and what I did with my time here. I want you to remember what is in this book always, as this is my advice to you, collectively, for your present and your future. All of you could never let me down, and I love you. To **Taj, Dashawn** and **Moses,** I love you all as well, and you are my family through and through, and this is also for YOU!

I had to reserve a spot for all of my workout partners that understand and allow the peace of mind that only hard steel and heavy weight can provide. Thank you so much for being next to me in my craziest of moments. **Big Ness, Drew, Khayyan, Rah,** and **Sha. Beast Mode is the only life!** We don't get older, only stronger, and I'll see you all at the gym!

The companies that I owe thanks to are as follows; **Wealthy Affiliate** for teaching me all there is to know about the creation of websites, which greatly enhanced my knowledge base. **Kaplan University** has a stellar group of caring professionals, and I have to say that the education provided is second to none. **RMT Coach Training, Walden University, Villanova University,** please never stop learning!

Minister James, I cannot express the warmth and love and spiritual fortitude. From the bottom of my heart, I thank you, and I love you. This is also for the inspiration of the entire congregation, know that with *His* Grace & Permission *ALL THINGS ARE POSSIBLE!*

FOREWORD

First let me provide a backdrop to this premise, for those of you who may not know what a prerequisite is. A prerequisite is something that is required of a person *before* the person can take part in the objective desired. Most often this term is used in the case of the college student. The student may want to take Clinical Psychology, for instance. The student would be told that before she can partake in a Clinical Psychology class, she will first have to enroll in and complete Psychology 101: A Basic Introduction to Psychology.

It is fully with this understanding that I sat down to write The 7 Prerequisites to Success. From my study of some of the most successful people in life, I've found that there are 7 prerequisites that resonate with all of these people. I will get to what these prerequisites are in a moment, my focus at this point is to solidify the idea of the prerequisite into the reader's psyche. Day is a prerequisite for night, 2:30 is a prerequisite for 3:00, and the number 4 is a prerequisite of the number 5, just to make it plain.

So if all of that is true, what could the prerequisites for success be? From Warren Buffet to Mark Zuckerberg, from Bob Proctor to Tony Robbins, the list remains one and the same. They have all had hard times at one point or another. They have all admitted to initial failings. They have experienced a state of acceptance, after initial disbelief and resistance. Then came the paradigm shift, this is when they had that Aha! Moment, and certain things were revealed to them.

Following this Aha! Moment, came belief, from this belief came dedication, and from dedication came the willingness to be persistent against seemingly insurmountable odds. There are many more subdivisions of each prerequisite; stages if you will, before each prerequisite is completed. For the sake of utilizing space as efficiently as possible, I will mention the subdivisions, with the detailed breakdown of each. However, the *flow* from one subdivision to the next is a topic for another book entirely.

This brings us to the last two Prerequisites to Success that is common to the highly successful, and those are Faith, and Tenacity. Faith does not doubt, and Tenacity does not relent. In the vision, or perspective of those destined for high achievements of success, doubt does not exist. There may be some question as to how, or when, or what will lead ultimately to the fruit, but there can be no question as to whether or not the fruit exists, or whether or not the fruit shall soon be in the possession of the seeker. No question. This is called Faith.

Tenacity is defined as the quality or fact of being able to grip something firmly; grip.[1] Again tenacity is defined as the quality or fact of being very determined; determination.[2] Tenacity is the ability to push forward, despite resistance. Tenacity does not allow you to give up, regardless to how hard the opposing forces may appear. Tenacity is that unyielding quality that simply does not – ever – take no for an answer. This is tenacity.

There are times when all 7 prerequisites will need to be employed at one time, and at different intervals, and points throughout one's quest. Still, there is a basic ladder which one must climb from one rung to the next, in order. This is true whether we are speaking of success in business, success in relationships, success in childrearing, or in the pursuit of higher education. All come with their particulars, but essentially the prerequisites remain the same. Observe now the similarities and correlations.

Take, for instance, a relationship. For sake of argument, a relationship between a man and a woman, any age will suffice. Very often there will be a communication break somewhere. This is usually in the first 3-4 years of the relationship.[3] This would be described as the hard time phase. The *only* time that this is not the case, is when one or both have experienced this inside the course of another relationship, and the lessons are brought along with that person, in order to manage the emotions and communication within the current relationship.

If that is the case, if a person has learned from past *Failure*, then that proves the second prerequisite. If not then there will most certainly be a period of failure after the *Hard Times*. This failure is often characterized as the overall lack of communication, temporary or permanent separation, or divorce, the proverbial 'time apart' or a resigning, as a sort of being there but not being there at the same time. This is characterized by sounds carried on by two people in regards to one another, as opposed to the formation and utterance of actual words.

Following *Failure* comes *Acceptance*. Now again, we are speaking in reference to a relationship between a man and a woman, but see if you cannot correlate situations between a person and their job, or a person and their mismanagement of finances. Acceptance is when someone sees that they have contributed to the mishap, wrong or error, and is mature enough to accept responsibility. It is that time when a person may realize that they need professional help. In the relationship example this may be when a couple seek out a Relationship Coach, Marriage Counselor, or a Relationship Therapist.

Once the Acceptance phase is initiated, structured learning takes place. Usually this learning is an introduction of the mind to new information. This is when old habits and ways of doing things are challenged, and replaced by new theories and practices. It is through the acceptance, that the old ways do not work, that new systems are allowed to enter into the realm of possibility. Acceptance requires a level of humility to exist. Without humility the *pride* will never allow the mind to *accept* that anything is wrong.

The people who never reach a level of humility are the ones who you can see that are obviously in a burning house. Figuratively, they are standing in the foyer area of a burning house, yet they will accept no water, nor rope to either put out the fire, or pull themselves out of the fire. They can do no wrong, and are always right. These are the personality types that blame everyone else for their predicament. It is the lack of acceptance that they could ever be at fault that denies them the ability to grow and be successful. It does not matter who they are with, they will run into the same problem, over and over again, as if the other person in the relationship is the same person that they just left.

These are the people who say that 'all men/women are the same'. It is not that all men/women are the same. No, it is that they find themselves in the same situation, regardless to whom they are around at any particular time in space, because they have not yet changed their interior design. It is like a filthy car interior. It does not matter if you are in a torn down ghetto, or the Grand Canyon, a person's enjoyment of their surroundings are going to be inhibited by their immediate interior situation. To fully enjoy, or even experience the outside of one's self, it takes an inner humility to first - accept when things are wrong, then to seek out the conditions and situations that will correct them.

Next, we have the Paradigm Shift. The *Paradigm Shift* is often times the result of the new information that one came into contact with following *acceptance* of their *failure*, which was obvious by the indicator of the *hard times* that they were experiencing. Do you see how it all flows in a line? The Paradigm Shift is a shift in perspective. It is defined as a fundamental change in approach or underlying assumptions.[4] This is when you, as a result of acceptance, are introduced to that which is so revolutionary, that a world you never knew existed opens up. In the relationship example, it is, perhaps, when a person sees how vastly their world changes from the consistency of seemingly unimportant gestures of appreciation.

Just taking the time to say the words, "I love you", or to ask "How was your day?" To someone whom you have never often said these words, will possibly open a whole new reality to you. I have counseled people who have used drugs and alcohol, and they did not know the beauty of a simple walk in the park, or the pleasure of holding hands under the moonlight. I know it may sound square to the uninitiated, but this is the result of a paradigm shift, because there was a time when all of that sounded corny to me as well. Then my paradigm shifted, and I'm so glad that it did!

Consider the relationship between an employee, and his place of employment or his employer. A paradigm shift may be as simple as realizing that his current situation does not have to be a permanent one, and is as temporary as he decides to make it. A paradigm shift could be the realization, and acceptance that, the manager could just be a poor soul who is in need of joy and fulfillment. It is not the employee's responsibility to take another human being's thinking or actions personal. I know I have gone from a tense perspective to a feeling of *sorrow* for people who used to agitate me. The view is much better and healthier over here as well, give it a gander.

So do we have an understanding of paradigm shift yet? This is the state, or experience that highly successful people go through when they see that something is not working for them. Maybe they need to hire people, instead of trying to do things solely on their own, or maybe they need to fire some unproductive people. Perhaps they need to trust people, perhaps they need not to trust people as much as they do. Maybe they need to stop working so much, and take their noses out of their work long enough to notice that their relationship is one-sided and suffering. Whatever the paradigm shift entails, it is usually a foreign idea that just totally overhauls and renews one's perspective, practice, and by default, potential for success.

Once the new information fills the void, or usurps the position of old beliefs and morals, the next step on the ladder to success is Belief. I have never read of a person who was/is highly successful, who did not *believe strongly* that they would be successful. Don't get me wrong. This is not to say that highly successful people have never had that thought, because most of them have. It was usually somewhere between hard times and failure. It took acceptance, and the paradigm shift, for them to be brought back to life and into the reinstatement of belief – the 5th Prerequisite to Success.

Back to the relationship scenario, there has to exist a *belief* that things can get better. There has to be a belief that the people involved in the relationship deserve for it to get better, and are worthy of a better relationship. I know that sounds obvious and simple enough, but believe it or not, the lack of this belief is at the core of most acts of self-sabotage. Some people just do not have the self-esteem required to believe that they are worthy of anything good in life. Of course, there are some exceptions to every rule, but generally speaking these are not going to be your highly successful people. At least, not for long.

These people need Coaching, counseling, or therapy, and sometimes they need to be monitored because they are not only a danger to others, but themselves as well. They are more apt to use drugs, be depressed and/or commit suicide. In most instances their feelings of low self-esteem result from a traumatic experience in their youth that remains unresolved, and surfaces anytime someone tries to care for them, or anytime they truly have a shot at overcoming their situation. The ghost of trauma past will resurface to deny the person the joy of fruit present, or a potentially fruitful future.

When Mark Zuckerberg created Facebook, he believed that it would be successful. Otherwise, why do it? No one does, or tries, that which they believe is going to fail. No, they believe that it will be successful, and then, if it is not, they try again. Belief is akin to hope, if a person has no hope, they will cease to attempt. We see this dilemma all of the time with those who do not see past their present circumstances. I am an expert in this area, because I, at one time, could not see past my former financial and demographic boundaries. Therefore I did not aspire to overcome my financial or demographic boundaries. I built a fortress in the muck and mire, and fooled myself into the *belief* that I loved it where I was at, deserved no more, and that it wasn't that bad after all.

This just resulted in pain, and years lost that cannot be regained. Ultimately, this is because when you are destined for a thing, and I truly believe this, when you are destined for a thing, that thing will become you whether you like it or not. It just may take some extra special conditions to borne you into your destiny. It may take some excruciating circumstances to shake you back in step with the plan designed for you. Some call this fate, duty, responsibility, or calling, regardless to your moniker I think you get the picture. There is something that you do, that you were made to, something that no one else can do, the way you do…but you.

Back to the relationship example, you must believe with all of your heart that your relationship is worth the work required to set aright. You must believe that your spouse or counterpart loves you, as much as you love them, and you must believe that you both can be successful in the area of your relationship, because if you do not truly, at your core, believe it will work, guess what? It won't. It never will, no matter how much you fake it, if you truly believe that it won't work, you're right. Let me assure you of this, if of no other thing; the person who believes they can do a thing, and the person who believes that they cannot - are both 100% correct! This is the inherent power of belief.

A subdivision of belief is purpose. Belief provides one with purpose, for example, I believe that a book on the prerequisites of success will be a great inspiration for those looking for success, but finding themselves stuck in one of the prerequisite stages. Thus, my *purpose* for this book is based on the *belief* that people who are in the prerequisite stages suffering with hard times and/or failure, etc. may come to understand that it is required of them to fail, it is required of them to experience hard times, let downs, confusion, frustration, and things that they think are not fair (subdivisions of hard times). My belief supplies me with purpose, it is my purpose that supplies me with desire, and it is desire that brings me to the next step, or prerequisite…

Faith. Faith and belief are very closely related, but I had to separate them because they are different angles of the same perspective. You can believe a thing and still resign to defeat, if you lack the *faith* required to carry you forward. Whereas, faith will not allow your belief to waiver if firmly rooted. Let me say it another way. Belief can be unlearned, faith cannot. Faith is belief in the things unseen, this is required of individuals when the going gets the hardest. When things make absolutely no sense, and defy all conventional belief, it is faith that strengthens one's resolve.

I said that belief can be unlearned. In Christopher Columbus' day people believed that the world was flat. The world unlearned that belief, when they were presented with fact. I don't want to go into religion, but think of a religious debate you may have heard. One side, usually the scientific side, has presented what they refer to as evidence to convince the person with faith that they are in error. Does this happen? All the time. Do they win the debate? Hardly ever, right? They can convert the person with belief, perhaps, because their beliefs can be replaced. It is much harder to replace a person's faith.

The believer believes based on what they regard as compulsive evidence. The faithful are faithful based on a *feeling* of certainty, an emotion, sometimes they cannot even describe it. They don't even say they believe such and such, do they? No, what do they say? They say, 'I just KNOW'. Now think of a relationship, if you suspect that a woman/man has been unfaithful to your friend, and you tell that friend for their own good, the person who just *believe* that their sweetheart is faithful may entertain your assertion. However, the person who has faith in their sweethearts' dedication to them will not hear of it. They will demand proof, and if provided proof, sometimes still will not accept it. You may even turn out to be the enemy for trying to be a good friend. Such is the compelling nature of faith.

Faith will make you go to the ends of the earth in order to bring life to your idea. The ideas of the faithful become a *mission*. You may not even believe, that after what you and a person has been through, that you could ever reconcile. But your faith to your God, and your vows will make you give it another try. Your faith in the institution of marriage will assure you that it is worth saving. Your *faith* in your relationship will ultimately determine its success at the end of the day.

Consider the respect for faith. Many things can be forgiven within the castle that is love. Many things are said that are hurtful, and done that are resented, but faithfulness is at the core of a relationship. Many times, if a woman/man know that their counterpart is faithful, there is room for work. When that faithfulness is broken, many times, there is no longer a sacredness.

A subdivision of faith is persistence. The faith that things are going to change is what brings about the element of persistence. This is definitely a prerequisite for success, because one can never give up, or quit, *and* be successful, it just will not work that way. It is this faith that drives one forward against all adversity, it is unrelenting faith that leads to victory after all resisting forces have been met and overcome. The faith will keep men convicted. You must have faith, you must not just believe, you must KNOW that if you continue on this path it will end in victory. In the same vein that belief is the counterpart of hope, faith is the counterpart of conviction.

Which brings me to my 7th and final Prerequisite for Success that we will discuss in this book; Tenacity. Tenacity is a noun that means persistent determination[5], and there is no more important element in success, than that of persistent determination. I am not saying that one must *work hard* to be successful. I will concede that changing one's self for true success is not the easiest task, at the same time. One must bring a conviction provided by faith, that one deserves to be successful and, ultimately, that one will achieve the object of their aspirations. Tenacity is the *will* to never give up.

In the analogy of the relationship, tenacity is to be unrelenting in the work towards resolution and repair. Tenacity is the untiring work towards the reunification of the spirits involved. Tenacity is that which will not allow you to forget your responsibility to your loved one, or to yourself, in regards to the relationship. Tenacity will allow you to overcome the burdensome opinions of others in regards to your relationship or dream. Tenacity is what will allow you to cut yourself off from frivolous distractions, and opposition to the goal. You have to be tenacious!

Tenacity, desire, and persistence of will, is what is required in the last leg of any race. It is when one is near to the end that they experience the most setbacks and disappointments. This is just the way it is set in the universe, so as to validate one's right to success. The only overnight successes are those of infants born into riches. The rest of us must earn it, and it is a process. Conditioning one's mind is a process, resisting negativity is a process, handling disappointments, and unfair situations is a process. Overcoming adversity, admitting and accepting when you're wrong, trying and applying new things, these are all processes. Processes that require tenacity.

In the case of the relationship, both partners must be equally tenacious in order for the relationship to really work. They must both be very energetic and creative when it comes to keeping the relationship fresh and new, because if not, if one is 100% tenacious about invigorating the relationship, and the other is only 30% - kind of tenacious – guess what? It's going to show. It's going to show and the person investing all of the work, and using all of the tools to implement improvement over time, is going to rightly feel shortchanged and resentful. So in the case of the relationship, can you see the need to be tenacious?

As a wrap up, how do these 7 elements look in the scope of success? I just loosely utilized the analogy of a relationship for an example, so that you could see the application to other areas, where success may be desired. Wherever one wants success, in whatever field one may be in, success is definitely attainable, and it's yours to claim. It is all yours, and that is true for every person alive, there is no boundary or limitations on who can achieve what. Racially, demographically, education level, all of the supposed barriers to success have been removed. The only thing that remains is the process. These 7 Prerequisites to Success are present in anyone's journey to success that you investigate. Once again, in order they are hard times, failure, acceptance, Paradigm Shift, belief, faith, and tenacity.

If used as a reference, this book can provide you with understanding as to why you may be experiencing one of these prerequisite classes. I'm going to use the analogy of classes, because it is like unto a course of study that one must undergo, and then pass the tests and quizzes presented, in order to graduate from that level to another. I have never known one successful person, and I know many, who have not gone through all 7 in the direct order that I present it to you. For another reader, let this be like a general overview of courses. Let this equip you and prepare you for these classes, so that when you end up consulting with what Les Brown refers to as the 'Messenger of Misery'[6] you can remain unemotional because you were prepared for it to come.

CHAPTER 1

Hard Times

WHY?

Why is the most commonly asked question by those who know not. Why does this happen? Why me? What did I do? Oh God, why hast thou forsaken me? Even Jesus is not beyond such reasoning. I have learned through the trials and triumphs of life not to ask the question 'why, but to ask the question 'how? How is this going to change me? What did I not learn prior to this, and how is this going to make me more equipped to handle what is upcoming in my life?

Preconceived Notions

These are the questions I ask, and by performing these small tweaks to your perspectives, that which naturally occurs in life is much easier to deal with. Hard times are a prerequisite to success, that none can go without experiencing on the face of this planet. Many look at the rich, the happy, those 'successful' in life, whatever that looks like for you. People look at others living *their* definition of success, and they believe that because these people have such and such, or since they are married to so and so, or because they have a Ph. D, they must not know what it's like to endure hardship. I would beg to differ.

The late great Bob Marley stated that, "every man thinks his burdens are the heaviest"[1]. I have found this to be true. People are only able to measure by the length of their own noses. By this I mean that a hungry man will look at someone who has abundance, and think that because that man is not physically hungry, he is not suffering, and has not had to face resistance. What the hungry man knows not, is that perhaps this man with abundance is walking to the corner to catch a cab, to take him to the coroner, because his wife and son were just killed in a car collision.

Perhaps the man with abundance just buried his mother the week prior, and perhaps a month prior to that, he was told that he had colorectal cancer, and had to begin undergoing chemo after 3 months on a tasteless, protein based, almost liquid diet because he had to detox from years of drinking, before he could begin the chemotherapy to save his life...maybe. The reason why I am displaying these possibilities, is to make known to the reader that you never know what another person is going through. Also, to add supporting arguments to my next statement.

Everyone goes through something. Yes, everyone does go through something(s) in life. Your burden may not be my own, and mine may not be yours, but everyone undergoes some form of hardship. If you think not, read. Read about your 'success' stories. I remember reading about Virgin Owner Richard Branson and how he stated that the head of a bank told him that he was going to shut Virgin down, the very next day if he did not produce some 600K. Richard said he had to physically push the head of the bank out of his home[2]. I wonder if you were aware of this story, the last time you began to sing the 'woe is me' melody.

No one is exempt from trial and measure. No one is exempt from the qualifying process of fire. Get used to it. The universe uses pressure to see if a person is ready for advance. Before a bodybuilder can lay down under 245 lbs. he first must struggle and succeed at lifting 225. This is his qualifier. You must go through hardship to prove yourself worthy for the next level. This is how it is done. It is akin to school, if you do not pass grade 7, how can you expect to be promoted to the 8th grade? Your successful endurance, the ability to withstand, and overcome adversity with grace is what qualifies you to graduate.

No Pain = No Gain

There is a process I want to talk to you about, this is the process of refinement. The process of refinement requires intense heat. "**Gold (Au) melts at a temperature of 1,064° C (1,947° F)**"[3]. This is pretty hot. This is a refinement (cleansing) process, in order for the gold to be purified. Within the fire all of the dross, dirt, and impurities are brought out of the original composition until the only thing left is pure gold. This is the gold that is qualified to go on to become the precious engagement ring. That which symbolizes a husband and wife's holy union before their God. What are *you* being qualified for?

This is the question I ask myself when undergoing some kind of calamity in life. What am I being prepared for, what is the lesson here? A lesson unlearned will oft be repeated. So I urge you to shift your focus, I urge you to take the bad with the good. When something of fortune befalls you, you do not ask "why me"? No, you enjoy, you relish, and you may even say to yourself that this good thing has come to me because of thus and so. I urge you to become creative when it seems like misfortune has befallen you. Many things are not what they appear to be.

Think about the examples given in the Bible. Think about Daniel, think about Moses, Abraham, and the qualifying process that they all had to go through. Think about the endurance, the character building endurance they had to exhibit, for God to deem them worthy of the undertaking at hand. How did they become God's chosen man? Think on Job. Think on all that was taken from him, and how he handled his adversity. Now think about yourself. How are you handling your adversity? Will you be deemed worthy?

The Silver Lining

All clouds bring with them a silver lining, all dusk comes before dawn. There is always a precipitator to any and all events worthy of mention. You are not exempt. You and I, no matter how much we may wish we were, will not be the exception to this rule. **Hard times are the qualifying stage for greatness**. It can also be the disqualifying stage, it is up to you. I urge you to choose wisely.

I have always been of the mind-set that the *greater the adversity*, the *greater the blessing* that lies ahead. I do not look at misfortune with a sneer, or hate in my eye, because I have lived long enough to accept it for what it is. Hard times did not come to stay, they came to pass, and when they do pass, there will be new growth to show. Just like a rain storm. When a rain storm takes place, and remains in a certain area for any amount of time, when it passes, there is new growth left behind, in the form of foliage.

You know what the ups and down prove to me? The same thing that they prove to a doctor, or a medical technician reading an EKG; that the person in question is still among the living. **You are still alive if you are going through the ups and downs**. When you cease to go through the ups and downs, the ebbs and flows that is life...you will be dead, and gone from this world. It will be over for you. You are going to suffer, you are going to celebrate. If you are suffering get ready to celebrate, and if you are celebrating, get ready to suffer. Welcome it, it shows that you are still here.

Hard times are a prerequisite for success, in that they prepare us for the next stages of life. Everyone has them, everyone's is their own. It is not to make a spectacle of yourself, and share with everyone else what you are going through, that makes us look weak. A symbol of strength, is to always have something good to say. Stop complaining. Stop whining. Always find the blessing, and expand your breast on that. Crying just reminds people of babies. *What are they going to do if you take their jobs?*

When someone works out, they tear muscle in order to make way for new growth, and what is the immediate response? Pain. When a child is in between one day and one year, when it is sleeping, sometimes it will scream out in pain, or wake up crying. Why? It is growing, and growth is painful. So when you go through it, embrace it. You are embracing greatness that is about to come your way. Do not prove yourself unworthy by crying yourself to sleep every night, or failing to rise to the occasion. Any people that you consider to be truly great, are people who have suffered and overcome much adversity. This is just your share, what will you do with it?

So the answer to the question *why*, in regards to hard times, is because it is a prerequisite of success. You must go through hard times to *qualify* you for the good. If you never knew hard times and was just born into the good times, and all you experienced were good times, when would you learn to reflect? When would you learn to meditate on God's grace and blessings? When would you be grateful, if you had no hard times by which to contrast the good? **It is said that a man is not educated until he has traveled**. Ponder that.

The Road Ahead

On this road we call life, there are going to be twists and turns, and there are definitely going to be rough patches, which you should be well acquainted with by now if you are past the age of 15. This is the education of travel, things are going to be different. It is not always going to be the same. Consider driving, aren't you appreciative when the fog clears, and the rain stops, and you can see again? What about when your tires come back into contact with a smooth surface, aren't you grateful? This is the purpose of the hard times.

I recall a speech by John Spence, who is now one of the top 100 Thought Leaders in America. I remember his speech on Ted Talks where he spoke about his college days[4]. His father was a member of the board in the college *he was thrown out of.* Yes, you read that right. One of the top 100 Thought Leaders of America, was thrown out of the college that his father was a board member of. John stated that he was almost never there, and when he did show up, he showed up hung over from the party the night prior. He said he had a 1. something GPA.

These were very hard character defining times for John. It was after this experience that he decided to shape up. It was after the experience of not being accepted into colleges after that, that he began to consider his future, and what it would look like if he continued down this path. It was his very narrow acceptance into a college after that, 'on probationary status' that allowed him to reinvent himself. It was after that experience that he formed a study group. It was after that experience that he graduated in the top 1% in the country.

It was after that experience that he was hired by a Rockefeller company fresh out of college, and then went on to head multiple million dollar multi-national companies before the age of 30. It was after that experience, that failure, that *hard time* in life, where he let everyone down, it was after that humbling crushing defeat, that he was able to rise back into the light of the sun, renewed with a fresh vigorous understanding. Many times our hard times come upon us by the work of our own hands. The question is what do we do with it once it is upon us? Let me say this, had John not undergone that experience and handled it the way that he did, do you think there is a good chance that he would not be one of the most sought after public speakers today? I think so too.

The Rule, Not the Exception

I can keep dishing them out. Success stories after the hard times saga. This is not a misnomer, this is the process, and this is how the greats are made. The greats are not *born*, no, the greats are *forged*. They are forged by the fires of life. Scars give you character, it gives you credibility. It lets the world know that you've been through something. Don't you dislike it when someone who you feel has never been through anything, tries to give you advice? I'm not saying that this is the right stance to take, as I've stated everyone has been through their own roads, but you do know the feeling of thinking someone is unqualified to advise you in a certain area, because they lack experience in that area, correct?

Well then, this is my point. How is God going to make an example of greatness out of you, if no hard times can be found in your *resume*? What is your pedigree? What qualifies you to be able to advise others? What makes you credible? How are you an authority? What is your background? Hard times are the backdrop to your life story. I know it is the hard part, but let me ask you, wouldn't you rather suffer now as opposed to later? I know if someone tells me they have good news, and bad news for me, I want the bad news first. Children in the doctor's office get the needle, *then* they get the lollipop, not the other way around.

Stages of Qualification

Before an architect lays a floor down, he puts a plank of wood in the corner. On this plank of wood he puts a generator. This generator creates weight. The architect must generate all of the weight that is to go on the entire floor – ever. The architect, or engineer, places a tremendous amount of weight on to the wood plank. If the plank breaks, then the engineer gets another kind of wood. Do you see where I'm going here? If the wood cannot stand the pressure of the job they are going to be assigned for, the architect must know, because the job must not fail. Before you are given a position in life, you must first be qualified to determine whether or not you are going to break, because the job cannot fail.

If you prove yourself unworthy and you break, you will be replaced, and there will be someone else assigned to the place and job that was yours to take, had you proven yourself reliable. That's what this is about, reliability. Can you be counted on? Can people rely on you? Think about athletes whose whole teams rely on them to make the spread, whose coaches look to them when they do not know the answer. Whose schools look to them to get the respect back for their school, whose teams count on them to bring the prestige back to their state.

Where are you in this assignment, what are your credentials, and where do you measure up? What have you been through? Who can trust you to lead them? These are the questions that hard times seek to find the answers to. Hard times probe for your weaknesses and exploit them, it is not the worst thing in the world to feel bad. Everyone at some point or another is going to feel bad, feel discouraged, wonder whether or not they are the right one for the job, or if they are able to be successful. The self-questioning is fine, it is natural, it is normal. The abandoning is not acceptable. **Abandoning your post in life is not acceptable**.

Not If, but How?

Running from your responsibilities in life will not be tolerated. Trying to escape from the reality that is your life, just will not work. All the drugs and alcohol in the world will not make your problems disappear, it will however, cause them to *intensify*. So do not run *from* them, but run *to* them head on. It's better to get the hard part out of the way first, and it is all about how you handle yourself, throughout the *process*. Never forget that, some tests are not meant to be passed, they are meant to gauge your strength dealing with loss. They are set up for you to fail. You are going to fail, that is guaranteed. In some things you are going to fail, the question asked by these particular forms of tests is not whether or not you are going to fail, but more importantly, *how* are you going to fail?

Are you going to lose yourself? Quit, give up, and not show up the next day? Are you going to let an *external occurrence*, destroy your *internal compass*, so that you know not what direction you are coming and going from anymore? These are called measures, what is your measure? Or better yet, what is your mettle? What are you made of? This is what hard times will make known. The answer inside of you cannot hide from revelation, everything in the dark will be brought to the light. Again, sometimes it is not whether or not you will fail, as that is a given. In these instances the honor with which you fail will be the determining sought after factor.

No Test, No Testimony

In the great words of Les Brown, "No test, no testimony[5]." If you have not been tested, then even you yourself, do not know yourself. Hard times bring out some ugly traits and habits, that people did not even know that they carried around with them. Vices, and diseases, that were just waiting for the appropriate hardship to show themselves in the midst of. I like to know where I stand personally, and I cannot stand with people on whom I cannot count. If life has not tested you, I will not be the one to do it, because I cannot risk your fail. You need to go and get some stripes, before I can make any use of you. It's not personal at all, life is serious business. **You may be a great personality, the world needs great people.**

With all of this having been said, one should have another question for the hard times. The question should no longer be *why*, maybe the question should be *why this long*? Why did it take this long for the hard times to come? Personally, I like to deal with the hard ones up front. In college, the tests that I knew were going to give me some extra resistance, these were the tests that I deliberately did first. The same thing applied to the harder classes, it's a principle of prioritization. I would see classes that I was not familiar or comfortable with, and I would request to have those classes first, and all together if possible. I just want to get that out of the way, so I can move on to the good stuff.

Since it's Going to Happen Anyway...

This is just an analogy, but life is no different. You're going to come up against challenges. Since this is known, why not challenge yourself? If you practice a life of self-challenge, then when something outside of you comes along to challenge your resolve, there will be no question as to your response, because you've been *practicing* up to this point for the occurrence. This will ensure that you should pass the test with flying colors. This is a state of ever readiness, preparedness. I always am in awe of how athletes appear during, and just after off season. I remember Emmitt Smith's appearance in a commercial after winning the Super Bowl in 1993, he said, **"All men are created equal, some just work harder in pre-season[6]"**.

Wow, some just work harder in pre-season. What would your life's pre-season be? What would your pre-season be, if you were not having hard times? Let me tell you, if you're not having hard times, if everything is good for you, if there are no challenges...**this *is* your pre-season**. This is your down time, this is your off-season. Now, in order to succeed come game time, come trial time, come hard time, you'd better do some inventory and take some assessments now. You'd be best to find some things about yourself that you could change, and change them. See, if hard times should appear, and you are already *built to endure* self-imposed restrictions, and you are used to doing things to overcome challenges, then the hard times will not make you blink.

Battle Tested

This is what soldier-ready means. Life needs a soldier-ready mind state to navigate the waters in any weather. Your husband/wife needs a soldier-ready companion, able to handle his/her self when calamity strikes. Your children need a soldier-ready mother/father ready to step up to the plate when it's disciplining time. Your business needs a soldier-ready

CEO/employee to be able to be counted upon in times of duress. Your finances need a soldier-ready executor to make the right financial decisions for the future, and not to be soft, and given to seduction.

See, what practice does is it brings you closer to perfection, it makes you sharp. It makes you prepared to weather the storm, should it ever arise. Think about the testing phase of anything in production. Think about all the tests that a car endures before it makes it off of the assembly line. It must be qualified by running simulations through multiple situations to ensure that it is not going to fall apart and get the whole family killed. This is a similar analogy to *your* preparedness test. Your simulated situations are the hard times that you must endure to ensure that you are not going to get the whole family, team, business, or financial situation slaughtered on the playing field. Oh yes, I said playing field, but it (Life) really is no game.

Spartan's Resolve

When you come up against hard times, you will be much more peaceful if you are, in fact, prepared. You will be proud of yourself, and calm under pressure, because pressure is nothing new to you, you will have what is known as a Spartan's resolve. If you take someone who has never worked out, and someone who regularly - works out to the gym together, and run them through a moderately demanding regimen, who do you think is going to be more equipped to handle it? Yes, the one who's been doing it on his own all this time. For him it is nothing new. However, the guy who has never stepped foot in a gym, or sat on a weight bench, he may just have some problems. Does that make sense?

Summary

So, here are some particulars about hard times. They are guaranteed, you will have them. Everyone does, you are not alone. **It is not personal,**

this is the business of qualification. Hard times are a refinement *process*, give yourself to the process. Do not think too hard. Sometimes it doesn't make sense, it does not have to. The point is to end up with a better you, work hard to ensure that you do. Prepare for hard times before they come, in order to be better equipped to handle them. They did not come to stay, they came to pass. **Keep a straight face, your future is watching**. Everything you will have tomorrow, will be a direct result of how well you handle yourself today. I believe in you.

WHY NOT?

This is also a commonly asked question, by those who know a little more about life than the person who asks, *why*? When a person comes and seeks Coaching from me about what they are going through, I empathize, I do not sympathize. I do not enable weakness, I do not aid and abet helplessness, or the inability to withstand. People are often under the false impression that because they do not hear of another's issues, that the person does not have any issues. The funny thing is that when it rains, it rains on everyone. Some people just handle it differently. Some carry an umbrella, some call a cab, some drive to work, and some don't show up at all. **When someone asks me why? I ask, why not?**

Why not you? Why should you be exempt? What makes you special? I may have undergone more than most people will ever know, because my life is not their business. So when people come to me with complaints that seem small in comparison to complaints I could have if I so chose, it definitely tells me something about their character. **Again, why not**? Who do you know in life who has never, I mean never, had something bad happen to them. Who is exempt from the qualification process? They say that God has mercy on the ignorant, and babies. Well, which one do you wish *you* were? Even better yet, which one do you think you *sound more like*?

Tough Talk

Who do you think that you are better than? Why? What about the generations that came before you? Did they exist free from challenges, free from hardship? I think you know the answer to that question. I think you would have to agree, that even though each generational evolution comes with its own unique challenges, overall life gets easier for each succeeding generation. I have to evoke a comment made by Eric Thomas, he said, "What if the slaves would have given up?" Where would all of the great black men and women be, what impact would they have made, had the generation that endured slavery just given up?

Now I'm going to invoke the stories of people you probably know, but whose stories of struggle you may not know. You know why? Because they don't ask, why? They just move forward, without looking back. **It is my aim to shock you into understanding that hard times are a prerequisite for success.** So that when you see them, or better yet, feel them, you know them for what they are, and do not see them as something designed to kill you, or break you. No, they were designed to make you, make you better, make you stronger, and make you smarter. Let's look into the stories of some people you've heard of, and some people you may not have, who have suffered all kinds of hard times before you got to know them.

Here's A Little Story...

Oprah Winfrey is where I'll begin. Oprah Winfrey is a woman that everyone knows, and she is a household authority. If Oprah says a thing is A, B and C, then it is trusted that the thing is A, B, and C. She is a famous actress, TV host, and now she has gone on to having her own cable channel; OWN (the Oprah Winfrey Network). However, Oprah's humble beginnings did not insinuate that she would be the powerhouse megastar that everyone knows now. Oprah Winfrey was *abused as a child* – sexually abused, and molested from ages 9 to 13. If this does not sound to you like hard times, then I don't know what hard times are. At age 14 she became pregnant and gave birth to a baby boy who would soon die in infancy. Sound like hard times to you? She is now regarded as one of the "most powerful woman in the world."[7]

Oprah was once fired, for 'becoming too emotionally involved' in the broadcasts. It was also said at one point that she was 'unfit for TV'. This was in Baltimore, where she had become an evening news anchor. Pretty big step up for a black woman who had endured such hard times at such a young age. Then getting fired was a pretty big step down. She did not say, "*Why me*"? Instead she forged ahead, kept her eyes planted on a goal that she had, and it was after this event that she took the role that would ultimately lead her into your home and mine, as an afternoon talk show host.

At this point there is so much that Oprah is known for, I do not need to rattle off her accomplishments, as many of you reading this book could most certainly teach me a thing or two about where she's been, all that she's done, who she's helped, and all that she's given to others. My point is just to make you look at the hard times. **The hard times that were, without question, one of her 7 prerequisites to success.**

What Would We Do Without...?

Who has ever heard of JK Rowling? JK Rowling is the author of the Harry Potter series, one of the most adored series of books and movies ever written or produced. However, what many may not know is how humble her beginnings were. In her own account, she felt like a *huge failure*. As a matter of fact she called herself the biggest failure that she knew. She was the proud owner of a failed marriage, the mother of a newborn baby daughter, and she was on welfare. She states that she, "felt worthless raising her baby alone"[8]. She did not have the money for a computer, so she typed the whole thing out on an old manual typewriter in Portugal.

JK sent the manuscript to many publishers and received negative result after negative result. One publisher went so far as to tell her to get a day job because 'children's books' don't make any money anyway. Does that sound like hard times to you? Here is a woman, whose mother just died by the way, sitting in Portugal, no money for a computer, and manually typing these pages out. No career, a brand new baby girl, and on welfare. She was just married, and had dreams and aspirations that had been dashed to pieces prior. Now, had she given into the, "*Why Me*" syndrome, then children and adults all over the world would not know about Harry, and all of the loveable characters. This is a literary work of art, children who do not like to read at all have read Harry Potter, and so it is also an instructional and educational tool. **An instructional and educational tool for which hard times was one of the 7 pre-requisites for success**.

Eye of the Tiger

Has anybody reading this ever watched a Rocky movie? No, how about Rambo? Just kidding, I know you've probably seen all of the above, and all of the sequels to all of the above. I'm trying to drive home a point, here. The first item you may not have known about Sly Stallone is that his unique sneer and speech comes from him having been born with the lower left side of his face paralyzed[9]. Stallone still had a dream to become an actor, and so he came to the state of New York with big dreams and was met with…*you guessed it*, hard times. Stallone was repeatedly rejected by studios that had no use for him. He was so broke, that at one point he slept in the New Jersey bus terminal for **THREE WEEKS**!

After this, times got even worse. So bad that he had to sell his best friend. Stallone had a dog, a dog named Butkus, and he sold the dog in New York for a measly $25 dollars. Money was very hard to come by, and times were getting harder. He was inspired to write the script for Rocky one night watching Muhammad Ali on TV. He writes the script and the movie executives want it, but they *do not want him*. He has a dream, his dream is to star in his movie, they offer him money to betray his dream, and *sell it* to them. Stallone refuses and remains broke and destitute with a mega million dollar movie script.

Finally they call him back and accept his terms, although the price that he was offered is severely cut down to a paltry 35K because he demanded to be the given the lead role. The first thing Sylvester did was track down the person he had sold the dog to, and numbers on this vary, but he is said to have paid between 3 and 15K to get the dog back. The dog is even in the movie, seen in Rocky when the lead character runs up the stairs. The rest is history, Sylvester Stallone's manuscript turned into a movie that grossed 200+ million in the box office. What was the prerequisite? **Hard times was one of the 7 prerequisites of this success story.**

When You Want to Succeed as Bad as You Want to Breathe...

Now I'm going to speak on someone who has been one of my more recent influencers by the name of Eric Thomas Ph.D. Eric Thomas is a motivational speaker who has been all around the world working with some of the most prestigious universities and corporations with the purpose of spreading his message of enhancing productivity, and completeness, within many institutions. He has many different institutions that he focuses on, such as the institution of marriage, scholastic preparation, performance, and excellence.

Of course he did not start out as a Ph.D. Eric Thomas started out as a youth in Detroit, Michigan. Eric speaks candidly about the *hard times that propelled him* to move forward out of his prior predicaments into the situation he now finds himself. Eric Thomas grew up not knowing who his father was, which is the story shared by many people in many different demographics. Eric talks about his mother working multiple jobs, his less than stellar performance in school, and his leaving home at a young age.

Eric speaks on being homeless, and sleeping on the streets of Michigan many nights. Sleeping in abandoned buildings, and if you know Michigan, you know how cold the nights, and mornings can be in the winters of Michigan. He speaks on *eating out of garbage cans*, and getting into trouble time and time again. At the age of 17, Eric came into contact with a preacher who began to influence and mentor him in the errors of terminal thinking, and helped him to see higher objectives. **Eric went back to school, got his GED and then set his sights on college.**[10]

While in college Eric started a nonprofit called Break the Cycle I Dare You, focusing on children with some of the same hard times that he himself endured. He has authored several books and has become a much sought after authority on success, and one of his many books is titled, The Secret to Success. A YouTube sensation, Eric Thomas is a prime example of breaking the cycle on many different levels. His motivational speeches has resonated with millions, but before The Secret to Success appeared to him he had to take a pre-requisite class. **The name of that class was Hard Times 101.**

Mr. Bad A$$

Who can say that they do not know Samuel L. Jackson? Samuel L Jackson is a premiere actor who has carved out a niche that no one can replicate. He is a sensation whose movies have made more money than any other actor alive, a whopping 7 billion dollars, and growing. What many may not know is that he was born in Chattanooga, Tennessee, the son of a factory working mother and a father who died of alcoholism. **He only met his father two times during his life**.

Samuel L. Jackson was a student who was very much engrossed into black activism during the 60's. He was an usher in Martin Luther King Jr.'s funeral procession in Atlanta, Georgia, at the age of 19. He was the recipient of a second degree felony, and a two year suspension from Morehouse College when he and several other students held members of the Board of Trustees hostage in demand of reforms at the school. He later graduated with a Bachelor's degree from that university. His first role in film was in 1972. Samuel L. Jackson had a very *intense addiction* to alcohol and cocaine. He had to be replaced in two plays because of his addiction, and he starred in Jungle Fever as a crack addict just days following his release from a cocaine rehab stint. I do not have to tell you, how successful he has become since then. **Notice his prerequisite to success…hard times.**[11]

Renaissance Man

Tony Robbins, to whom every **Life Coach** owes so much, as he basically fathered the industry, has had his own story of hardship and despair before he became the personality that everyone came to for advice. Tony Robbins is the eldest of three, who was born to an alcoholic and a very abusive mother. He related that his mother was married four times throughout his childhood, and even her husbands were not allowed in his mothers' room unless they were '*handling their business*' as he put it one time during a Thanksgiving Oprah episode.

He lived with his tumultuous family in a 1200 sq. ft. home, where he would always see and hear his mother and these men fighting, screaming, and breaking things. When he became the object of his mother's fury, she would pour liquid soap down his throat until he would throw up. She would use hangers on him, and beat his head against the nearest wall at times. He recalled one time having no food for Thanksgiving, and a complete stranger showing up and providing food for his family for Thanksgiving. His father, at the time, tried to deny the food, saying that he did not take charity.

The man informed his 'father' that he was just the delivery guy, insisted that he take the food, and said something along the lines of not allowing his pride to starve his family. Tony related that soon thereafter his 'father' left them on their own, but this act of kindness resonated with Tony, and changed his life as he took it upon himself to begin to feed others as he was once fed. To this date he has fed more than 2 million people for Thanksgiving and he states that the idea came from this initial act of selfless giving. **Talk about hard times being a prerequisite for success!** Tony has grown to be a super servant, he has advised everyone from US Presidents to regular everyday people and treats everyone the same, as a child of God. As stated, there was no such thing as a '**Life Coach**' before Tony Robbins gave it a name.[12]

Recap

I provide all of these different examples so that the reader can pick where they are, and see correlations. Whether you are presently in a state of poverty, lack and want, or suffering in a marriage that could use some help. Whether you are in school, perhaps failing, or in what you see as a dead-end job, you are not alone. People have been there before you, and people will come after you. It is not something that you have done wrong if you were born into this situation. Even if you have put yourself into the hard times that you are experiencing now, **you can do something about it**, and it all begins with accepting the situation for what it is…a prerequisite.

First, do not look to others as a form of averting your eyes from your own situation, look at them for *investigative purposes*. Pick the most inspiring person in your life, those whom you consider to measure up to your definition of success. Investigate their lives, and you will certainly find some hardship. How do I know? This is what is called a **universal truth**, you are going to endure some hardships, before you go on to be rewarded for your tenacity (another prerequisite). **Success does not come to those who give up.** Had any of the preceding examples took their hard times as a reason to stop moving forward, I could not have used them as examples that you could investigate or use as a reference, because *no one would have known them.*

For every Oprah, there is a Sally, who endured the same, less or more. The difference between the Oprahs and the Sallys, is that the Sallys view of their hard times were unconquerable. They could not see a chance for advance, and as long as you are alive, there is a chance for advance. The difference between the Tonys, the Samuel L. Jacksons, and the Peters, Pauls and Toms that you do not know, is that the Peters, Pauls and the Toms gave up. They faced less, more, or equal resistance, and chose to bow to it. They chose not to press on relentlessly, instead they caved and accepted the mundane existence that they saw as being the best that they could produce with that which God had given to them.

The people that I spoke about earlier did not have 5 arms, they were not born with two brains, the difference between them and yourself is that they had different *perspectives*. They saw things differently. I think many people can relate to one or two of the obstacles that people I used as examples faced in their lives. That was the purpose of the exercise, for you to see *relationship* between situations. For you to then see what they made out of the same things that you, yourself have faced, because ultimately if they can do it, then you can too. All it requires is the change of perspective. Some see rain as a reason to stay inside, others see rain as a reason to dress for the occasion, and show up anyway.

How do you show up to life? This is a very important question. How do you show up? Regardless to what goes on in your home, regardless to where your finances may be at the present moment, regardless to what the past that you were, or were not responsible for, presented? How do you show up? Do you show up saying *'woe is me'*, or do you show up saying 'glory be to God'? This is the pertinent question, and many times the only question that needs to be answered correctly in order to change your situation.

One thing you cannot do, one thing I urge you to seriously not do, is focus on the present. Do not become resigned to your current situation, because **the present will become the past when you let go** of it. However, if you choose to hold on to it, it will become permanent because you will bring it along with you into the realm of your tomorrow. Your tomorrow will resemble your today, unless you *let it go* so it can fade away. Very simple concept, yet it takes practice to **shift the habits of thinking**. The purpose of this book, is to help you do just that. So when you find yourself leaning towards self-pity, and asking yourself *"Why Me"*, think of all of these people I have referenced, then reference the people that you can add to this short list, and ask yourself instead…*Why Not?*

WHAT YOU CAN DO

Mentally - What you can do mentally in these instances of hard times is be presently aware of the situation. Think of how you got in this predicament. Did you have any part in its presentation? Are you responsible for any part of it's coming to be? And if so, alter your course. If you are experiencing hard times due to anything that you can change, then change that which you can, accept what you cannot (change), and move forward. As long as you move forward, *closer to your destiny, further from you past*, your reality will reflect your progress.

Do You Remember?

Do you remember role playing? When you used to play cops and robbers, house, or cowboys and Indians? Then look at this as an active cognitive (thinking) exercise. I want you role play, I want you to think of a forecaster. What does a forecaster do? A forecaster says that, "This week is going to be full of rain, storms and thunder from the north. Next week will be full of sunshine." Right? Isn't that what they do? Don't you get dressed, or plan your affairs based on the forecast? Ok, can you see where I'm headed? It's perfectly fine if you cannot. I just have the imagination of a child sometimes, bear with me please, it will make sense in the end.

I want you to become the forecaster of your life. I want you to say something along the lines of, "It's raining today, but tomorrow's forecast is sunny, clear skies, happiness, wealth, and an abundance of optimal health!" Practice that every day, no matter what you've been through today, say it's going to be better tomorrow. Actively, say that it's going to be sunny with a high of a cool 85*, and then visualize it. Feel the forecasted sunshine on your face, smile because of it, become emotional, the energy in sunshine makes you smile. Another lesson, for another book.

Now once you have mastered that, I want you to begin to interject other things into your forecast. Interject peace, interject money, success, abundant health, relationship improvement, and forecast a new job, a better situation at your present job, or a new car. A forecast should sound something like this, "Well, it's been pretty rough today, with the bill collector calling, and the shortness of funding, but tomorrow looks great, with money coming in early, from a *presently unknown source*, and wiping out all of that debt. Paving the way for a great week, and month ahead!" Now that is a positive forecast, isn't it?

Positive Visualization

This is referred to as positive visualization, positive imaging, and positive reinforcement. If you have ever read *As a Man Thinketh*, by James Allen, this will resonate with you, and if not that is fine, and I highly recommend this book for reading. **As a man thinketh, so shall he be**. If you think about being poor, you will attract that energy. If you think about being rich, you will attract that energy. Do you know about the factor of de ja vue? You may have thought or dreamt about a thing, saw it in your mind's eye, and then the next thing you know it is present. The same way that you think about a person or think about talking to a person, and then you see the person, or the person calls you.

This is the same thing when it comes to positive imagery and forecasting. I want you to try it, try it on something small, don't trust me on face value, and put it to the test. Presently project an image in your mind, something light, by light I mean small time, minor. Think of a smell or a sound, think of a movie, this is practice. People who buy a certain car, turn around and begin to see the car everywhere. I laugh all the time when I hear people say that they bought, let's say, a Lexus. They bought the Lexus, because they did not see that particular Lexus anywhere, and they wanted to be unique. However, **once they purchase the Lexus, since it is now their car, they begin to see the same model Lexus everywhere**. The joke is on them.

Subconscious Conscious

This is the same way that you can focus the subconscious mind on something, through the present training of your conscious mind on something. **Read that again.** I suggest that you can change the object of your subconscious, suggestive, or subjective conscious which is also the seat of creation, through the active focusing on more positive, affluent situations or acquisitions. This is so real. I must add emphasis to this factor. If the mind can conceive it and believe it, the mind can achieve it. So, *conceive yourself coming into success*. See yourself coming into a new job, see yourself and your loved one overcoming obstacles in your relationship, and compromising into a state of blissful peace. See never arguing again with your parents, boss, or loved one, then work towards it actively, and watch as these tensions begin to subside. At least in degree of severity, until they cease to exist altogether.

Make It Physical

This is the point of creating what people refer to as a vision board. Replacing your current situation with the situation that you foresee as being your own. Even if you cannot quite visualize yourself there now, that is fine. I want you to expand your vision, see yourself in the scenery of your forecast. If you want to relax on a beach, take a mental image of it, then find a correlating physical picture of your image. Find it, draw it, cut it out of a magazine, and paste it onto a board and look at it. When we were young we used to do these things. We had no problem buying posters of things that we would like to have, and putting them on our walls.

Now the present realities that we have to deal with; work, bills, loss, stress, etc. have become so influential in our lives that we no longer *project*. We no longer imagine, we have lost our creative imagination, it has been arrested, along with our development, and we have become resigned. Resigned to what we call a dead-end job, resigned to poverty, lack and want, resigned to doing what we have to do, as opposed to *having what we would like to have*. It is a stunting process that we have taken on as our own. Usually this comes from being around people who complain all the time. 'I'll never have this', or 'I hate this job', or 'I wouldn't do it if I had the choice, but what other choices do I have'?

These outlooks have become our own, we enter into a job, get into or out of school, we have such big dreams, but we allow our dreams to become muddied with other's lack of dreams and aspirations, and we end up settling for less. This is the purpose behind the creation of a dream/vision board. To *replace our complacency* with cognitive activity. When you feed your mind with the food that it needs, it replicates what it sees. **The eyes are the mouth of the mind, and what we see, or focus on, is our mental diet.** It is very important to feed our minds with that which is good for us, the same way in that people diet to change their physical composition, we must go on a mental diet to change our present realities.

These are some of the things that we can do, in order to cease being sideline observers in our situation. When we begin to actively change the things that we think of, or look at, we become the creators of the backdrop to our lives. We set the stage for the play that is our lives. We are no longer idle in accepting things, but we become active participants and dictators of our lives, because that is the role that we were destined to have in our lives. Hence the saying, **your life is what you make it**. This is true.

Become Purpose Oriented

I challenge you, I challenge you to create your dream board, no matter how silly this may sound, this can be your first step in purpose orientation. I need you to return to the innocence of your childhood, this is the emotional part of it. Remember how emotionally driven your youth used to be? Remember how you just knew that when you grew up, you were going to have the big house, the two car garage, the grass was green, and the sky was a deep blue? Now it seems like the reality that has become yours is one of insurmountable debt, relationship troubles, and worries about the future. The grass has turned to brown dirt, or grey concrete, the car has become a leased car whose payments are tied to your neck, and the skies have become clouded with uncertainty. **I need you to release your present.**

I need you to release your present, and your future does too. **Release your present and embrace your future**, embrace your future situation, embrace your future position as the executive of whatever business allows your dream and passion to flourish. Embrace the pay grade that will allow you to spend more time with your family, your wife, nature and/or the things that bring you the most sense of fulfillment. *I need you to make peace with your present* no matter how hard the times may presently be, if you are reading this book it symbolizes the opportunity that is now yours to change. To change the present situation, into the desired future reality. Now that future can be later today, tomorrow, next week, month or year, the change begins once you begin to act on these things that you are learning. Create your vision board.

Physically - What you can physically do in these hard times is rid yourself of as many toxic circumstances as possible. Ask yourself, what are you doing now that you could improve upon? Are you working out, eating right, and remaining as healthy as possible? Are you keeping good wholesome company? Are you around company that subjects you to stress, arguments, and short sightedness? Are the people that you keep around you optimistic, or are they weak, and given to complaining all the time about what they do not have?

Power of Association

This area is the focal point of the sound advice to surround yourself with people who are doing the kinds of things that you want to be doing. The old adage that if you find yourself in a room with nine broke people, you're bound to be the tenth, holds true. You do not want to surround yourself with a toxic environment, and you want to cut out as much idleness as possible. Idle time should be filled with productive steps. Productive steps which take you closer to your goals and further away from your current situation. When you lay down to sleep, you should be pleased. Pleased in knowing that you are closer to your goals than you were when you woke up in the morning. If this is not the case, then you have some inventory to do.

What are you investing? This is not a trick question, even the people with no financial means have very substantial worthy investments that they could be making. What kind of investments can one make when one has no money? I'm glad that you asked, what do you have an abundance of, even when you have no money? It is something you were born with, something you do not know the limit to, and something that is completely under your control as to how you spend it? Have you guessed it? The answer is ... *time.*

What are you investing your time in? Do you watch a lot of TV? I should certainly hope not, especially if you are nowhere near where you would like to be. Do you spend time on social media? Who doesn't, right? I'll tell you who doesn't, people who are actively present in the mind state of achieving their goals, that's who doesn't. If you are reading, yes, I said reading. If you are reading, I'll say it a third time, *if* you *are* reading, *what* is it that you *are* reading? Are you reading the sports statistics? Who struck out, or triple doubled last night? All right, let me know how that is going to help you achieve your wants and dreams.

Energy is a Slave to Focus

If it is not going to help you achieve your wants and dreams, it is an irresponsible waste of time. Your energy is a slave to your focus. This is in the case of those who are not living the life that they want to live, those who are not successful...yet. Those who are not successful by their own measure should be actively present in the changing of their reality, not actively pursuing useless information about trivial things, as a way to escape from their mundane existence. If you were to educate yourself, if you were to invest in your mind and your thought process, if you became educated in these areas, you would be that much closer to living the life that you wish to someday have. **I applaud everyone who is reading this book.** This is a positive step in the right direction.

This shows that you are ready to begin the process of changing. Just being attracted to a book with this kind of title says to me that you are interested in learning something that you do not already know. So, let me tell you, your *time is the most precious asset* that you have on this earth. If not, why do you think there are trillions of dollars spent yearly trying to take your attention from other things? Every TV commercial that you see, every ad in the paper, every billboard, every email that is centered on soliciting, is based on the stealing of your time. It is estimated that if you spend time looking at car commercials, you will be *seduced into purchasing* a car, and from who? Whoever's ads are more effective, and the ones that you see the most of, that's who.

How Are You Investing the Majority of Your Time?

This is a science. Everyone wants your time, everyone wants you to spend more and more time with them. Mentally first, because wherever the mind leads, the body will catch on and follow. So, if you spend time watching TV for a certain amount of time, at some point you are going to become hungry, and if you've seen four McDonald's advertisements in teo hours, it is safe to estimate that when you get hungry you're going to be in the mood for a Big Mac. There are people who get paid millions of dollars to study the purchasing practices of the public. *Why do you think this is?*

This is because it is not an assumption or a hypothesis, this is a proven fact. If you invest time reading about how to think better and more effectively, then as a by-product of such learning you will assume a more enhanced thought process, just by default. Show me who you associate with and I'll show you who you are, it's simple. Where do you invest most of your time? Is it invested working to make someone else's dreams come true? Is someone else living a luxurious life due to your 40+ hour work week? Interesting, well tell me, **what are you doing with the *other 124?*** Are you upset that someone else is profiting so well from your work? While you receive no more than enough to barely show up for the next 40+ hour cycle with your shirt on – barely.

Who Profits From Your Peril?

This would be hard to believe unless you are spending the rest of your time to offset this situation. If you are in a relationship that could use some work, are you working, actively working, to make it better? How? Is it guess work, or are you reading? Receiving Coaching? Listening? Learning? Are you aware that students are investing years of education behind the notion that *you will never learn* the essentials on how to make your relationship work? It's true, they are doing what you refuse to. They are reading, and investing endless hours in school to become Divorce Attorneys, Marriage Counselors, and Marriage Therapists because they know that the field is lucrative. Why is the field lucrative? Because people refuse to read.

So how is your time invested? Who is your time invested with, and what is your time invested focused on? This is very important to anyone who is looking to get out of hard times. **Hard times, you may find is just a result of your misallocation of time.** I always wonder to myself, when I hear someone complain about they don't have enough money to do such and such, but they have no job. That is a misallocation of time. I always wonder when I hear someone complain they don't have enough time to enjoy their lives, and then they ask me if I'm on Facebook. This is a misallocation of time.

T + E = C

Time plus the energy put behind it equals change. I'm going to say it again. Time plus the energy invested behind it equals change. You can have anything in this world that you want, if you're willing to sacrifice the time and put some energy behind it. The criminal, and the engineer, both put time and energy into honing their craft. They may both be experts in their respective fields, so the third factor to consider is the area of focus where they are dedicating their time and energy. Ask yourself this, what am I focusing my time and energy on? Is it going to take me where I want to be in life? Is it going to put me into the seat in which I wish to sit? How long will this take, and *is it worth it?*

Are your dreams worthy of you going back to school? Are your dreams worthy of you learning a trade? Are your dreams worthy of you investing time and energy into acquiring a Coach or a mentor? I'm going to introduce a new idea to many people that they may not be expecting. I know I said time plus the energy put behind it equals change. Yes, I did. I know a couple of people read the beginning of this paragraph and said to themselves, "well, going back to school, learning a trade, and acquiring a coach all require money." You know what? You're *absolutely correct*. **The energy that I'm speaking of investing, along with the time in these cases, is money.**

Curren(t)cy

I know I lost some people, they are saying energy isn't money. Then why is it referred to in instances of curren(t)cy? Why would it be called currency, if there was no current? See some things require more *energy* than others. Riding a bike requires a certain amount of time and energy to learn. Performing brain surgery requires even more time, and a lot more energy (money, curren(t)cy) to learn. This is all based on what you are willing to sacrifice, or as Eric Thomas so eloquently states it, "How bad do you want it?"[14] Books cost money, well most of them do. If you're reading this on the internet, the power that fuels the internet system in your house is provided by a what? A current. This current takes what? Money! Ah, now we're arriving at an understanding.

What does your boss pay you for? You may think time. This is somewhat true. However, if you do not *perform* adequately on the job, will you retain the position? Not for long right? So is he paying you for your time, or is he paying you for your *energy*? Then, what exactly is he paying you for your energy and time, and why? This is a capitalist profit based society, so chances are, unless he's on his way out of business, your boss is paying you a certain amount for your time and energy, because he is able to make *more* money off of your time and energy than he pays you *for* your time and energy. Don't you wish you knew what he knew?

You want to know something? You can. You can learn exactly what he knows and more, if you were to more wisely invest your time and energy. It may require some money, there is nothing for free but air, and peace of mind. Education costs, a high standard of living costs more, of course it is going to cost you **time, energy, and money** to make the transition from where you currently are to where you want to be. How much time, energy and money? That is up to you, and you alone.

Wrap Up

How long is it going to take you to get out of the prerequisite hard time class? *Less than some and more than others*, no two situations or minds are the same. I may want to be a mixologist, you may want to be a brain surgeon. It would not take me as long to learn to make a mean, clean martini, as it would take you to learn how to perform a life-saving procedure. Does that make sense? Good. Still the answer is up to you. Hard times does not mean that you cannot find the money (energy) to invest in your times going from bad to good. It starts with stopping.

How does it start with stopping? The *beginning* of taking responsibility, is the *end* of being irresponsible. The beginning of investing in yourself is the end of wantonly wasting your resources. Remember, as a man thinketh – concentrate on the good, and good will come, focus on the goals, and the means will make themselves accessible. Many people who you would call successful today had no idea they would be where they are now, or how they would get there. They just had a picture in their mind, and they were **given the proper steps after taking the first**.

I'm going to say that again. *You may've missed it.* Many of the people that you would consider to be successful today had no idea they would be where they are now, or how they would get there. They just had a picture in their mind and they were *given* the proper steps after taking the first. Meaning they had another prerequisite I shall more thoroughly delve into later – Faith. That is not the focus here, the focus here is that someone, something, some *force* met them halfway. They were shown, or *given* the proper steps after taking the first steps. The first step is the what? Hardest. Especially when one is currently enduring hard times. Remember though, this is just a prerequisite class, and you won't believe what comes next.

CHAPTER 2

Failure

Now here we are, in the realm of a subject I know so much about. No seriously, I could write an endless tome on the art of failure, so large it would fill two libraries. This is something I am an expert on. I am a **certified authority** on the *art of failure*, so when you read this you can rest assured that you are reading literature from someone who knows what they are talking about. I am not going to go into particulars because I would turn this book into a five epic movie tirade. With that being said, I can't wait to delve into this subject material, it's like reading from *the back of my hand*.

Failure is a thing we all experience, some more than others, as I alluded to earlier. You are going to have to get you some of this in order to move forward. It is an acquired taste, of that be certain, but at the same time it is a good dish. This is because it is a humbling dish. It is required, it is a prerequisite. You do not know what you like, until you know what you do not like. You do not know what will work, until you are well aware of that which does not work. Be sure of this, you will not be able to succeed until well after you have weathered some failures.

Take Baby Steps

Imagine a baby trying to walk, those of you who have children know what I'm referring to. Children attempt to walk so many times before they actually get the art down pat, and even after they do you are going to be a witness to marvelous failures. Pay attention to what is taking place though, as you contrast this phenomena against your own attempts to walk on onto the stage of success. What is taking place is commonly referred to as the *learning curve*. The more steps, or the more failures that a child makes, the quicker it will be able to stand and walk on its own. I am reminded of a friend of mine, we share a common background, and when we entered into the realm of business, he stated that he, "couldn't wait to learn how to walk in this world."

New Experience Orientation

This was such a groundbreaking analogy for what we were attempting to do. Of course we could walk, but walking into a new world, or realm, is a situation in which one must do just that. We call it 'getting your legs under you'. I want you to envision a child trying to learn to ride a bike. How many times do they fail? Fall? End up scraped up, and crying? Just like the toddler expressing new strengths, they are always venturing further and further, and when they reach that new distance, hold on, because they are going to crash. *You* are going to crash.

Hopefully, you do not have to crash and burn, but even that is expected a couple of times on your road to glory. **You are going to have some miraculous fails**. Just when you think you've got it, *here it comes…wait for it…Wham!* Guaranteed. There is no exception to this rule, the only exceptions are the failures that no one wants to te ll you about. Observe the process and what happens though. Each time a child pulls away from its guardian and attempts to do it on their own, they are exhibiting a unique boldness. This is key.

The Process of Growth

Every time that they do it, much like ourselves, they are expecting victory. Each time that we begin a new process on the path to success, we expect to succeed and when we go...*Wham!* it's painful. We have to lick our wounds and we may tear up a bit, depending on who saw us fall and how much we invested, but it is to be expected. You cannot expect to fly without learning how to first run, we can't run without first walking, and we will not learn how to walk without busting our lips a couple of times. *Some more than others.*

Now this is what you want to be careful not to do. We don't want to get scared or give up. I have seen some 4 -5 year olds in strollers, because they don't want to learn to walk, they always want someone to carry them. Have you ever seen a large child being carried by their parent, who starts to cry when the parent tries to put them on the floor? You do not want this to be you. You don't want to grow fearful of exploration or the attempt taking process.

It is going to hurt, but get back up on the proverbial horse, *at all costs*, because you want to take immediate advantage of all the information you have gathered. Every time a baby falls, it learns something that does not work. Ok, so sticking my leg out this far and tucking the other one under that ankle there is a no-no. Once you have that knowledge down pat, with a busted lip to keep you mindful and honest, chances are you are not going to fail the exact same way twice. So your chances for success are greatly enhanced by this learning experience. **Therefore, failure = learning experience.**

What is the Definition of Insanity?

Some are more hard headed than others, and they have to learn the same thing over and over again until they are convinced that it is not going to work….*that way*. Do you know someone like this? So hard headed and stubborn that they continue to do the same thing over and over again, the same way, expecting different results? Have you ever heard that this is the definition of insanity? **Doing the same thing and expecting different results**, is the classic explicit definition of insanity. The point is that every time that you fall, you are going to learn lessons that you cannot pay for out of your pocket. *Failure is priceless*, if you have not experienced any, you better go get you some.

Without failure you will not be able to define success, or recognize it, if you were to see it. It is by the clear distinction of knowing what failure is, that we are able to properly discern success. Failure is essential to the process of the attainment of success, it is a prerequisite. If the child never attempts to walk, thereby failing, it will never learn to walk. It just will not happen without this crucial stage. This is the way that it is done, and there is no getting around it. So get used to it and accept it for what it is. It is a given.

UNDERSTANDING

To fail is to understand. To understand what? To understand that which does not work. When you understand what does not work, you are going to try another way at achieving your success. You get closer to obtaining your goals every time that you fail. Failure is not a permanent thing, unless you make it permanent. To meet with temporary failure does not insinuate permanent defeat. *To accept permanent defeat is not honorable, whereas to try and to fail is honorable.* It shows that you are on the path, and as long as you stay steadfastly upon the path, that in and of itself is success.

Initiation

Think of any undertaking, like writing your name. Try to remember when you were in school and you had to learn how to write your name. At first you could not hold the crayon, marker, pencil, or whatever instrument you were initially taught to write your name with. First you had to become accustomed to gripping the instrument correctly. What did that take? It took practice. It takes practice to properly hold a writing instrument, no matter what hand you write with.

No one starts out perfectly doing anything. There are learning curves. Some children drop the pencil, some press too hard and rip the paper. I look at some people's handwriting to this day and they are grown, and still have not mastered the art of penmanship, that is fine. Whenever I have to get a check-up, I cannot, for the life of me, understand the doctor's scrawl. I am sure that others can relate to what it is that I am saying. These people have become very successful, though their handwriting is still, for the most part, illegible.

So let's follow this analogy for some time, bear with me, this is rudimentary. Do you remember writing your name over and over again? Can you recall having to write your name on it, over and over again, perhaps two or three times across, skip a line, the same three names, skip a line and so forth? Every line got better and better, every line and every paper started to actually resemble your name, *somewhat*. More and more, until you began to actually be able to write your name comfortably with no assistance. **Success follows this very same process.**

Repetition Deepens the Impression

You are going to have to start over and over again in life. You are going to commit to an undertaking, and it is going to look terrible, because you do not know what you are doing, especially if it your first foray into the endeavor. You are going to stink at it. *Terribly.* You are going to resemble that infant trying to stand on rickety knees. Your plan for success is going to be well thought out, so you think, until you make some progress, back up and take a look, and it looks like that child trying to write its name for the first time. It's going to make no sense at all.

The next attempt at success will be better than the first, and so on, and so on, until you begin to crack the surface. Do you know that it is said, that it takes some 10,000 hours to be able to assert *mastery* in any given area? Yes, 10,000 hours. Do you know what that equates to? 10 years. 10 years of trying to do something, should garner you competent proficiency in any given field of study. Even when you learn something on a surface level, this is like writing your first name correctly and then being given your last name to write after it. *Whoa*, a whole new situation. You must then begin the process over.

This is what learning is, this is just what it is like. So you get to the point where you have your first and last name down pat, and you're proud, and then the teacher says, "That's great Johnny now we're going to learn how to write a full sentence." Whoa, a whole new situation. This is the process of life, first you learn the basics, basically what does not work, so that you can begin the process of learning what does.

The better someone is at grasping this concept, the quicker they are going to be able to accept the prerequisite failures, and by default the quicker they will begin to realize success. It is said that the prize is in the process, and not the actual attainment of any goal. This is due to *the process being the place where you learn* such valuable life lessons. This is why every successful person sounds like a sage and reservoir of wisdom. It was not the actual success that makes them sound this way. It is the process that they had to go through, that changes their state, and leaves them with such indispensable insights.

God is in the Details

The prize is in the details. Many people have to go on to succeed in another area, after the attainment of the initial goal, because it is in the striving that they actually feel the most alive. To have arrived is good, it's a great feeling, but where do you go from there? If you discontinue learning, you discontinue *growing*. This is why some people can never feel like they have learned enough to quit school. They go all the way to Ph. D, because they can not see themselves at a time when they have stopped learning. These are people who have fallen in love with the *process*.

Get Acquainted

I welcome failure, it is my close friend. I alluded earlier to how long we have been acquainted. There was a time when failure was recognized as my twin brother, always lurking in the shadows, ready to come and sweep me off of my feet whenever I thought I had been planted on solid ground. Now I like to be challenged. My wife calls me an enthusiast for all things. She says I *have to* have a project, if there is none to have, or no reason to have one, I will create one. For me, it is life! Without failure, there is no growth. If you are not encountering failure, then you have become resigned to a safe zone. I dare you to stretch.

The analogy that comes to mind in reference to a stunted growth, is the *over-protective* parent. The parent who does not allow the child to venture out into higher learning. The sheltering and protective, burdensome parent who always calls the child's name, and comes and catches them, before they were about to fall on their face and learn a valuable lesson. This parent robs the child of knowledge, they rob them of information gathering, they rob them of learning, and if they do it too long they *rob them of spirit*.

Deer in the Headlights

How many people know someone who does not like anything about their job, relationship, current status in life, or the state that they are in, but make no moves whatsoever to venture forward? This is fear. Fear of the unknown. The results of stunted growth, many times it is the fear of the overprotective parent that the child has absorbed and made their very own. This is one of the saddest things to encounter. This person is afraid of failure, and a person who is afraid of failure has no chance to ever encounter success, because they refuse to detach themselves from their comfort zone.

These people make statements like, "this is all I know", or "this is all I've ever done." There is a big wall, seemingly insurmountable, between them and their dreams. Sometimes these people do not even *have* dreams they have become so conditioned. They are malleable, and easily impacted. I do not mean anything negative by it, this is just information. If this sounds like you, then you need to practice breaking the tether.

We cannot change the way that we were raised, but once we become responsible for ourselves it is time to evaluate the values that we were brought up with. If they make sense to you and allow for personal enrichment, that is fine, but if they leave a sense of longing and fear of the unknown, it is our responsibility to take responsibility for ourselves, because we are no longer children and there is only us to blame.

Hero Area

Imagine for a second if the Wright brothers had been too fearful of failure to try. If you're too afraid to fly then this will not resonate with you, but for the rest of us, imagine it. Imagine how many times they failed in their lives, trying to give life, or *flight*, to their vision. There are those who only achieve the success of the process, and the actual attainment of their dreams are fulfilled by someone who takes ownership of the vision long after they are dead and gone. The one who fulfilled the dream gets the credit, but he stands on the shoulders of those who started. Those who never gave up, those who were willing to push the envelope no matter the cost. **Can you see that this is the hero area?**

The Hero area is reserved for those who never give up, enduring failure after failure, because they had in their possession another prerequisite that we will expand on later. A prerequisite to success called *Belief.* They believed that it was worth it, to dedicate their time and efforts, their energy and their money to something that they failed to do, many times over. That did not stop them, they never betrayed their belief, and they stayed true. Then someone, maybe a generation or two behind them comes and tweaks their model and *look at us now*, we have flight!

Back to the Drawing Board

What is a common saying after failure? "Back to the drawing board." This is the refinement process, where faulty reasoning is purged and new found knowledge is implemented, resulting in the birth of new possibilities. This is the arena of great minds and will, that do not know discouragement, who do not accept defeat, and call setbacks by another name… *understanding*. This is the process of evolution. The evolution of an idea is a breathtakingly beautiful thing. This is known by any proud parent who has watched their child go from not knowing how to walk or talk, to teaching their own children how to walk, and waiting for them to talk. This is the beauty of life. There is nothing like it. Failure is a prerequisite.

Did I mention that failure is priceless? There are things that are of immense value, such as education, that require vast amounts of energy expenditure and sacrifice, that can be bought. Training courses can be purchased, and paid for, but have you ever heard that there are things that you learn through *experience*, that cannot be taught in the classroom? This is true. You never know if something sticks unless you throw it against the wall. I can remember being told by a supervisor of mine that, "**when you take the test, you want to answer the questions with the knowledge that you learned in school, not what you have learned on the job.**" That is because they are two entirely different things.

Teaching vs. Training

There is knowledge of an educational background, and then there is knowledge of an experiential nature. Which one would you base your children's lives on, if a car swerves in front of you, and you have to make a split hair decision? No question, right? I am not going to defer to what the driving manual says, as opposed to what I learned from the last time a similar situation took place, because the writer of the driving manual was speaking theoretically. There is an inherent difference between knowledge of a theoretical nature and that of an applicable nature. If you pause to recall what is stated in the manual, that may be all the time it takes to wipe yourself off of the face of the Earth. *I defer to application.*

Don't get me wrong, the educational prepares you for the experiential, the theoretical prepares you for the applicable. Look at it like this, let's break it down. You spend 12 years in formal education. This is grade school. From there you graduate into undergraduate learning for 4 more years. Then you graduate and go on to graduate school, this is learning, this is education. Then when you graduate from there you get what is referred to as *training*. Different ball game entirely. This, many times, takes place as an on-the-job internship, to prepare you to make the transition from school, into the field of your choice, and active *practice*.

Active Practice

Do you know why this takes place? Because there are things, there are situations, that are going to present themselves on a job, that no book in any level of education are going to adequately inform you on how to handle correctly. This is why your training is provided under the tutelage of one who has so and so many years on the job, a supervisor, not a teacher. Do you know what you are expected to do during your internship? You are expected to fail, over and over again, because it is a learning process. A learning curve designed to take you from an **educational perspective, to an experienced perspective.**

Through this period of constant failure you are able to refine your *understanding* of what to apply, when, and what to let fly. The people on the job know that you are going to fail, that you are guaranteed to fail! This is why you are under constant supervision so that you do not kill anyone in the process of learning. The people who do not go too far in life are the ones who are too rigid to learn, and the ones who are *afraid to fail*. Those people do not venture far into the world, and they stay in the comfort of the familiar. **The thing with the familiar is that it is a certain size, there is not much space for growth in the comfort of the familiar.**

To become great, you are going to have to venture beyond the boundaries of the safe and secure, you are going to have to *take some risks*. Like the baby learning how to walk, if left to its own nature it will attempt this on its own. It is the stifling from the outside that counters this otherwise natural process. A child can be taught, let's say *conditioned*, not to explore, but by nature the child is an explorer. Everything that it sees, it wants to hold. Everything that it gets into its hands goes where? That's right, everything that a child gets into its hands goes straight into its mouth.

Now I'm not saying to let a child touch an open stove, or swallow Clorox, though I'm not sure how a child would get its hands onto a bottle of Clorox if the home is properly child proofed. What I am saying is be mindful, be mindful of the future, and that your child is going to have to find its way one day without you. Do not destroy their imagination, do not make it fearful and clingy. I feel like telling women to put their children down all the time, take that baby out of the stroller, *let them run, let them play, let them learn, let them live!*

The Proverbial Inch Gained

Relax, they are going to be alright, the learning is going to take place. It is going to hurt you more than it is going to hurt them, because they are going to be right back up, wiping their tears, dusting themselves off and trying again. This is what they have to do in life. Imagine Henry Ford, imagine if Henry Ford's mother would have stifled his imaginative nature, if she would have held him close, not let him venture, and not let him fail. We may still be using horse drawn carriages to go to and fro. People, please do not be afraid to fail, get good at it. Fail constantly, as much as you can, because *for every failure there is a proverbial inch gained.*

For every failure there is a new groove born in the brain physically. Once you have experienced or learned something it cannot be un-learned. It is your property, your intellectual property that you can now draw upon for reference in times of need. What you may not be aware of, is that while you go forward from failure to failure, or from unful-filled venture to unrealized success, is that you are actively partaking in the creation of your blueprint. You are drawing out the diagnostics for your success as you fail – as long as you do not throw in the towel there is promise.

The Promise

There is promise in showing up. Showing up is priceless. Who do you know of, who is successful, that could have won, had they not shown up? I agree. Not a one. Therefore, if you are consistently showing up, you are halfway there. **You just need to iron out some rudimentary particulars.** This is the part that can cause some to forsake the path, because it is so mundane. It *hurts* to be in the arena, but in the back row, or the nosebleed section, concealed by obscurity. What you need to realize however, is that everyone that you know of, who defines what the meaning of success is to you, started in those nosebleed seats. With every failure they gained ground. With every temporary setback they moved *up* a seat, *over* a seat. They worked their way to the front and center stage, by fail and recovery, over and over again. So take pride in your failure. You're in the arena.

The Story of The Miners

Your time is coming, no one but you can deny yourself of that hard fought victory that belongs to you. It is yours for the taking, you are but one or two failures away from glory. Do not stop now. I saw a cartoon depiction once that tells this story perfectly. I love these things because of the simplicity with which an artist can capture such a stunning, and sometimes painful, reality. The cartoon I saw was of two Miners. One Miner is digging a tunnel, above the other Miner who is also digging a tunnel. The two miners are unaware of each other, but they are both mining for diamonds. You see the diamonds available for the Miner on top maybe two to three pickaxe swings away.

The Miner on top is closer than the other, but he has turned away in disgust. I guess each of his failed swings has *taken the fight out of him*, so he is no longer persisting in the face of the resistance, and he has turned away. He is walking the opposite direction from the diamonds that are only two swings away from his acquisition, with the pickaxe over his shoulder and a look of disgust, and defeat on his face. The Miner under him gives no signs of slowing down or stopping, you can see sweat dripping from his brow and he is furiously swinging the pickaxe.

I don't know how heavy those pickaxes are, but this one *looks heavy*, and the Miner has a certain confident look of determination about him. He's actually further away from the diamonds that the Miner who has given up was, but he is continuing his fight. He correctly sees each fruitless swing of the pickaxe, not as a failure but a success, because it's bringing him closer to the goal, and he is correct. The picture is depicted in a way to make the reader understand, that the Miner who is persistent is the one who is going to inevitably retrieve the treasure, while the one who has given up could have been the one to lay claim to untold riches, had he just stayed the course and been able to weather the adversity of 2 – 3 more swings. The caption simply states to: **Never Give Up.**

Then there is another one, almost the same as the first one, except there is no competition. This cartoon is of one Miner, same pickaxe, same diamond patch, the only thing with this cartoon is that the wall between the Miner and the diamonds look so thin all he would need to do is kick the wall, *all of the hard work has already been done.* But instead he has resigned. He has given up and is on his way in the other direction. The depiction with this cartoon states: '**You never know how close you are...Never give up on your dreams**'.

The Principle

I love these cartoons, because they give such a resounding voice to what I am trying to convey. One never knows how truly close they are until they give up, once they give up they know how far they are from their dreams. They are so far that they will obviously never reach their goals, because no matter how close they were they have ceased all efforts. You never know whether you are going to win or not until you quit. That action of quitting is resolute. It is an absolute certainty that you will never win once you quit. That you can bet on. **Quitting must never be an option.**

Have you ever heard that it is better to have loved and lost, than never to have...can you finish the statement? Never to have... *loved at all.* If one is so fearful of failure, that they never try, then why try anything. Understand that the *gift of experience* is the one thing that we are definitely meant to have in this life. I don't know what your faith is, and that is not my concern, however, if you believe in anything, you have to believe that we were given life to *live.* To experience, to enjoy, to love, to lose, to win, to fail, etc. This is life. Fear will keep you from the experience of the purpose of your existence. Of course you are going to lose.

The First Loss

What is the first thing you will lose in life? Think about it. The first thing that we lose when we come into this world is the security of our mother's womb. Was it intentional? Was it meant to happen? I *believe* so, as I've never seen it happen any other way. What is the last thing we lose? Our own lives. We die. Is it intentional? I *believe* so, as I've never seen it happen any other way. What do we win, or gain when we lose our mother's womb? We get the prize of life. What do we win, or gain when we lose our lives, that is up to you to determine for yourself.

My point is what's the worst that can happen when we fail? What is the worst thing that can happen, that we actually *learn* something? We may get hurt, it may make you sore for a little while, that is alright, it will subside. It is supposed to be painful, by the way, to remind you not to do it again. **Your victory, your success, is drawing you towards itself, the same way you are drawing yourself towards your success.** In order for this thing to work, you're going to have to have some reminders along the way of wrong directions and danger.

The Purpose of Scars

This is the purpose of scars. What do people refer to when they think of scars? I can remember a scar I received long ago from being somewhere I had no business being, and doing something I had no business doing. You know what my mother said about the scar? She said it was *'character defining'*, and you know what? She was right. It defined my character enough so, that I made sure that I was never present to receive the same kind of scar, from doing the same thing, in the same place, or anywhere that resembled it, for that matter. It served me, as a reminder. **This is what failure does for you, it provides you with a point of reference. It bestows upon the receiver the gift of understanding.**

AWARENESS ENHANCEMENT

The part of failure that is the most essential is its *inherent awareness enhancement component*. You see failure has a way of automatically enhancing one's awareness immediately. You *know* that something must be done when the repo men show up for your car. Why? Because whatever you thought was going to be the mechanism, by which you were going to pay your car note failed. This failure will enhance your awareness that something else must be done, in real time.

Enter: Complete Failures

What I am going to do here for this segment is to enhance your awareness about some pretty lousy ideas, and complete total losses, created by some very famous and equally successful people I know you will have no problem recognizing. If, by any chance, you do not know the person by name you will know what they are famous for, and where they found their success, and the fact that they *absolutely aced* the prerequisite class for failure before they graduated on to the University of Success. This is not with the intent of revealing people's dirty laundry, as a matter of fact, the majority of this information is widely public record.

So let us begin with someone everybody knows and loves, Mr. Bill Gates. You know Mr. Bill Gates as one of the founders of Microsoft. You know, the computer software that is the powerhouse software behind the Windows program? Yes, that Microsoft. Heard of this fellow, correct? Very good, what you may not know about though, is Traf-O-Data. Traf-O-Data was an idea and creation, that Bill and his partner Paul Allen came up with. Before they came up with Microsoft, they had Traf-O-Data.

Traf-O-Data failed miserably. This failure was used as an awareness enhancement tool. "Bill had contracted with a company that measured traffic patterns by counting the car wheels that ran over pressure-sensitive rubber tubes".[1] The plan was to sell this data to the government, but they just couldn't get it to work right. Later, Bill Gates *dropped out* of Harvard University. It was after these two failures that Bill Gates and Paul Allen would come together, yet again, and with their awareness enhanced by the Traf-O-Data failure, they created Microsoft, and the rest is history.

Bill Gates and Paul Allen have created one of the most innovative stand-alone programs that have become a household name across the world. Bill has gone on to become a leading spokesman for independent thought, and has become a philanthropist, donating millions of dollars to different charities that benefit millions of people. Now my question is, have you ever heard of Traf-O-Data? If you have not had to do a school project on Bill Gates, and are not into the independent study of successful entrepreneurs and their history, probably not. What if he would have been scared of failing, or paralyzed with fear after having failed so miserably? The world would be different. This man has been said to have a net worth of 79.2 billion dollars. Food for thought.

We learn from our mistakes. One of the primary differences between a person, if that person is striving for success, and a certified success story, is that the person striving has not failed enough yet. He still has some failing to do, so if this sounds like you, if you are not successful, get out there and get some failures under your belt. I don't mean to go out there shooting for failure, always expect to win, and put forth the best possible effort, and you'll know when you've crossed that failure finish. How will you know? When you've learned from enough failures to put together something that people need, and something that they are willing to pay for, then you will be successful. Use Bill's story for motivation, if he would have never learned what he needed to from the failure of Traf-O-Data, he would have never created Microsoft. What will *you* create?

K. F. (Failure) C.

Have you ever had one of those 15 piece family meals from Kentucky Fried Chicken? How about the biscuits and fries? Those were my favorite, man…with some butter and grape jelly. You know what that was right? That was the fruit of failure. The Colonel as you know him, or Harland David Sanders was an immense failure. So much so that he failed at getting backing for his now infamous recipe for chicken and secret sauce recipe, *more* than 1 thousand times. That's right, 1 thousand plus times he walked into an office, gave his presentation, and 1 thousand plus times he was shown the exit, with no money or deal to show for it.

KFC states that 'The Colonel" traveled with his secret sauce mixture in his car looking for partners, now that's tenacious. Those were pretty hard times, and here was a man who was destined not to take the word 'no' seriously. Regardless to how many times he failed, he continued on with a desire and an expectation in his heart that he would be vindicated. They didn't know what they were talking about, and I'm sure he told them just that on more than one of those thousand plus meetings. He was 65 years old when he finally failed enough to be granted permission into the University of Success[2].

Now, I don't want to say, "Here's an old man", but here is an older man, willing to look temporary defeat in the face and label it justly. He did not whine and moan, he did not quit and drop his pickaxe, he was carried on by his faith, and from every failed meeting, he *innovated his presentation from the information* he had obtained through that experience. Once a man has learned every way how not to do something, by having his awareness enhanced consistently, he's going to get it right. Personally, I'm glad he did get it right, I used to be in love with those butter biscuits and gravy!

Recognize the name Rowland Hussey Macy? How about the MACY*S department store, are you familiar with that? Yes? Great, did you know that the MACY*S on 34th street in downtown Manhattan, New York was his fifth store? All of the first four failed, and failed miserably. His first store was opened in Massachusetts, and there was no high demand so the lackluster sales did him in. That time, and the following three times was the prerequisite. Finally, the lessons he was learning kicked him into an *enhanced state of awareness*, and he realized what he needed was prime real estate.

He tried the old road over and over again, failing each time between the years of 1843 and 1855. He never gave up though, he never quit, and he never allowed his failures to become his forecast, as they became his *rear view image*. He continued to learn until it clicked, I mean four times in a row? That would give most dedicated people doubts. This is the point of failure, it will test you, and if put in the proper context and perspective, it will teach you. I think the flagship store and subsequent massive success is the product of some pretty serious learning[3]. What do you think?

Detroit Automobile Company

Who remembers Detroit Automobile Company? You remember, they came out with that new black ... no, I'm just joking. They didn't come out with anything. Well, they didn't come out with anything that was received as acceptable, what they did do was close their doors in 1901. The Detroit Automobile Company was the first automobile company that Henry Ford had. Yes, the great Henry Ford of the Ford Motor Company had to go through the prerequisite class of failure 101 as well. As a matter of fact, he enrolled a couple of times[4].

The key to sales is to become the voice of the market. Mr. Henry Ford was deaf to the voice of the market, and so he did not meet his market's demand. He made cars that people felt were much too expensive and of low quality. So he had to close his doors a couple more times, before he could get a passing grade on his fourth attempt, which we now know as the Ford Motor Company. I hope you are seeing a pattern here. Most companies fail within their first 90 days, the majority of the rest in their first 2 years, and more than half of those that are left over in their first 5.

You can however, *change the world*. You can however, succeed *beyond* your wildest imaginations and make your name become a household brand, talked about at dinner tables for centuries to come, if you but allow yourself to fail enough times. Have mercy on yourself, you already failed, **why quit on top of that**? Why not get what you came for? What's the worst that can happen? You, fail? I thought that happened already. Get over it. If these people I have provided, as an example to edify the credibility of the failure prerequisite to success, prove anything to you, they should prove that it can be done. Against all odds it can be done. Do it!

Swimming With the Sharks

Mark Cuban is the owner of the Dallas Mavericks, and TV personality on the Shark tank series. He is also a businessman, author, film producer, investor and philanthropist. In 1999 he sold his Broadcast.com video portal to Yahoo for 5.7 billion dollars. Yes, Million, with a B. Before this, however, he was an avowed failure. Mark states that he failed as a cook, failed as a carpenter, and had a brief stint as a waiter. He states that he failed in that arena due to his inability to open a wine bottle.

He is very successful now, by anyone's judgement, and he spends his time pretty much as he pleases. He has learned very much from his prior failures, and he gives them credit for his present day successes. In his own words, "I've learned that it doesn't matter how many times you failed. **You only have to be right once.** I tried to sell powdered milk. I was an *idiot* lots of times, and I learned from them all[5]." Right on Mark!

Listen, I am not making the power of the prerequisite class of failure up. This is proven time and time again, by the most successful people we know of today. There are no exceptions to this rule. **True success finds the dedicated,** it finds those who want it, and it finds who is willing to go to bat for it. Success is like a woman, if you are willing to fight for her, and give all you have for her, she will be yours. It may not be easy to get her, there may be a lot of chasing, courting, and flirting in the preliminary stages, but if you are willing to demonstrate that she means enough to you, for you to endure some trials, and temporary failures, in the end *she will be yours.* How bad do you want it? What are you willing to give? What are you willing to do?

Disney World

How about fail? Are you willing to fail as in the cases of the examples I've given, are you still not convinced? Let's look at the case of Walt Disney, one of my favorites, since I've grown up on his movies and characters. Well, did you know that Walt Disney was a high school dropout? Yes, he dropped out of high school. So don't think just because you failed a few classes, or dropped out of high school, that you have to fail at *changing the world*. No, the choice to leave your mark on the world is yours to make, and the chance to change the world is yours to take. It's just going to require some failure on your part. Let's go further into this.

Walt Disney was once fired by an editor who said he, get this, "lacked imagination, and had no original ideas[6]". Whoa! How wrong was that guy? Now, had Walt allowed that to discourage him from moving forward, there would be no Mickey, Donald, or Goofy. Another failure was his first animation studio. In this venture he committed absolute failure after failure, but he learned, and got better from every single one. Eventually he had to shut the doors, and he went bankrupt. Walt is responsible for so many first attempts it is shocking because, as you know, most first attempts end up in failure.

I want to go through some. In his first studio one of his productions included a human going into a cartoon world. It was a little girl. At this time the common theme was for cartoon characters to roll off of the page that they were drawn on, and interact with humans in a human world. Well, Walt tried to do the exact opposite and he paid for it, he failed. No one was interested, and it was shortly thereafter that he went bankrupt. However, when he failed he came back in the same field with improvements to his *understanding*. It was after this that he came up with Mickey, well actually *Mortimer* was the name of the mouse character he had created, until his wife saved him from failure, and convinced him that the name Mickey would be more marketable than a mouse named Mortimer. What do you think?

Walt was the first voice of Mickey, and he said he created these productions on a shoestring budget. Soon thereafter he had a hunch to add color to what was to become the first animated cartoon in color. That was a success. To try something so revolutionary and new, *again*, so shortly after failing speaks to his relentless lack of fear. This cartoon actually won him an academy award. The first academy award *ever presented* to anyone for an animated picture.

Here's another example of the fear of failure being non-present in the minds and hearts of the innovative. He wanted to produce a full length film. His peers and advisors laughed at the idea and tried to dissuade him. He would not hear of it, and later came out with Snow White. Full blown success, he chose to follow that with Cinderella, another full blown, stratospheric, smash success story. He followed that up with Alice in Wonderland, and people hated it. He stated that it 'did a complete nosedive'. What he learned from that was that in order to be successful, the character he created had to be *full of heart* in order to galvanize the public. From then on, it seems he fell into a stream of successes culminating in the creation of the infamous Disney World, where everyone in the world wants to go after a successful accomplishment.

Almost Losing Virginity

I want to talk to you now for a moment about Richard Branson. If you don't know who Richard Branson is, that may be your first problem. No, I'm joking, but seriously, **if you want to succeed it would be wise to learn all that you can about those who have become successful.** So, Richard Branson is the owner of Virgin Group, which is a consortium of about 200 companies. Virgin has recently come out with a mobile phone line, and Virgin Galactic, which is a space tour rocket ship company, it's just miraculous the thoughts that can be put into action, and the lives that can be lived, if there is no fear of failure.

Richard has also heralded the Virgin Megastores, Virgin Record Company that had stars like Culture Club and the Rolling Stones, as well as Virgin Atlantic Airline Company and Voyager Group, which was a terrestrial travel company. Richard also however, before realizing all of his successes, had a nice amount of failures to lead him to the promised land of entrepreneurship. He once *rode a tank* into Times Square, Manhattan, to challenge Coca Cola to a square off with his Virgin Cola, which failed miserably.

Richard has also come out with a line of Bridal shops entitled Virgin Brides. I don't know if it was the name or something, but that idea did not end up flying. Understand when people who have enjoyed success fail at something, it usually costs them at least hundreds of thousands of dollars, if not millions. I say this to express that there is more at risk to lose than just '*face*', when they fail, and still they are well aware that it is a prerequisite of success. So you will see them do it over and over again, without fail! As a matter of fact, he has some words to say about the different view on failure taken the world round.

Richard stated in an interview, "In Britain, people who try things and then fail are actually well-respected. People like the underdog[7]". After which point he goes on to admit several failures, one being actually sinking in a ship on his first voyage, while testing his first vessel. He says he was literally saved by men on a banana boat. Still he concludes with, "But it was things like that, where we tried and *failed*, that put Virgin on the map, gave it a sexier image than our bigger rivals, and turned us into an adventurous company and brand[8]".

In some instances it is best to let the people behind the situations edify it for themselves, "At Virgin, we don't spend much time regretting the past, and we don't let mistakes or failures get to us, and we certainly don't fear failure[9]". This is Branson after being asked how he felt about his lackluster decision to take on the Heavyweight Soft Drink Champion of the World, in Coca-Cola. I generally do not like to use quotes as often as I have in the case of Richard Branson, but this is one case example where I cannot say it better that those who I am referencing, so in the case of when Richard left high school. Oh, yes, he dropped out at the age of 16. When he did his headmaster (British equivalent of a principle) wrote to him and said, among other things, "**Congratulations, Branson. I predict that you will either go to prison or become a millionaire[10]**". Luckily, we see how it turned out!

Numbers Don't Lie

This man is a prime example of how we cannot be fearful of that which feeds us. We should eat experiences, we should dine on disasters, we should study our moments of stupidity and take notes, so that we never fail the same way twice. See, therein would lie a problem. Have you ever heard, fool me once, shame on you, and fool me twice, shame on me? I will not be met by the Messenger of Misery because I went down the same wrong road the same way again. It just won't happen. It will take something new to trip me up, every time, and I'll keep coming until I figure them all out.

Hopefully you can see the importance of failure from the examples I've provided. Do not, by any means take my word for it, but I would definitely listen to a combined real time net worth of over **490.4 Billion dollars**. Numbers don't lie, and neither does real success, they validate, and edify one another. The stories detailed here can be found with the speed of lightning, just look for it. The point of this was to introduce you to a class that you are going to have to take. That is, if you want to succeed in life.

Summary

You do not have to want to become a billionaire. That is not what success is measured by. **Success is not measured by money.** Success defined means the accomplishment of an aim or purpose[11]. That aim for you may look like a healthy marriage, the purpose may be more time with the kids, or beating an illness, obtaining financial freedom, etc. In writing this, I present an accumulation of right information, based on intense study and experience. These are 7 Prerequisites to Success in whatever arena you choose. You *will* bump into these, each one of them, at one point or another on your way to the glory.

Before we close this subdivision, I would like to speak on why people are afraid to fail, why they are afraid to take chances that could bring them success ultimately. It is fear, *fear of what others* will think. *Fear of who's* going to know that they failed. *Fear of being* laughed at, this is such a vain society. People are always preoccupied with the way in which they appear to other people, who couldn't care less anyway. This is why everyone is up to their eyebrows in debt. They are fearful of what others with think of them if they exercise economic education, which is delayed gratification. They are scared to jump into possibility with both feet, because they are *afraid of* what *others* will say or think if they fail. They may be embarrassed.

SO WHAT?

o what if we fail? So what if people think that we are slightly off, or out of our realms because we do something that they cannot see the genius in? Does that mean that there is something wrong with us? *Or them?* I have only the clues I have found, and what I have found is that everyone that has some genius in them, was at one time labeled by low achievers as out of their minds, or crazy. Some still are labeled this way after having achieved success. What if you choose to stop because of others perceptions? **That is being scared to live, because you are worried about what others** *perceive.*

Who is Qualified to Judge?

Are we all aware of what color blindness is? Color blindness is defined as: *"A defect in perception of colors, caused by a deficiency of certain specialized cells in the retina that are sensitive to different colors*[12]*"*. Again, I asked in the preceding paragraph, who was wrong for the labels cast upon some by others. The one who wears the label, or the one who stigmatizes. We learn from the definition of color blindness that there is a defect. There is a defect caused by a deficiency of specialized cells, cells that are *sensitive.* If I am wearing a green shirt, and you call it black, because that is how you perceive it, *I am not the one in error.* I'm going to make a connection here.

Let's say we are in school, I love to use the school analogy, because we are always in a learning setting no matter where we are. So here we are in school, and let's suppose a classmate catches your eye. They catch your eye, and they are attractive to you. You do not know, or question *why* they are attractive to you, you just know how you feel. So you introduce yourself to them, and you go on a date later in the week. Of course, no one knows because you met in a school setting, and it is no one's business.

Now let's say that you have gone on a series of dates for several months, and now you're sure that they are the one that you want to have in your life, for the rest of your life. You get along so well, they are so caring. You feel like the qualities of this person will enhance, and add on to your own set of qualities, and that if you could just combine the two, or be able to draw reference from the other, there would be no denying either of you. You can realize your desires, wants and dreams, and you see a beautiful future together. Now let's propose you have some friends and family with whom you share your aspirations, so you let them in on this info. Let us now say that their collective mouths drop.

Their collective mouths drop, and they say, "You can't be talking about that person, that SKINNY person!" "*Oh no*", they go on to berate people who are slim figured, and have nothing nice to say. They go on to explain to you that you are so much better looking than they are, and that you are judged by the physical qualities of the people you keep around you. So if you are with them, and they are perceived as unattractive, that will make you unattractive as well. What do you do?

How Does This Relate?

Here is the analogy. You have a dream, a desire, a longing, and a gut instinct. Something you feel like you should be doing. Convention, however, will tell you not to make any sudden moves, *convention will* *tell you not to stray from the well-worn path.* Convention, will tell you that you are crazy, that you're chasing something that cannot be caught. They will tell you how many countless thousands before you tried and failed, and that you couldn't possibly be better than all of them. They will go as far as to tell you that you are destined to fail, and if you even continue to pursue this dream they will disassociate with you.

This is where we allow others to *influence* us, and by default, **we allow them to write our story**. I know that a biography is intended to be done by the person whose life is under the lens, or at least at the bequest of the person whose life is under the lens. I could not write anyone's biography, accurately, but my own, or maybe someone else's with their guidance word for word. I could not interject my own beliefs or suppositions into someone else experiences. *Why do we let other people's perceptions, write our biographies?* Many times it is not even founded. It is our fear, our belief of what their perceptions may be that we do not even begin to pursue our dreams, our true loves, etc.

This is where destinies become sacrifices. It is upon the altar of the fear of others, that our future lives are sacrificed. The fear of having failed in the eyes of someone else. I have personally made many a mistake that I could have avoided, had I listened to the advice of others. I could not for the life of me, however, have felt comfortable with the decision, had I not found out for myself. Many a time they were absolutely correct, but it is a scientist's job to test a hypothesis. **Life is a science, and if you have no qualities of a scientist, you are going to live the life of a plant.**

So back to the analogy. Do you break your loved ones heart? Do you begin to ignore them, or *shift your feelings* and actions around them? Do you walk like you do not know them when you see other people that you know? Do you tell them you're sorry, but you're going to have to break it off with them? Do you convince yourself that they are too slim, and that you are going to be regarded as less attractive in their company? Do you know just how superficial a world this is? Do you know that you, or no one else, will ever satisfy *everyone*? It just will not happen, it is not meant to, as everyone sees things differently, what is important to pay attention to, and follow, is the way that *you* perceive things.

Follow Your Heart

Everything is not for everyone, no two people are built exactly alike. Even twins who look identical, and share many of the same beliefs and principles, may differ in some areas further than the divide separating New York and Texas. **This is what makes us unique.** You have a chosen path, *you have a talent that only you can perform the way that you do.* Something that you derive a more fulfilling sense of pleasure from than anything else the world over. Are you going to allow others the pleasure of your misery? Are you going to forsake your happiness, your possible only shot? Will you stay true to yourself and your dream, your loved one?

This analogy can be used with a crippled child. You, for whatever reason have been blessed to be the parent of a child who is disabled. Everyone tells you how hard it is going to be to raise a disabled baby. They were concerned about you being a parent before, and now that the baby has arrived disabled, they are very scared for you. They tell you how expensive it is, and that there are places where the child can be cared for by people who have dealt with these situations for years. There are people who have gone to school for this.

Don't Abort Your Affinities

You're young, you don't have to do this. You can drop your baby off at the hospital, or precinct, and wash your hands of the whole situation. This can be forgotten, no one has to know. **But they would be wrong,**

wouldn't they? They would be wrong to think that you are the kind of person that is heartless and does not care about your own child, so much so that you can go sacrifice him to the whims of strangers. They would be wrong in assuming that you have a character that lacks nobility, wouldn't they.

Don't get me wrong, I'm not by any means saying that if you give your children up for adoption, whether they are disabled or not, is significant of a lack of character nobility. That's not what I'm saying. What I'm saying is *how could you allow someone else to dictate your actions, and there by your feeling and future?* You may as well cease to exist. You may as well change your name to theirs, have them write you an itinerary, and live for them. What I am saying is make up your own mind, and stop living as a victim to other's perception deficits. It doesn't make a difference how anyone *but you* perceives anything that has to do with your life.

Now Starring.....

You are the producer of your life movie, you are the narrator, and you are the lead role. Consider the finished product, consider what things you want your character to go through, and decide how you want them to handle the situation, and then *do it*. People are always going to talk, some do it because they have mouths, some people do it do see if they can control your life. Some people do it because they are nosy, and love to meddle. Some people do it because they genuinely care, and still others do it because they are bored and have no lives of their own.

Misery also loves company, and so, **some are the proud recipients of a disaster of a life.** All because they allowed themselves to be directed by other people, and now they are miserable. The only way that they see themselves of being any consequence at all, ever, is to do the same thing to someone else. *Do not let that someone else be you.* Do not let someone scare you into falling out of love, with your girlfriend, with your dreams, ambitions and pursuits. Of course, everything you do is not going to be the right move in someone else's mind. That would make them you. So when someone feels like telling you what you should be doing with your life, or who you should be doing it with, listen to yourself.

When someone comes along, because they will, and imparts their defects of perception on to you because *their vision is short* term and they cannot see your long term goal, politely tell them to keep their opinions to themselves because they are distracting. At least, if you do this you'll be able to tell whether they even respect you.

Strive to Thrive!

Also, let me provide this wisdom that men and women both should be aware of. When you change for someone else, when you allow yourself to become their willing project, you show how little you stand for. You show just how little you think of yourself, and they stop respecting you anyway. **No one respects someone who has no respect for themselves.**

Let me state this clearly, I *want to fail* in the eyes of others. I want to be so far away from the 'average' in life, that they do not even see me. I have very little tolerance for the mundane, and I believe the same should hold true for anyone in pursuit of the great. **In pursuit of the great, you cannot associate with the lackluster**. Those who even concern themselves with having an opinion other than supportive for what anyone else is trying to do. One of the pre-requisites for success is failure, now that can also mean the *failure to notice* those who do not matter.

Not saying a failure to acknowledge someone's presence. No, we are all human and on that note everyone should be given an amount of acknowledgement. What I mean is when you begin to be overly preoccupied with the opinions or judgements of someone who is not where you want to be in life, why would you listen to that anyway, it just makes no sense to me. **I seek out the opinions of those who have succeeded in the areas I am attempting to succeed within.** It is these people that I seek out for counsel. It just seems more safe and sensible. I could care less what a slacker thinks of my new innovation, they don't have the experience to make a proper assessment anyway. **So what?**

So what, someone thinks your loved one is too slim or unattractive, or different, they should be different, they are *your* mate. Just like your talent and dream, and your talents and your dreams. Your mate should not please everyone, because if they tried to, they would not be trying to satisfy you, which should rightly be their only concern. Am I making sense? I'm trying to *shake you of the fear* of failure in the eyes of others. I'm trying to enhance your awareness, by enlightening you as to the behaviors of others. **The behaviors of others is to, get this, be preoccupied with the behaviors of others.** It's the blind being led by the blind, when an unsuccessful slacker, tells someone else who is equally unsuccessful that they should be doing such and such. It is the last nail into the coffin of mundane existence when a person takes their opinion for anything other than their opinion. **So what?**

You Can't Please All the People All the Time

The moment you give too much concern to the opinions of others, prepare for loss. Prepare for loss, prepare for pain, and prepare for misery. Much suffering comes at the expense of trying to please others. Many people are so busy running to and fro, trying to please this one and that one, that *they do not even know what is pleasing to the one that matters most... themselves.* They have been wearing what others say look good on them, and doing what others say that they should be doing for so long, that they would be lost having to dress themselves, or having to decide what to do on their own. **That is the worst failure of all, losing one's self.**

This is a chapter to give you further grounding, this should put things into perspective for you in regards to failure. Look at your *alumni*, look at the people listed who have failed, over and over again, in excessive amounts. They did not set out to *please* anyone. **Success cannot be attained by those who want to be liked by everyone, those liked by everyone are respected by none**. They are wishy washy, they say/do one thing in front of one group, and then say/do another thing in front of another group. There is a word for this kind of person: hypocrite. You do not want to be labeled a hypocrite, because that will surely lessen your chances of becoming successful.

Back to Being Principle-Centered

People want to do business with someone they can trust, someone with integrity. People want to be in a relationship with someone on whom they can rely, someone with *boundaries*. People want to enter into situations with someone they can depend on, someone with *loyalty*. These qualities, among others are highly sought after qualities retained by people who are successful. Some successful people do not have these qualities, they also do not have the *quality* of success, of those who are regarded as having these traits. This quality of success cannot be obtained by he who is concerned with the opinions of others. People pleasers are liable to do anything, at any given moment, depending on the crowd.

Imagine your child trying to ride a bike. Imagine your child telling you that they are afraid to attempt to ride the bike, because they do not want other *people to see them* if they fall. What would you say? What would your advice to your child be? *Your advice to your child should be the same advice you give to yourself* whenever you encounter reluctance about trying something new. I will offer that you are grown as well, so what you say should be formatted to your age and tailored to your responsibilities.

There is no viable reason to be intimidated by the eyes and opinions of others. Remember what Richard Branson said about the people of Britain. They respect people who have failed, after giving 100% in an attempt. It is honorable. The only stupid question is the one that remains unasked, as the only funny failures are the ones that were not given 100%, and the ones that are not immediately followed up with another attempt. *So what*, someone thinks that you are going to continue to fail? After Michael Jordan got cut from the team, who saw him with all those rings, and superstardom? Exactly! They just don't know the class that you're in, and who has graduated before you. They don't know whose successes you have to refer to.

Don't Let Other Mind Your Business

So what, someone judges your relationship as being less than stellar. Does the person in question make you happy, and support you? Do you love one another, and is there trust and honor present? These are the only questions that count. **Do not let someone ruin for you something which they wish they had.** Don't fall for it. *Many a time a person will try, by all means, to separate you from that which they wish they had for themselves.* The reason is if they can separate you from it, they don't have to be reminded of what they have not anymore. So hurting you, or causing you pain is sparing them from further pain and humiliation. That's so *what*!

Do not be fooled by your own limiting beliefs, do not give insignificant people power over you. Do not give significant people power over you, or your decisions. Do not care for someone else's opinion so much that you fail to realize that you are the only one you have to live with for the rest of your life. *You want to be comfortable in your own skin, for the remainder of the ride.* You do not want to be haunted by forsaken possibilities.

You do not want to be chased in your sleep by the things you could have done but did not. If there are some things that you are not able to do, at least let the reason be your own, and have no one else to blame. The worst thing is to realize that you did not do something because of someone *who is no longer in your life anyway*. That is a terrible realization, I state this from a point of experience.

Take Ownership!

Let your life be your own. Take ownership! From this day forward promise yourself to care more about yourself than the opinions of others. It's ok to be able to laugh at yourself. You're going to make some mistakes, that's what people do. Remember the infant learning to walk. The only babies that never failed are the grown people who cannot walk. Failure is a prerequisite to success, there is no ifs, ands or buts. There simply is no way around it, so *toughen up.*

Toughen up, get ready for some scrapes, and get ready for some bruises. Especially if what you want to accomplish in life is of a high nature, such as something that will be of benefit to others. Oh yes, get ready for some massive opposition, get ready for some vicious opinions. They are going to descend upon your happy head, and if you are unsuspecting, unprepared, or naive, they are going to fly away with your hat, and your dream, between their beaks, and in their talons. Do not let temporary failure take you out of the game, do not let it end your season. All seasons do not come back around. Not team wins all the games, all the time! For some the end is final, and you're too good for that. For you to have endured this far means you have some potential.

I truly believe, no, I know, that for every person reading this book, there is some quality that only they possess. There is some dream that they have that only they can fulfill. There is some service that only they can provide, to the extent that they are able to provide it. There are millions of people that would benefit from those of you who read this book if you choose to never give up. *If you solemnly vow, to never allow, another opinion to perform an incision, separating you from your dreams, in that moment alone, you become the most important to your team.* A little disappointment and discouragement is permissible, what is not permissible, however, is the forsaking of your responsibility.

Keep Your Candle Lit

You were created with a vision, your *vision will evolve into a purpose* if it is allowed to grow. You must guard your garden with your *soldiers of intent*. You must not allow rabbits to trespass. Those rodents that would pull up the newly planted ideas at the roots. You cannot allow the roaches to encroach upon your field of dreams. For, from your field of dreams could be produced the cure to cancer, you could be the person who develops the cure to AIDS, the answer to pollution could be waiting for you behind your next corner of failures. Have faith, and never give up on your dreams. **They want to be had by you, as much as you want to have them.**

You are never more than a few failures away from your aspirations. Regardless to how lofty your dreams may be, the loftier *the better.* It is best to shoot for the moon, because if and when you fail, at least you can be counted among the stars. That is a take on a statement by Les Brown. Never fail to give people credit for their work, chances are you'll be given credit for yours. Never fail to be respectful and open to opportunity, chances are you'll always be respected and the doors of opportunity will never be closed. Never be fearful of failure or the opinions of others, one doesn't make any difference at all, while the other can make all the difference in the world. Make sure you know which is which, and make sure you tell the next person who just has the need to inform you of their unsolicited negative opinion, *"thank you, but so what?"*

So what if the love of your life does not look attractive to your friends, or like someone they saw you being with. So what if they don't think that they are the right one for you. They are not supposed to. They are not the ones who have to be with this person, they are not the ones whom this person chose. *You are*! You know how much they love you, you know the dedication, and you know the promise, the late nights, the selflessness, the generosity. You know them and that is all that matters. *Nothing else.* Your parents do not have to live with this person, they do not have to go about creating a life. **They already have theirs, yours is your own, and you are the one that is going to have to live in your skin.**

Summary

The exact same applies to your pursuits. You are the one who is going to have to live in a 9 to 5, doing whatever it is that you elect to do. If that is fine with you, then so be it, never stray. However, if you want more out of your life, if you want *your time to be your time*, then you may have to approach things from a more unconventional stance. Again, let no one deter you from your vision and your dream. Let no one's lack of self-esteem or belief, rub off on you. Allow no one to tell you how to get out of your situation, *if they are not the example of it.* That is general lunacy. **We cannot take the advice of a chicken hawk on how to become an eagle.**

We cannot take the advice of someone who is making 9-20$'s an hour on how to become a millionaire, if that is your aspiration. If your aspiration is to become a millionaire, would you seek out the advice of someone who is on welfare? *Ah, you now may begin to see my point.* A person's opinion, or their observation of your situation or predicament *once voiced*, becomes unsolicited advice. If you did not ask for such a person's advice, why would you take it once offered? They may genuinely want the best for you, but *if* they had the correct blueprint *don't you think* they would use it for themselves? I certainly do, and this is why I could not care less if I was paid to. When handling affairs of a higher nature and calling, it does harm to the cause when you consider the opinions of low achievers as important. So what!? *Of course you're going to look crazy to them, you're supposed to*! You want more out of life, and are willing to take the prerequisite classes to get there. **Failure notwithstanding.**

CHAPTER 3

Acceptance

Acceptance - "*acceptance is the action of consenting to receive or undertake something offered*[1]". Look at the power behind this definition. Most people think of acceptance as being able to deal with something, but look at this definition. Acceptance is the 'action of consenting to *receive* or *undertake* something *offered*'. Otherworldly understanding results from this definition.

If acceptance means *consenting* to *receive* or *undertake* something *offered*, the next question is, *what?* What is being offered in exchange for the acceptance? Remember the last two chapters. **So the questions are, what is being offered, and what has to be accepted?** The prior chapters were Hard Times, and also Failure. These are two situations that people cannot accept easily. People cannot accept hard times, and others cannot accept failure. Again, the second question is what is being offered? Peace, greatness and success.

Love, Peace & Happiness

Peace results from the acceptance of hard times, and we just learned, that success comes as a result of failure. Both are prerequisites to success, and both come in the time that they are supposed to, the objective is not to be resistant. The objective is to accept. **Openness**. Openness is what is inferred by acceptance. An openness to what comes, be it completion or calamity, a mental state of acceptance regards both as the same, and thereby, sets oneself up for the best results that the world has to offer.

I was listening to Bob Proctor yesterday, and he was talking about the **Law of Attraction** being a secondary Law, and the primary Law being the **Law of Vibration**[2]. The Law of Vibration is a *mental frequency and attitude*, most noticeable in one's response to the things that one cannot change. There may be some who remember this from the Serenity Prayer. The acceptance of things that one cannot change is crucial to one's success. If only, to ensure that one does not further complicate one's situation, by a less than stellar response to that which is undesirable.

Locus of Control

There are going to be things that are out of your Locus of Control. Let me explain this premise. **Your Locus of Control are the things that you can exert control over**[3]. You can control what clothes you are wearing, so that is within your Locus of Control. However, you do not control the weather in your area, so that is outside of your Locus of Control. Another example would be the banks closing in times of a natural disaster. I'm going to go into financial readiness, and show you the relationship for a moment.

When Hurricane Katrina took place, the banks were shuttered and no one could get their hands on any money. Was that within their Locus of Control, the banks being closed? No, it was not, they had no control over this. However, the fact that the people had no access to money was of their own doing. *Why do I say such a thing?* I say such a thing because it was inside of their Locus of Control to keep some money physically on hand for emergency. They chose to give away their Locus of Control. This is very important for you to understand.

Whatever measures are within your Locus of Control you are going to want to take responsibility for, and maintain control of. Of course the bills have to be paid, so it seems sensible to put your money in the bank, and a lot of people were not in expectation of a natural disaster, so they did what they do naturally, give away their Locus of Control. It did not prove to be the right choice, and something the people regretted and suffered for, when the Messenger of Misery did arrive.

That was just an analogy to illustrate what the Locus of Control is. Now that you know what the Locus of Control is, what is outside of your Locus of Control? Let's take insurance. Is that outside of your Locus of Control? Yes, it is, you can have a stellar driving record for 20 years and better. Are you still going to be expected, legally, to have insurance? Yes. That law is outside of your Locus of Control. *Whether you pay for it or not*, is well within your Locus of Control. You can drive uninsured and hope that you do not experience the unexpected, or hope that no cruiser pulls up behind you and runs your plates, but what would be the best thing to do? **Control what is inside of your Locus of Control**.

Now that the picture is resolute in your mind, a natural question would be are hard times under your Locus of Control? Some are, others are not. What is always, *absolutely*, without question, subject to your Locus of Control? **Your attitude. Your perception. Your response,** your stress levels, your peace, your Zen, and your outlook on the situation. This is always irrefutably within the realm of your Locus of Control. This is where the Law of Vibration comes in. You do not have to allow something *physical* to impact your *mental* or *spiritual faculties*. The mental and spiritual faculties are that which are integral in the attainment of success. Therefore it is of the utmost import that no matter what takes place outside of us, we maintain control over *what takes place within us*[4].

The Power in Letting Go

Some people of a lower frequency encounter the seemingly unfair, and respond with anger or despair. Does that change the seemingly unfair from having taken place? No. What has happened, has happened. It is in the past the second after it has happened, *however, you bring it into the present, and do not allow it to fade by your response to it*. This is why acceptance is one of the pre-requisites to success, it is also one of the most powerful steps in the process to Peace, because of the power inside the act of letting go.

It makes sense to say that if your hands are full, there is no room for anything else to be added. Now *what if your mind and your heart are full?* Full of contempt, full of apathy, and full of anger for how you have been wronged by the world. Where is there left any room in your mind for *high frequencies, fresh new ideas, revelations, and the seeds of creation?* Where is there any room in your heart for *compassion, consideration, and understanding?* This is why people who are freshly free from a tumultuous relationship are strongly advised to avoid relationships to allow for acceptance to set in, before transferring old energy into a new relationship.

Out With the Old, In With the New

Acceptance allows room to be cleared for the new to come into being. Acceptance does not harbor enmity, and does not allow for things that are old to remain encased in your psyche. Are you aware that *negative thoughts carry a frequency* that leave a negative *residual* effect in your body? Yes, they do. This is why stress ultimately debilitates and kills. The physical form of stress is a sludge like substance similar to tar from nicotine. This will attach itself to your back and accumulate. This is why people who are stressed out feel like they are "*weighed down*" or like they carry the "*weight of the world upon their shoulders*", it is due to the accumulation of this tar like substance.

I can remember while learning **Transcendental Meditation**, that our instructor told our class, that this accumulation of toxic waste is a poison that is carcinogenic in nature, and it can actually be scraped off of the back of the rib cage like butter and spread on a piece of bread like apple butter[5]. Pretty disgusting isn't it? This is why there is so much money in relaxation therapy, because *people refuse to let go of the past*, and it is their refusal that is *killing their present*, and *destroying their future*. In order to be successful, one of the most important pre-requisites is acceptance. Acceptance will leave you feeling light, like a child. Able to smile, to play, to be genuine, to accept the blessings that follow.

Release & Relax

Blessings follow the act of letting go. When you empty your mind, you allow space for the new fresh ideas and creative energy to take root. You *allow for the present* to be used for the creation of a beautiful future. When things cease to bother and frustrate you, they will cease to make fruitless attempts, and their frequent happenings will dissipate. They will cease to exist. It is like being afraid of the dark, once you accept that there is no inherent danger concealed within darkness, it will loosen its grip on you and your nervous system will relax. Thereby allowing you to enjoy a peaceful nights rest and to wake up rejuvenated, and adequately *prepared for the present.*

The same thing holds true for the past negativity that you have been subject to. Some things happen to us that are not of our own doing. Perhaps you were born into poverty, perhaps your parents died in a car accident. Perhaps you were born with an illness that requires constant maintenance, maybe you were molested, or raped as a child. You had no control over that. It was/is not fair, and you have had to face some more difficult challenges than others growing up. It is fair to say that under these circumstances, correct? I think so too. However, after you grow up, after you become of age to understand, *when do you take possession of what is within your Locus of Control?*

When do you take the power back from your prior circumstances? A lot of bad things happen to people for no *apparent* reason, the keyword here is *apparent*. It is not *'apparent'*, why some people are born into abject poverty, born unto drug addicts, born with a chemical imbalance, but maybe it is to prove the indomitable spirit of the human being. Perhaps it is to prove how terrible circumstances can be overcome, through the will and through determination. Everything that you go through becomes an ingredient to the recipe of who you are, and so your experiences become beneficial to others. That is if you can overcome them.

Terrible things happen, trust me, I get it. I really get it, however these things are mostly out of our control. What is in our control though is how we respond to them. OK, we had abusive parents, do we in turn become abusive because of it? It is proposed that serial killers were molested and abused as children, my response to this is what about all of the children who were molested and abused who turned out to be great responsible citizens who would no more hurt a fly than to hurt a child, and have turned their experience from that which inhibits them to that which empowers them?

Energy Tranformation

Acceptance gives the person who is practicing the art of it special powers. When you possess the power to accept, you possess the ability to expect. When you can accept, you can expect to receive, remember this carries an energy component. When you accept the negative, you can expect the positive. Do not forget that acceptance is the action of consenting to receive, or undertake something offered. When you are faced with hard times and failure, you are actually being offered something. That gesture of acceptance is the action of *consent* to receive.

The influence of acceptance allows one to utilize the *powers of perception*. Perception instantaneously has the transformative powers to change a thing from negative to positive in the blink of an eye. Think about the energy of people who do not become stressed under duress, are they successful? If you were to ask them they would without doubt reply in the positive, because they have mastered their emotions. When one has mastered their emotions, regardless to whatever takes place, they put a positive spin on it, genuinely, and positive energy flows. Aren't these people attractive? The ones who know no misery? Aren't their energies intoxicating? Don't you want to be around them?

Positive vs. Negative

Now, contrast that positive energy with the energy of the negative worry wart. The miser. If you were to ask them whether or not they are successful in their eyes, you would get a resounding no. These are the people who never have enough and never feel secure, no matter what they have. In business they are always looking for ways to crush and cripple the competition, in relationships they are fiercely disloyal, and given to charades. To them a successful relationship is having at least one person who is unaware of their philandering, while they sleep with all whom they can. They are never satisfied in any section of their lives, nor do they trust, primarily **because they subconsciously know that no one can trust them**. These people have no control of their emotion, and go from hot to cold in the blink of an eye.

They will never accept any unjust activity from anyone else, intentional or not, regardless to the fact that they do people wrong all the time. These people have a very hard time reconciling the fact that what they do to others has been done to them. They hold on to the feeling of wrath and fury, they know no mercy or forgiveness, they will hold a grudge until death, no matter what happens. *They will never know success, no matter how much money they have.* They will never know love, no matter how many mates they may have. Nothing will satiate their appetites. These people are very cold.

They will recall stories from decades ago, when someone crossed them and what they did about it. These people harbor resentment, and you will hear emotions in their telling of a story, no matter how old it is. They may have left and remarried three times, they will recall the reason for the first divorce bitterly, and no matter what the facts were they will never paint themselves in a negative light. They are always the victims in every episode, and will never take responsibility. *They know no acceptance, therefore they know no legitimate success.* When you notice these traits in a person run, fast. They will bring all that they can down with them.

If these traits are recognizable, because they are your own, hope is not lost. You learned to be this way and things can change for you. *If you change your perspective, your reality changes with it immediately.* So we are going to delve into the realm of **cognitive reframing.** You must begin to see things that you think happened "*to*" you, as things that happened "*for*" you. Now your job is to find out why. Why would you have been born in poverty, to an abusive parent? Remember what Tony Robbins did under these circumstances. Perhaps your purpose is to do great things for others, or to help others become financially free. Perhaps you had to go through what you went through to understand the need for, and importance of, selfless service.

Hurt People Hurt People

Many people who were hurt and no longer are, return the favor of healing to others who are still hurting. Hurt people hurt people, and healed people heal people. This is why you'll find those who were victimized by, and lost everything to, the throes of addiction, in substance abuse facilities across the nation *providing substance abuse services* to others, trying to advocate to them the virtues of sobriety. Think of your most enthusiastic diet and health gurus. They were most likely obese at one time of another, or they healed themselves from diabetes and other ailments through the gifts of nutrition and exercise.

This is why they are such staunch proponents of the saving grace that they represent. Perhaps this is the reason for your sacrifice. Number one, because you were strong enough to endure, number two, because you are strong enough to go back and get others. Maybe you are the one who will bring awareness to the situation and, in doing so, make the future better for others because of your idea, or *resilience*. They say that it takes one to know one, so maybe you had to *become one to become a savior to many*. The reality is that you are the narrator of your story. I just know a lot of people who are active, and successful, in their fields because of their unique experiences, good or bad, which made them ideally suited for that field.

The Master of Your Fate

Only you can decide why a thing happened to you. No one can tell you why a thing takes place, unless you give them your Locus of Control. Remember, your story is your Locus of Control. You may not be able to control all that happens *to* you, but you should be able to control all that happens *because of* you. Just take ownership of what you can, and prove proficiency at that, and more will be entrusted unto you. If you can prove mastery over yourself, the control over things outside of you, will be yours to exert.

Actually, that sounds easier than it is. See, this is the training ground. *It is actually easier to control others than it is to control yourself.* This is where the Sages are made, this is the realm of the enlightened. The dispensers of wisdom that come from this highly evolved set of people are those who have proven that they can control themselves.

Why is it that they are highly regarded? Due to the fact that most of humanity is controlled by *desire, appetite, anger, lust and emotion.* The greats of our time are those who are concerned with things of a higher nature. Those who *resonate on a high frequency* consistently, and are not governed by that which happens outside of themselves.

One of the hardest things that a person will endeavor to learn is how to master themselves. This begins with extreme unpleasant situations, this begins with denial and disappointment. This is why many of the first searchers for inner understanding, and other-worldly information and enlightenment would fast and leave the comfort of their homes. They would subject themselves to hunger and poverty, for the purpose of obtaining the *jewels of wisdom* contained therein. Monks would sit still for hours on end, and accept the aches of their bodies, still their minds, and deny themselves ephemeral pleasures. Think on this.

Denial = Acceptance

Think on the power obtained through the acceptance of the unpleasant. The firm resolve not to be moved by that which brings some to tears and others to *anger, hostility, disappointment, drug use, aberrant behavior, depression, eating disorders, and/or suicide.* Think on this. Think on how there is another calamity always present to overpower, and take the place of the last one. Think of how the media, and government will foster for you a new reason for panic, and distress every 72 hours, if not 24. Think of how your attention is taken, and stretched to the point of consistent distraction in the attempts just to keep up with what is going on *around* you.

Now think of the healthiest response possible. Would not the healthiest response be denial? Denial of the world's woes into your area of concern. Don't you have a great reason to reject distraction and become focused on your goal? Wouldn't the best response be to discontinue that erratic substance from your menu? Just take it out of your diet. There are some things that we are fond of, that bring us immediate pleasure, that we just have to accept are not good for us in the long term. Things that are actually detrimental to our productivity and livelihood.

Long Term Thinking

We must forego the immediate for the long term. We must learn how to have *delayed gratification*. We must be accepting, and we must have patience. **Patience makes us perfect, or helps us to come as close to being perfect as possible.** How do we become well versed in an undertaking? Through practice. This is the purpose of meditation and fasting. Fasting is the practice of exerting discipline over one's wants, cravings and appetites. There is a saying that we *dig our graves with our teeth.* Meditation is the practice of calming ourselves, regulating our heart's rhythm, our blood pressure and thought patterns. With repetition and reinforcement the subject of our practice becomes second nature. It becomes a natural reflex or response to a stimuli.

Think of what you do when you awaken. Most of us awaken and jump in the shower *immediately*, perform our refinement ritual, come out of the bathroom and maybe *fix coffee* (a stimulant), some *smoke cigarettes* (a stimulant akin to cocaine), and others *review* the plan for the day ahead with some anxiety. Still others review the night prior with anxiety, what they did wrong, what they should not have, did not have to do, etc. Very few pray, or meditate, and those who do rarely do it before they jump into the ritualistic cycle of theirs.

Be Still Danielson

This is the point of the 20 minute meditation immediately upon waking that *Transcendental Meditation* is the proponent of. This is what I do, but *Tai Chi* is similar, as is any form of mindfulness on mind emptiness, or *deep breathing awareness exercise of quietness and stillness.* We have forgotten how to sit still, and there is no awareness of anything inside of us, only on the outside of us. This we need to change. We do not readily acknowledge, or build a relationship with that which is inside of our Locus of Control (*our bodies, breath, blood pressure, thoughts, etc.*), yet that is what allows us to be present for that which is outside of our Locus of Control. We have misplaced our priorities.

Through a mindful mediation we are able to control our frequencies better. When we wake up, usually it is with the aid of an alarm, or with a preoccupation with the time. *Are we too late?* Will we arrive to our destinations on time, factoring in 5 minutes to brush teeth, 20 minutes to shower, 5 minute coffee, etc.? These distracting thoughts, and the sound of the alarm intensifies our frequency, which finds a peaceful maximum efficiency regulation within our restful state, while we are at peace asleep. What an immediate meditation allows us to do is regain, retain, and retrain that optimum frequency for longer and longer periods throughout the day.

Through the constant practice of this calm, transcendent emotional state, we become harmonious, we become able to invoke calm and peace into our being at will. *Why would we want to do that?* When we are confronted with disaster, calamity, some interpreted emergency, if we have a stillness and a peace present within us, if we have practiced the harnessing of that state, then we can summon it when we begin to get stressed. When we meet with an event that brings anxiety upon us we can invoke the calm, and respond with thoughtfulness and awareness as opposed to panic, and a sense of hurry and distress.

Results Orientation

What will this do for us? This will earn us a deeply rooted sense of respect from others who have not mastered this ability. This will cause others to seek you out when they find themselves overwhelmed, because you never seem to be overwhelmed. This will catapult you into a position of leadership, because you can be relied upon, and because you are calm under pressure. *Anxiety is not sexy* at all, it is annoying. No one wants it in their office, on their team, above them in a position of authority or below them in a position of servitude. It makes people nauseous. Especially if they are in the practice of becoming calmer within themselves, **erratic personalities amongst calm calculating personalities clash like water and oil.**

I urge you to try to accept. Practice acceptance, mindfully and daily through the medium of meditation. This will not only open your energy *receptors,* and clear *repositories,* for the *entrance* of success. This will also *enhance* your state of *spiritual, mental, physical health and well-being* so that once the success becomes yours, *you will be around long enough to enjoy it.* This is vital to the world that we live in right now, because so many people are *achieving their dreams at the expense of their livelihoods.* People strive and strive in their respective fields for accomplishment, promotions, bonuses and graduations or acquisitions, only to obtain them, and once they obtain the object of their desires they fall violently, sometimes terminally ill.

In Sum...

So practice acceptance, and do not destroy yourself in the process. In *any* process. Many people would trade, at the end, their success for a second shot at their health. Still others realize that they were successful at life, as long as they were successfully in good health and good spirits. Success is not something all people need, *some people are not ready for it.* This is why life presents us with these natural prerequisites, with the intention of preparing us for the *retention* of success, after the *acquisition* of success. We shall delve further now into the subdivisions or units of this prerequisite, and what you can expect to learn from successfully passing these stages; *humility, growth, and possibility.*

HUMILITY

"*Humility is a modest or low view of one's own importance; humbleness[6]*". Now don't get me wrong, I'm imparting the importance of things other than your own importance, not just downplaying your importance. What I am stating is that there are **principles** that are more important than one's creature comforts, for instance. You will find yourself in a blessed position, when you place yourself in a *position to be a blessing* unto others.

Universal Principle

There is a major misunderstanding in the views of most people, and this is one of the reasons why many people will not be able to tell you that they are successful, and the ones who may tell you that they are, are secretly cursing under their breath, because they are trying to convince themselves more than they are you. The part of acceptance that comprises humility is the universal principle that *in order to receive, you have to first let go*. In order for the universe to deem you important, your focus must be on the importance of others. You win in the game of life by default.

If you provide others with a service that is needed and time appropriate, you will be successful. People are paid, generally, for the time that they spend, multiplied by the service that they provide. This is why, when you are less experienced you earn a lower wage than someone with ten plus years of experience, even though you both turn in a 40 hour work week. The *quality* of your service will not be the same quality of the service that is provided by a veteran. *So the culmination of your pay grade is determined by two things; quality and quantity.*

Now, when you are performing an astronomical quality of services, you will be astronomically compensated for the service that you are providing. This is why the most successful people of our time are servants. They are people who provide a much required service to humanity. Many times a service that cannot be achieved when going to someone else. So you must be *singular in service*, **meaning that none can duplicate that which you bring to the table.**

Passion Patent Pending

You have to patent your passion. Let me repeat, you have to *patent your passion*. There is something that you are able to do, something that you, and only you, bring to the table. Specialized knowledge can be learned, this is where you must interject your own '*special sauce*' into the mix. See, anyone can flip a burger, but there is just something that you get when you go to your favorite burger joint that you do not get elsewhere. Perhaps it's the service, maybe it's the servers, maybe the cause is the cleanliness with which they perform their service, or maybe it's the olfactory (smell) factors. Whatever it is, you get what I am saying.

Create your patent, some servers do not serve with smiles, some talk too much and are genuinely phony. Some people are arrogant and deem themselves more important than their clientele. Wherever you find yourself, it is always best to be humble. You do not want to be in a hostile environment that is stressful. You want to be humble and exalt the virtues of others. This is how your virtues will get noticed. You may say, "Shawn, how do I succeed by directing the attention *away* from myself?" and to that I would answer, "Easily." By directing the attention to someone else, everyone is directing their attention to you initially, and they will remember that it was important to you to point out the virtues in another human being.

People do not do that anymore. **Chivalry is dead**, people do not hold doors, say thank you, yes ma'am, and no sir - these are all *calling cards of the ancient*. So when you breathe life into humility it is a ray of sunshine, a fresh breath of air, it provides people with hope. You will be the favorite employee, CEO, janitor, dishwasher, driver, pilot, attorney, judge, police officer, etc., if you just employ a little humility. I don't know why, this is just a well-studied and passed down for generations upon generations fact of science, *'you must let go in order to receive.'* To receive what it is you want, you must first demonstrate the ability to give it away.

Principle of Charity

This is what is said of charity all the time. **If you are hurting financially, you are not financially helping others**. If you have no money to spend, it is because you are not giving money away. *Things flow in a circle* and in order for them to flow, you must keep up. If the universe is providing you with money for your well-being, who else's well-being are you helping with that money? We are *stewards* of success, and *stewards* of economic enrichment. To whom much is given much is required, that was not said on the movie Spider-Man for the first time, no, not at all. That is an old quote that was perfect for the scene because there was an opportunity to drive that principle home.

Do you know that it is a blessing to be able to think straight, to calculate, and to comprehend? The next time that you're feeling personally responsible for the faculties you were born with, it would be good humbling exercise for you to go to a nearby *developmentally disabled center*, and become acquainted with those were not born as *lucky* as you were. We become very arrogant, and we exalt ourselves for things we should not take responsibility for. We should be happy that we are healthy, not *prideful and condescending*. We should be appreciative of our features, if we think we look 'good', etc., we should not be haughty, and snobbish. We should be very humble if we were born into a family that had money, that blessing should not be used as a weapon with which to cripple and injure others who were not as fortunate.

Stewardship

Irresponsible stewardship will lead to your loss of that which has been entrusted unto you. What does this mean? This means that if you *misappropriate your blessings* you will wake up one day to find them gone. This means that if you have an abundance of wealth and do not provide charitable relief to anyone but yourself, you may soon find yourself relieved of all that which you were never able to give. I saw a video one day. The video was done by some European students. They wanted to see who had the biggest heart, and willingness to share.

They positioned one of the students outside of a pizzeria, the customers were coming and going, as it was mid-afternoon. The student was not dressed haggardly, he was just dressed plainly, like he was not rich, but he did keep a look of general malaise on his face. As the people are coming out of the pizzeria with their pizza pies and their suits on, coming from, and going back to work, the young guy is asking them to feed him if possible. He is informing them that he is hungry. Do you know not one of these '*civilized*' well-to-doers were compelled to spare a couple of dollars, or to go and order a slice of pizza for the young man? I mean, pizza slices are not $50.00 last time I checked.

Then the students up the ante when they see a man of African

American descent who is obviously homeless, disheveled and down on his luck. They see this guy sitting on the floor next to a building, and they want to see what kind of heart *he* has. So a new student goes and buys a pizza pie, and brings the pie to him. The man thinks it is just someone's kind gesture of charity, and he thanks the new student for it, says a prayer and begins to eat. As he is onto his second slice, here comes the first student, he is walking slowly and listlessly. He sits down about three feet from the homeless man and looks out into the sky, wiping his face. He just looks tired.

A couple of moments go by and he looks at the homeless man, and the homeless man stops eating. He gestures to the homeless man, and the *homeless man offers the student* a slice of pizza, the student takes the pizza, thanks him for it and they enjoy the pizza together. When the student finishes and says thank you, the homeless man asks him if he wants another slice, he tries to say no and the homeless man insists, saying, "We have to eat when we can, never know when the next meal is coming," and *forces another* slice upon the student.

Moral of The Story

Now here is a man who has *nothing*, no job, no decent clothes, who does not know when his next meal is coming, and we have no idea as to the last time that he has eaten. Yet, when he is blessed with something very small – he understands the *principle*. He understands the principle that if he wishes for the universe to provide more, *even he* must provide out of the blessings bestowed upon him, no matter how small. This was such a powerful experiment, because it displayed the cold indifference of *affluent mankind*, and it showed the warm, generosity of those who have not.

The student thanks him kindly and eats the second slice of pizza, and then gets up, brushes himself off, thanks the homeless man again and then walks down the block. A few minutes later he comes back around the corner with some of his classmates and bags full of shoes, clothes, undergarments, soap, shampoo, deodorant, and toothpaste, and they tell the homeless man what he has been a part of. They thank him for his kindness and his caring nature and they each, there was five of them, give him a $100.00 bill!

This is an example of the aforementioned principle, in order to expect, or wish to receive, you had better get into the business of giving away. Why do you think every religion that there has ever been, extolled the virtues of charity? I'm not saying that you are going to be blessed with $1000.00 for giving away two slices of pizza, and you should not *give for the explicit reason* of the reciprocation of the donation, **that is not how this works.** When you give, sincerely for no reason other than the sake of giving, **you crack the code.** *You tap into the reservoir of abundance.*

I have never seen this principle fail, it even extends generation. You can *build up an account* of goodwill for your children to reap the rewards from after you leave. *People* remember how kind and generous a person you were, how much more the **universal principles**? Some call it Karma, and there have been many other names given to this phenomena, still the precepts remain the same. Give good to the world, and receive well in return.

Assets vs. Liabilities

Humility is one of the best assets that a person can have. When you think in terms of success, try to think of what could be an asset or liability in your pursuit of it, this will give you an idea as to whether or not you are on the right path. An asset is something that constantly brings in revenue, and a liability is that which draws out revenue. In this example the revenue, or curren(t)cy that we are speaking on is *energy*, so *good energy* is that which we are in pursuit of, so, an asset would be any characteristic or practice which draws in good energy. This is what humility does for us.

Humility is a form of acceptance, and our aim is to maintain a frequency of a high nature, whose residual effect is good will. For this to take full effect humility is a prerequisite. If a person does not maintain a level of humility, then everything that happens will be met with resistance. The resistance will take shape in the form of the question *why?* Humility, again, asks the question *how?* How is this going to benefit me? How can this be used for the better? Humility will keep you in a state of searching, searching for the good that you can do, which will be returned to you in the form of different services that you can provide to others.

Law of Alchemy

All of the examples I've used in this book are of people who practice alchemy. Alchemy is defined as *"the medieval forerunner of chemistry, based on the supposed **transformation** of matter. It was concerned particularly with attempts to **convert** base metals into gold or to find a universal elixir[7]"*. It is also defined as *"a seemingly **magical process of transformation, creation, or combination**[8]"*. So for the purpose of this analogy we will utilize the latter definition, in that the examples were able to transform a situation that left much to be desired, into their *uncovering of a service that they could provide* to others that was much desired, which left them *reaping the benefits of that service* which they provided, and continue to provide for the betterment of humanity.

Can you see how the element of humility was a prerequisite in this equation? If they had not been humble and accepting of their circumstances, in order to ultimately overcome them, what then? This is the science. **The science is becoming like water.** *Water is humble*, it does not stop at an impasse. Instead it looks to find its balance around whatever element is blocking its progress. That's what we must be like. Water does not ask, *"Why is this thing in my way?"* It does not waste the time, it just finds ways around it, quickly. Humility will allow you to do this. We cannot be choked up with pride, this does not allow for understanding, and resolution.

Be Like Water, My Friend

Have you ever watched a person resist the wave of events? They are the ones who we always see beating their heads against the wall, so frustrated that they cannot think straight. They are the ones who consistently try to do things the same way. Everyone else can see the root of their situation, and ways they could implement to eliminate the opposing force. However, they are blind to this reasoning, they see things in black and white. Their *viewpoints do not allow* for humility, therefore their points of view do not allow for growth. I want you to think back to a baby. The baby's bones have to be humble, they must allow for the natural process of growth.

Imagine a child's bone structure. A child's bones are soft and malleable, this is *how they are able to grow* and stretch. If their bones were hard and rigid, they would not allow for growth and the baby would be in tremendous amounts of pain as the structure begins to stretch, grow and take on new shape. The hard bones would *suffocate* this process. They will be stiff and brittle. They will break. The great martial artist Bruce Lee was proficient in this understanding, let us look at his analogies:

"Be like water making its way through cracks. Do not be assertive, but adjust to the object, and you shall find a way around or through it. If nothing within you stays rigid, outward things will disclose themselves.[9]*"*

"Empty your mind, be formless. Shapeless, like water. If you put water into a cup, it becomes the cup. You put water into a bottle and it becomes

the bottle. You put it in a teapot, it becomes the teapot. Now, water can flow or it can crash. Be water, my friend.[10]" - Bruce Lee

Bruce Lee knew exactly what he was talking about. We cannot be firmly *attached* to that which is static, or *stagnant, fixed* in time, *permanent* with no room for growth. I am not saying do not stand for something, because *cause* gives our lives a sense of purpose, so we must be principled and motivated by the force of our cause, or our **why**. I ask that you just allow for the evolution of your understanding. The ability to add addendums to your understanding as new situations and information introduce themselves to your reality.

Without this ability to adapt, one would surely be broken, or stuck in one reality. What our experiences allow us to do is innovate, to evolve, in effect we learn what does and does not work and we update our efforts accordingly. **Remember there was a time in which the great navigators believed that the world was flat.** Imagine how they had to upgrade their views and practices. Again, Bruce Lee advises:

"Notice that the stiffest tree is most easily cracked, while the bamboo or willow survives by bending with the wind.[11]"

"Adapt what is useful, reject what is useless, and add what is specifically your own.[12]"

"If you always put limits on everything you do, physical or anything else, it will spread into your work and into your life. There are no limits. There are only plateaus, and you must not stay there, you must go beyond them.[13]" - Bruce Lee

His viewpoints are as timeless as the universe itself. These are the laws of which we speak, as being able to crack the code to success. If you are properly utilizing the prerequisite of acceptance, with humility, *you are already successful, you may just be waiting for the money to catch on.* Don't concern yourself with it. It will come. Guaranteed. *It will find its way to you, just like water.*

"Humility is the true key to success. Successful people lose their way

at times. They often embrace and overindulge from the fruits of success. Humility halts this arrogance and self-indulging trap. Humble people share the credit and wealth, remaining focused and hungry to continue the journey of success.[14]" - Rick Pitino

"I tell my kids and I tell protégés, always have humility when you create and grace when you succeed, because it's not about you. You are a terminal for a higher power. As soon as you accept that, you can do it forever.[15]" - Quincy Jones

In Sum

Humility is one of those virtues that one must have in order to be successful. Many times we will have a person who has amassed much in the forms of material wealth and success. If this person is not humble, if he is arrogant, prideful, and boastful, a great calamity will befall him. This usually will instill in him humility, *from the outside.* How much better is it to have humility from the understanding inside, than to have to have it *imposed upon you?* This is like one who has had his diploma snatched away from him, because he did not complete one of the prerequisite courses.

This is the purpose of humiliation. Humiliation will cause one to become humble. *Arrogance* is an ugly possession, he who wields it is surely in for a rude awakening. There is no virtue to be found in debasing others, and taking credit for that which one has been blessed to receive. To He whom much is given, much is required. So find the blessing in the little that you have, and use a portion for the benefit of others so that you may be entrusted with more. **This is the art of stewardship.**

GROWTH

cceptance allows for one to grow. Imagine a cantankerous soul who is stubborn, and always thinks that they are correct, regardless to how wrong everyone else knows that they are. I shudder at the thought of teachers having the duty of imparting understanding to those who refuse to be taught. I'm sure at some point you have tried to give someone the benefit of your wisdom, only to be refuted and then watched in dismay as they went through some horrific tragedy that they could have easily avoided had they only had the ability to accept what you tried to tell them.

Information Changes the Situation

Information changes the situation, however there are those who refuse the information that is afforded them by others, and life itself. If you find that you are not living the life that you would like to, or think that you ought to, you may be required to accept that you have more learning to do. You have to study others, and accept the information of others, to apply to your specific situation in order to change it. If you are not able to execute this basic function you are definitely in for a rocky road ahead.

It takes a degree of humility for one to be able to be taught, this is why the humility segment came prior this one. This is a prerequisite of a prerequisite, if that makes sense to you. If you have a degree of humility then you can grow, remember the softness of the baby's bones. **Growth is vital to the survival of an organism,** it must evolve, and it must mature. Growth is necessary, **without growth one begins to decay.** This is true of all aspects of a human being. Notice how even the fingernails and hair continues to grow, even after a person has been pronounced deceased. Now imagine if your fingernails and hair stop growing, what would the verdict be? The verdict would be that you were no longer alive. So can we agree that growth is a determinant that something, or someone, is still alive? Good. Now we're getting somewhere.

If you agree that with life there is growth, and because you are reading this you must be alive, is it safe for me to assume that *you understand that you must continue to grow?* Fantastic! Now there are many aspects to a human being as I just mentioned. There is the *spiritual, the physical, the mental, the health, the relationship, the occupation…*these are all components of a human being, and there are a vast amount of more aspects, but for the sake of this topic we shall focus on these aspects. *What does it take for an organism to grow?*

Developmental Necessities

In the case of the baby, the baby would need the *proper nourishment*. What I propose is that the same is true, for the other aspects that we have mentioned in the case of an adult. There is the spiritual. Are you growing spiritually, or are you receiving the *spiritual nourishment* in order to grow in this area? If not, why? Are you involved in a body of worship, do you practice habits of a spiritual nature? If not, you can expect to see stagnation in the development of this area.

In the case of the body, if you were to starve yourself and deny yourself food and drink, the required nourishment of the body to grow, could you expect to retain life in this area for a long period of time? I would guess not. So the question *in regards to your success* is; **are you providing your mind with the nourishment required to flourish in this area?** Are you developing, or are you in a state of decline and decay. *Why?* Many times it is because you are not allowing yourself to be taught that which you need to know, in order to grow.

Higher Degrees of Information

If your specific knowledge has gotten you to a certain place, and you know not how to progress further in this area, it is time for you to expose yourself to a *higher level of knowledge.* **It is time for you to proceed beyond the limits of your information.** Meaning you will need to seek out new bodies of knowledge that you have yet to become acquainted with. You might have to go back to school. In the case of a relationship that is on its proverbial deathbed, you may have to seek out a Relationship Coach, Conflict Resolution Specialist, or a marriage counselor.

This is how one grows, remember there are no limits, only plateaus that will impede progress. *Many times it is one's own success that will ensure his failure.* If a person meets with early successes in life, he may be inclined to believe that he has all the answers, and does not need assistance to continue to grow. This is not true. Take for example a company that starts out very good because they are new to the market. After a while the initial excitement wears thin and the company is no longer new. How do they regain their footing?

Organizational Turnaround

The company regains its footing and stays alive through the input of new and fresh aspects to add to the company to keep them on the cutting edge. If there were no need for specialists in this area then the field of consultation would not exist. Consultation does exist because companies are well aware that if they do not consistently grow, or breathe new life into their company they will cease to expand, they will cease to grow, *i.e. they will die*. They will pass away because they became obsolete. They became old and outdated because they were unable to reinvent themselves.

If this were not true then companies like Apple, for instance, would not always be releasing the next new IPhones, and IPads.. The fact that they do this allows you to know that this is akin to success. *What is?* **Growth is.** The sooner you accept that, the sooner you can go and *recruit the specialized forms of knowledge that you need to continue to be in demand*. The sooner you can compete in an ever growing multi-national capitalist society. There is so much going on, and always some company is rolling out the next new whatever. *What is the shelf life of an idea?*

Idea Innovation

The shelf life of an idea is very short, as a matter of fact the moment that an idea becomes known, someone begins to go to work on cultivating an add-on. People constantly are adding to and taking from an idea, and making it better than the original, *smaller, faster, cheaper, stronger, smarter, etc*. So you must understand that the shelf life of an idea is very short. As a matter of fact it begins to die as soon as people find out about it. It's life as merely an idea ceases to exist *the moment* someone else comes into contact with it.

Life Process of an Idea

The idea becomes a discussion, becomes an agreement, becomes a plan, becomes a product, becomes a commodity, and the idea is dead. The *idea is dead*, it has become a static object. It has life, but now it is no longer in the idea form, now it is a line item. Next thing to do to remain vital, is to come up with another idea. Long before Apple came out with the IPhone 6, they have had people hard at work on the IPhone 7, and 8. This is a fact, and this is so that they remain relevant and in demand. **The moment you take a break in learning, the standard operating formats update.**

Think of a person who went to college in 1995. They went in 1995, they got their Associate's Degree in 1997. They took some time off and got a job. Now some 19 years later, *things have what?* Things have changed. In order to stay relevant, *they must what?* **They must grow.** How do they grow? There are various ways, but let's say for this chapter they decide to go back to college for some further education. What is the first thing that they are going to notice? They are going to notice how different college has become. *Why?* Because everything changes.

The Speed of Change

The speed with which things change is blurring and hard to conceive. The moment you purchase something the next thing is on its way. Who remembers *Nintendo?* There was a time when that was the freshest gaming console on the market, is that true now? Not hardly, now it is a classic, it has been put out to pasture and replaced by something that people who mastered the games in Nintendo, could not even begin to understand *unless they kept up* with the progression and evolution. So I am saying all of this to impress in your mind that, by all means, you must continue to grow to remain relevant. **If not you will be left behind.**

This is why education is a continual process, it never stops just because you graduated. When you graduate *from the theoretical,* you graduate *to the applicable.* It is no longer book study, now you are practicing with human lives, real programs, or whatever it is that you went to school for. **Growth is constant, it is as consistent as time.** It will not stop or slow down, as a matter of fact the speed at which things get done will continue to escalate. So your efficiency at absorbing information and producing results from this newly encountered information must accelerate as well. If not, *you are done for.* The world does not account for those who cannot keep up.

The Point of Obscurity

No, let me take that back, and explain. The way in which the world accounts for those who cannot keep up with innovation is in the form of dead end jobs that require *past tense thinking.* Those, however, will not exist beyond the **point of obscurity.** Need an example of the point of obscurity? There used to be what were called 'pinsetters'. Have you ever bowled? You know the machine that puts the pins back in place after a strike? *This used to be a job* that people got paid for. Before there were alarm clocks, there were people who were called '*knocker uppers*'. Funny name, right? They would knock on windows above their heights with rods that would extend, or they would throw *pebbles at windows* to wake people up.

Another job that has past the point of obscurity that no longer exists is the elevator operators. There used to be a person inside of every elevator operating it. Have you ever heard of a *milk man*? Before refrigerators were a household item, there was no way to keep milk from spoiling, therefore the milkman would show up every morning with fresh, cold milk for consumption. Can you believe that there was time when this occupation was absolutely vital to society? However, society has outgrown the need for this occupation. Therefore, **by default they have outgrown the need for people who can only operate up to the level of function that such a job required.**

Your modern day *podcast*, or satellite radio used to be a *Lecture.* A

Lecture would come into a factory and read to the people as they did mundane work, that they would tire from. The Lecture's job was to entertain, and keep people focused on their work by providing a *'zone'* for people to *'get into'*. Just the same as your IPod does today. Interesting stuff, huh? Obsolete? *I think so.* Before TV, people were *employed* as radio actors. They performed skits and plays, one is called to remember the **War of the Worlds skit** wherein people thought the world was really being invaded by aliens due to Orson Wells convincing voice on the skit. *Google it!*

This world that we live in used to employ people as *'rat catchers'.* I know you may think I'm joking, but before poisons and traps were made for rats, people in the inner cities made very good money by physically catching these varmints and putting them to rest! *Were you aware that in the not-so-distant past that there were computers?* I know that may cause some of you to laugh because you may be reading this on a computer. Well not so long ago there were people, usually women, who were employed as *'computers'.* What did they do? They *'computed'*, crunching numbers and figures by hand. This job boomed during WWI and WWII.

Switchboard operators, as they were called, used to connect every single phone call by hand, this also was a major employer for women. They connected every single phone call, wire to wire, so people could have a conversation with their loved one, there was no call waiting. It is now done digitally, and used to be done manually, hint-hint.

"According to a recent report by the BLS, over the next decade 10 types of industries will be phased out of the economy and deemed no longer viable or profitable. Why you ask? Well, for the most part it is because these are industries with jobs that can either be performed by a computer or outsourced to another country where labor is cheaper, thereby making people-our own human resources- the obsolete entity that no longer serves a purpose or function in these specific roles[16]*".*

These industries that were discussed were gas stations, newspaper publishers, semiconductors, department stores, the postal service, wired telecom, etc. The reasons for this being afore mentioned innovations in technology.

Let Me Upgrade You

I cannot stress enough how important that it is that people continue to *update, improve, and continually grow* in their knowledge, in order to remain relevant. Do you know what happens to people whose occupation becomes obsolete? If they have not updated their **mental software** (*brains*), they become obsolete with the outdated occupation, and become a *burden on society* as they can no longer provide for themselves or their families. It is a scary reality, but one that you can be prepared for if you take the appropriate measures. **Therefore, growth is a prerequisite of not only success, but it is a prerequisite of survival in general.**

Do you want to be the proverbial Captain that goes down with the ship, or are you smart enough to recognize when something is a lost cause? Are you able to recognize and accept what is a lost cause when it becomes apparent? Or are you like unto the person who acted as if there was no fire until they were finally engulfed by it? This is what is meant by *acceptance and growth*. Those who are unable to recognize or accept the necessity of growth have chosen to wither and pass away as obsolete. This is a prerequisite class, the fundamentals of this class must be introduced, acquired, and mastered before success can be realized.

The Truth About Maintenance

This is because the world does not stop. It travels around the sun at the terrific speed of 1,037 and 1/3 miles per hour. So those who have a habit of saying that 'they're maintaining' when you ask them how they are doing, are in reality not 'maintaining', they are *going backwards*. As the Earth spins forward, if you are not moving forward with it, you are actually going backwards, when you think that you are standing still. Laws of nature do not take into account your laziness, complacency, or your comfortability level.

Every year that you have been alive there has been a constant process going on, a growth. Every season the plant life is born, reaches maturity, and every winter it dies or goes into a state of hibernation. Then when spring comes and the sun's light touches its surface, it awakens and *begins the process of growth anew.* How about you? Have you grown every year? Perhaps physically, but have you grown *mentally, physically, spiritually, and within the scope of your profession*? **Have you updated *your* database?** Your database would be your brain, your thoughts, your understanding of things. This is why many wise people refer to knowledge as being infinite. This is because it is ever growing, ever renewing, and ever changing.

To Infinity & Beyond

That which worked today, may not work as efficiently tomorrow. **That which you do for a livelihood, may not exist as worthy of a paycheck, or even be mentioned tomorrow.** Do you know people that are grown, but still operate as if they were teenagers and have their whole lives ahead of them? Like they have time to drink, party and lay around all day? *What happens to these people later in life?* How do they fit-in? They don't fare too well, do they? They are people, whom, when spoken in reference to, are said to have let '*the world pass them by*'.

I remember a beautiful speech given by the great Dr., and motivational visionary, Eric Thomas. He was standing in front of a large crown and talking about the topic that I am speaking about now. To borrow a point from him, he said to the crowd that "*you are not updating, you are not growing*", he said, "*you buy every new phone that comes out, you line up in front of the store, but you have failed to upgrade yourself*". He said, "*You're still working with the system that you had back in 1995*[17]". That was epic. It still rings true. Every day the Earth goes through what is called a revolution. This is the 24 hr. revolution around the sun causing day and night to alternate. Can you say the same about yourself? Have you gone through a '*revolution*'? **If not you are behind, and better catch up.**

The Ant & The Grasshopper

This is why some people who '*wasted their time*', have to do a *week's work in a day, a day's work in a hour, a month's work in a week, and a year's work in a month.* They are trying to catch up. Think about falling behind on your bills, you may have to find two months worth of money in one month, or you continue to what? Fall behind. You do not want to fall too far behind, on any level, because there is what is known as '*too late*'. I know people do not like to think of things in this way, but think on the ant and the grasshopper.

Who is the ant and the grasshopper? Oh, I am so glad you asked. Some people believe that some forms of information are outdated, and no longer need to be related to the next generation. I disagree with this rationale, *every generation can learn from the prior generation's wisdom gained through experience.* There is even some wisdom that transcends time and space, like the wisdom which elaborates on, and adds understanding to, **universal principles**. Such as the great African philosopher Aesop, who was responsible for the body of work that the world has come to know as Aesop's Fables.

One of Aesop's fables had to do with the ant and the grasshopper[18], these were the main characters. The story goes something like this, and your situation in life compared to others will give light to who has studied this timeless wisdom and applied it. One day during the spring a grasshopper was playing and singing, just as he always did. When he saw an ant carrying a large leaf. The grasshopper said to the ant, "what are you doing"? The ant said, "I'm gathering protection and building my home for the winter." The grasshopper laughed at the ant, and told the ant, "It's only spring, why don't you laugh, play with me, and do fun things?" The ant told the grasshopper, "No, I don't think so, the winter is coming and it will bring with it the cold, and a slot of snow".

At this the grasshopper said, "All you ants do is work and worry, slow down, don't be in such a hurry". But this did not distract the ant, who continued to go about his gathering of plants. When summer came the grasshopper was playing and singing, just like he always did, when he saw the ant again. This time the ant was carrying some wheat. So the grasshopper says to the ant, "What are you doing now?" The ant tells the grasshopper, "I'm done building my home, so now I'm working on storing some food for the winter", and advised him to do the same. The grasshopper laughed, as he chewed a blade of grass, and said, "It is summer, there is food everywhere, I would rather have fun, and when the winter comes I'll do what has to be done." So the ant went on working and the grasshopper went on playing.

Alas, as it does every single year, the winter fell upon the Earth, and it was cold, and there was a lot of snow. The grasshopper was in trouble, as he had built no shelter for himself, and all of the plant life he used for food was gone, withered and decayed, or frozen. The ant, however, was warm and well fed, as he had prepared for the harsh season. The grasshopper remembered that the ant had built a shelter and had stored food, so he went to look for the ant. He finally found the ant, and pleaded with the ant for some food and shelter. The ant let the grasshopper come in and gave him some food, but told him, "It is true I have stored food, but if I feed you all winter, then I'll die too." *At some point the grasshopper had to leave and find food for himself.*

Now we are aware as adults, that the winter is the death season for most insects who do not prepare for the winter. However, this fable is meant for children, to teach them morals. So the fable goes that when the next spring came, the grasshopper was more than willing to join the ants in the shelter preparation, and the storing of food for the winter to come. He had learned his lesson.

Moral of The Story

The morals imparted are that '*hard work always pays*'. Also to '*work for today for what you will need tomorrow*'. How many of you are as wise as the ant, or as doomed and destined for self-imposed hard times as the grasshopper? Did you know that only 59% of the North American population has at least $500 dollars in their savings? Do you have money invested in gold, escrow accounts, stocks and bonds, or real estate? Are you properly prepared for the season of calamity, should it ever come?

If an emergency took place, if something happened to the car, or you could no longer work for a period of time, would you be well off? If you needed $2,000 for some unforeseen accident would you be able to afford it, without having to borrow from someone who was as wise as the ant, because you are unprepared? I'll write a book focused on financial literacy and what to do with your money to ensure its staying ability later, I promise. *This book is designed to help you to obtain the success, right now.* This is the purpose of this book. There is a similitude of a *spiritual nature, a health and wellness component, as well as occupational correlation to the lesson learned here as well.* This is for you to compare, and contrast, against the analogy of the preparation principle on display in the story of the ant and the grasshopper.

Preparation is a prerequisite for growth and survival. If you have not prepared by keeping yourself, your skill set, and your education up to date, what will you do when your current occupation becomes obsolete? What will you do as the demands for your job continue to grow and escalate? *Will you grow with the demand, or will you starve like unto the grasshopper?*

POSSIBILITY

Without preparation, without growth, there is no possibility for success or survival.* If you are able to adequately accept the need for growth and preparation, there is a distinct possibility that you may be successful. There is certainly a better possibility than if you fail to grow. So now we are going to enter into the realm of possibility, I welcome you...

Once you have gone through the prerequisite stages we have already discussed, given that you are able to pass these tests, you graduate unto the realm of possibility.

Acceptance affords possibility. Nothing is possible without acceptance, and I'll tell you why. If you do not *accept* a job, chances are you will not do very well on that job, correct? My point exactly. If you do not *accept* that it is your birthright to be wealthy, your birthright to be healthy, and your birthright to be successful, chances are you never will. It is not possible, because you will not *accept* that such a possibility exists. However, once you open your mind to the fact that anything is possible, it is within that act alone, that all becomes possible. You cannot do what you do not know how to. As a man thinketh, so shall he be. **If the mind can conceive (*accept*) it, and believe it, with work the mind can achieve it.**

The Power of Possible...

Synonyms for this act are "*belief in, trust in, faith in, confidence in, credence in, giving of credence to, etc.*[19]". If you can believe and trust, if you can have faith and confidence, if you can give credence to your ability to do something, whether or not you have ever done it before, or know how to, or where to start is irrelevant. As long as you accept that *it is possible*, at that point it becomes so. So now you know that something is possible, you have accepted that, what do you do? Acceptance of the possibility allows you to move forward with faith. You will have much more self-esteem in the undertaking of anything at all once you see it as being possible.

Let me now impart upon you this grand truth, the person who thinks something is impossible, and the person who think that something *is* possible are both correct. How can that be, you ask? Easily, if I *think* I can do a particular thing, I am correct. However if I *think* that I cannot, I will not even try, or give a lackluster effort, again proving that if I *think* I cannot do something, I am also correct in that assumption. Where does that leave us? That leaves us knowing the importance of acceptance.

On this note, I will bring to your attention the fact that, **if someone else has done a thing that means that you can as well.** You may just need the *skills, training, tools, etc.* You may need these things to be successful, but these are things that can be acquired in order to facilitate proficiency and ability. It becomes possible once it is accepted. Simple and plain. How many of you ever did a thing that you thought you could not do? How many people believed that they could not do math, for instance? How many people never thought they would see the day when they would not be tempted to have a drink, smoke a cigarette, argue, or be unfaithful? These are real time problems that take work to overcome. My point is that when a person *accepts the possibility, and* *begins to give an effort*, the object of their acceptance many times becomes their reward.

Some people have a phobia about public speaking. They do not believe that they can stand and speak in front of a crowd. Of course we know that they can they just have to do it. Stand there and talk. However, until they accept the fact that it is a possibility, due to the fact that people do it every day, they are correct, *they* cannot do such a thing. Their limitations do not stop the person who has accepted the fact that *they* can do such a thing from doing it. For the person who has accepted that they can, regardless to the fear that they used to harbor, for that person, **the possibilities are endless.**

Steps & Stages

First must come the acceptance, in the realm of success. One must accept that they can be successful before they ever try to become successful. Those who do not think that it is within their birthright, or within their power to become successful, to save their marriage, to elevate their understanding of finances, to have better communication with their child, to get along better with their boss, these people never will. It is their lack of acceptance that make these things unattainable. **My point is that our limitations are self-imposed,** and can be removed as easily as removing the dark from a room by turning on the light.

I know that may be harder to accept for some than for others, and that is fine. Things come to people at varying levels. *People come to awareness at varying levels.* That is to be accepted, some have longer track records of a more intense disbelief than other, but **everyone has the possibility to become whatever he or she wishes and believes.** There was a time when women did not believe that they could be in the military, that is, except in the capacity of nurse or hand maid. Others, men, thought the same thing too. ***Note:*** *Sometimes it is our own disbelief* *of a thing that allows others to think the same.* When women began to think that they could be in the military, many men were still of the assumption that they could not. They could not *accept* it.

They could not accept it because they could not wrap their heads around it, they could not picture it. Once women accepted the possibility, what happened? They began to try, didn't they? They began to try, and this simple act of *effort*, equipped with *belief*, changed the landscape of the armed forces forever. This is not subject to the opinion of others. **No one else's thoughts on any matter make it any more true or false that as a man (woman) perceives, so shall he (she) achieve, it all becomes just a matter of time.**

Opinions Notwithstanding

Once the women began to accept the possibility that they could become soldiers, and then prepared themselves and applied energy to the belief, *it became so.* Regardless to how many men and other women thought it an impossibility, it became a reality. Now there are women all over the military in every capacity imaginable. This is not to say that there are not still men and women who are resistant to the situation and think it improper. That is just fine, **it does not matter what another person perceives as being possible or 'proper'.** This is heavy information. I hope you're paying attention.

It does not matter what *another person's acceptance level is,* if you accept that you can do a thing, at that moment it becomes a possibility *for you* to do, *regardless* of what others think. Imagine if the opinions of others were fact. Imagine, there would be no women doctors, there would be no female police, slavery would never have ended, many of you would not be reading this now, *and I certainly would never have written it,* if the opinions of others were reality and more than just opinions. Even our own for that matter, the opinions and reservations that we may have had in the past, have no effect on that which we can accomplish, from the very moment that we accept it as a possibility. I'm going to say that again.

The opinions and reservations that we may have had in the past, do not have any effect that which we can accomplish, from the very moment that we accept it as a possibility. This is why *yesterday's failure can become today's triumph.* We just have to change our thought processes. That is all, the moment that we *change our thinking, our possibilities change.* This is why it is pertinent that you never cease to learn. Information changes the situation. If you thought that you could not do such a thing because you never became acquainted with the information that enlightens you as to the possibility of a thing, you can change that limitation as soon as you *access and accept* the new information. How fascinating is that? I love education.

The Wonderful World of Education

I love education because it opens up new worlds of possibility. Now let me be clear, I am a student of life who does love formal education, however I am not using, for sake of reference, formal education as the example in this case. I love the **continual process of the accessing of new information.** I love continued learning. It does not matter *where* you are learning this information. I accept, school is not for everyone, *it was not for me, until I became mature enough to settle down.* Still, after I left school in my younger years, I did not drop out of the **University of Life.** There is no better teacher than experience. I stayed studious, and I loved to read and learn, I just had to do it on my own terms when I was younger.

So if you find yourself out of a formal educational setting, do not think that you have to abandon the continual accessing of information. You can study as much as you want, whenever you want, about whatever you want. *This is the beauty of freedom.* There was a time, when certain things were forbidden, definitely for certain people, but even from the general masses, there was a time that you could not access some topics without a certain amount of money, years in school, or being accepted into a certain circle. With the explosion of the information/technological age, that is no longer the case.

Anyone can study anything, pretty much anywhere. There are so many educational mediums, so many possibilities for people of any background, people of any race and geographical setting. The only thing that stops a person in this day and time is their own **limiting belief system.** Of course, I know that there are others who try to limit people's abilities and aspirations, especially if they are of a population deemed unfavorable by the powers that be, but that has always been the case. Also, it is to be noted, that even though it has always been the case, it has always been conquerable. The people who have been held down by other people have always ended up on top, *history validates my last statement.*

For the Sake of Clarity

Let me, for the record, address shortly that I am not oblivious to either historical or present *inequalities.* There has always been an oppressive factor for every people on this planet. At one point or another, *every people have been subjected to less than equitable opportunity.* **This however, does not validate the existence of an excuse.** There is no excuse for a person or a people to give up, on anything, simply because of subjugation. An in depth assessment and study of history will prove me correct that, at one point or another, every group of people were once the target of less than optimal opportunity. Some have used it as an impetus for achievement, and others have used it for an excuse as to why they cannot accomplish whatever they want in life. *However, as an excuse, it simply does not suffice.*

As soon as a human being accepts the possibility that they can accomplish something that has never been accomplished before, for that person it becomes possible. If not, we would not have innovation, if not, we would not have world changing events. Presuppositions are changed as soon as someone dares do what others refuse to believe is possible. The funny thing about this is that as soon as someone sees it done, their prior doubts are denied credence, they now know that it can be done, and as a result everyone starts to do it. This is true for everything.

It was once supposed that the world was flat, and could not be navigated from one end, back to the beginning point. *That has changed.* It was once believed that man could not break the sound barrier, and *that has changed.* It was once believed that a person could not run a mile in under four minutes, and once it was done, *everyone began to do it.* This is the nature of man. It is natural to be fearful of the unknown, until one becomes acquainted with an overpowering belief. **This is why more information is a prerequisite of understanding.** It is absolutely necessary that we continue on the path to the acquisition of knowledge, because it is ultimately information that changes the situation.

Education = Empowerment + Freedom x Responsibility

There was a time when people had never flown, or let me say that people were unaware of any example of human flight. Did that detour the Wright brothers from innovating, or Amelia Earhart from being the first female to fly across the Atlantic Ocean? No, it just fueled their beliefs that they could be the first to do it. To prove that it could be done. Now there are trans-continental flights that take off only minutes after one another, endlessly, all over the planet. So *the seemingly impossible, is now done by everyone*, and the fruits of other people's beliefs are enjoyed by the entire human race. **Get you some resolve.**

What will you be the first to do? What will you do that you will be the first in your family to do? What will others be inspired to do from your example? Who will you free from fear? Who will you set the example for? Who will you show that there is nothing to fear but fear itself? **Accept your responsibility,** you are not a plant, you are not a bee, and each of these forms of life has a responsibility, how much more so yourself? How much more are you responsible for? What is your duty, what is your gift, your contribution, your charity? What will you bring to the table to show forth your ability to overcome adversity? **Make your choice and get started now!**

Do you accept that it is *our responsibility* to leave the planet Earth a better place than when we were born into it? Do you believe that we each *have a gift*? Something that we have *been blessed with the ability to do* better than anyone else in our time on this Earth? Well then, don't you think you had better *get started?* **Do you feel that you could strive to be the best that you can be, and do the best for the human population that you know how to do, and not be blessed with success for your endeavoring?** This is not the success purely of a materialistic nature. This is a higher level of success, befitting of one on a higher plane of existence. When one feels fulfilled and satisfied, there is a physical affect.

Never Have to Work Day in Your Life

There is the physical effect of a reduced heart beat, lowering of blood pressure, heart disease reduction and a calmer, more serene state of mind when one feels they are doing something that they were born to do. This is why people say to find something that you like to do that you can be compensated for, so you never have to feel like you have to *work a day in your life*. Accept your calling and handle your business. Again, success is not measured by material, so do not think that I am saying that a person is not successful if they are working a regular 9 to 5. If no one worked a regular 9 to 5 and we all aspired to be entrepreneurs/business owners, where would that leave us if we had to go and get a regular check-up?

Accept what is right for you, what makes sense for you to be doing, that which brings you **peace and contentment.** Never let anyone else dictate or design the story of your life for you. Remember you have to live *in your skin and with the decisions that you make.* You do not want to blame your unhappiness on your parents, for one day they will be gone, and you will not have them to blame. Then you will realize that **it is you**. It always *was you*, and then you will feel great remorse, at not having followed your own dreams and accepting someone else's dreams as your own. **This is criminal.**

The Influence (Sabotage) of Others

I want to expound on this premise for a moment as it is very serious, especially for our younger generation, in the form of **peer pressure.** How many people have chosen an act or a course of action that was not of their own design? How many people can say that they made choices that they wish they would not have, and how many people can say that this was done in the presence, and under the influence of others? That would be pretty much everyone reading this book I suppose. I know that I have suffered from this lack of resolve. Many times, in fact.

There are many occasions in which the *inner voice* of man will warn against an action, only to be overpowered by the feeling of having to *satisfy others.* The same can be said of *looking a certain way* to others, a *reluctance to disappoint.* You don't want to disappoint the company you're in, or have them look at you a certain kind of way, so you do some things that you know you have no business doing, and that you know you would not do, were you not in their company. This is why parents try to warn children about the company that they keep. **Humans are social creatures, we wish to belong.**

Internal Resolve

We have a longing for association, we wish to belong, and we do not want to disappoint the company that we are amongst. If this means disappointing the voice within us, then so be it. **It truly speaks to the strength of an individual to turn away from people,** and abstain from actions that they know are not good for them. Very rarely will a client of mine say that they just *chose* to start using drugs. No, most of the time they were introduced to it *by someone else.* When I ask if they felt any kind of apprehension towards indulging they affirm. They just felt a *stronger compulsion* to indulge, due to the influence of the people or the person that they had around them at the time. This is serious business.

We must have the strength to accept our inherent intelligence, our inner voice, the voice of something greater than ourselves, within ourselves. It is that voice which is never incorrect. Many people have died *without the opportunity* to come back and tell the living, that just before they did that which resulted in their death, that they '*had a feeling*', or '*sensed something*' that told them not to do what they were doing. There are so many single mothers and aborted children, due to this act of just '*going along*' with something. **The danger with this is that a single wrong decision can easily change or even end your life.** It can definitely alter your future, and the sad thing about it is that people cannot say that they honestly did not know better.

Why can they not say such a thing? Because God, or the Universal Principle or whatever you wish to refer to that essence as being, instilled in us all an ***internal voice***. Like a GPS, it tells us, "*you have turned down a dead end, make the first legal U-turn*", but how many of us accept this direction? The stronger, more grounded of us do. These are the ones who have a high sense of *morals and values*, the ones who have a strong sense of *connection and responsibility* to their parents, and loved ones. This is why you will find most children who are involved in gang activity come from a relatively broken home. This is why most alcoholics and drug addicts can tell you where their home life left much to be desired, and they found *companionship and consolation* within the effects of the foreign substances, or within the wrong crowd.

WARNING!

This is definitely not the path to success. Not saying that one who has suffered from this sort of thing does not have the ability to succeed, they do. They just have to *accept* the inner voice as their own *higher nature and subconscious intelligence*, trying to save them from the negative paths that they are on. **This is the danger of submitting to peer pressure.** When we accept the voice or compulsory force of someone or something outside of ourselves to dictate our actions, we are in real danger. **We become subject to the fate that is meant for others.** It may be their destiny to drive drunk and kill themselves and everyone else in the car, it *becomes your destiny upon your choice to get into the vehicle.*

As adults, coming into contact with danger or regrets is much more possible, if you choose to go down a path that you know you should not. It is not the fault of others. It is your own choice, for which you will be held responsible. You have the same **inner GPS** as everyone else, do not allow someone else's *navigation of the negative*, allow you to take faith that a thing is safe for you, if you hear the *voice telling you to alternate courses*. Do not stay in a career, location, or relationship because that's what everyone else is doing. **Run, run fast, and run to your own.**

CHAPTER 4

Paradigm Shift

PARA-WHO?

Para-Who? Prada-What? Paradigm Shift. A paradigm can be simply defined as a typical example or pattern of something; a model[1]. A paradigm shift can be defined as being a *"significant change in the paradigm of any discipline or group[2]"*. Ok, so we can put the two together and, in layman's terms say that a paradigm shift is a significant change in the example or pattern of something. This can take more forms than one may think.

Can you remember the first time that you were introduced to the concept of God? One day you're just thinking that you are on this planet, and perhaps you may have learned a thing or two about Darwin's Theory of evolution. This usually comes to a student's awareness around the third or fourth grade, typically in science class. Then someone interjects with the idea of a creator (if you were not raised in a particular faith), who has created everything according to the book of Genesis, a little bit contrary to the Darwinian explanation of life.

This presents two diametrically opposed bodies of thought. On the one hand there is an all-powerful creator who created the heavens and the Earth, and everything that we see and hear. On the other hand life began as a formless liquid, then the liquid evolved, got washed up on shore and began to have thought, legs following fins, and so forth. **A Paradigm Shift can be explained as going from one thought or ideology, to the next.**

Shift in Understanding

How does this equate to success? Within life this is going to happen from time to time, as one sets out upon his quest of learning. I have had a great many of these in my life, one example being that of going from school (*theoretical*) to actual practice (*applicable*). There were things that were taught in school that did not apply whatsoever in the scope of practice that I was in. I am certified as an Alcohol & Substance Abuse Counselor.

However, you are going to find that this is the case in the scope of whatever practice that you are in. Another example is when a child is under the assumption that they are almighty themselves, because they have never been hurt, or cannot recall the time. The first time that they become cautious, or aware of the reality of physical pain, is *after hurting themselves*. So we can infer, that **the alternation from preconceived knowledge to newly acquired and accepted knowledge is definitive of a paradigm shift.**

A Paradigm Shift can be subtle, or it can be more powerful than that. Many children come up saying they want to be police and firemen. Upon learning that fire burns, and police many times come under fire on the job and are not that well paid, one's initial aspirations change sometimes, *don't they?* Usually they do, sometimes they do not. Whenever you find out that something does not work as previously thought, there is a shift in paradigm. How many of these have you had?

Why is PS a Prerequisite?

This is so revolutionary in both concept and application, it is a prerequisite to success because things are not always going to work the way that we plan them to, or think that they should. Paradigm Shift is the old, proverbial '*back to the drawing board*' analogy that causes us to take a closer look at prior notions. **Whenever you learn a thing that replaces older knowledge with new knowledge, this is a paradigm shift.** It is so interesting because, like unto learning it is an ongoing process that does not cease.

If you are actively seeking out information, you are going to come across that which contradicts previously held beliefs. That is fine, it *refines one's perspective.* Imagine how the grasshopper's paradigm shifted after having faced the first winter in the cold, while the ant he saw had built a home and stored food for himself in Aesop's fable. Pretty revolutionary, right?

I would think so, the same thing happened when people became aware that they live on a planet that is round as opposed to the previous held notion that it was flat.

A paradigm shift is that which challenges you to see things another way due to evidence of possible error. I will give one more personal example, have you ever tried to hide something from someone, and found out how hard that can be. Well, upon finding out that one lie leads to another, which leads to another, one may become of the mindset that *whatever doesn't come out in the wash comes out in the rinse,* and it is just better to tell the truth in all matters, than to try to deceive people and hide things from them. You may find this out after stealing some cookies from the cookie jar, and telling mother that you did not, with chocolate all over your hands and face. *Doesn't work that well does it?*

Refinement Perspective

As stated, this refines perspective makes us better. The same concept is applicable in terms of technology, we've spoken about failure and how things become obsolete. Well, until things began to descend through the process of decline, these were things that people thought *could not, and would not* happen. Man became more adapted to change from the reality though. **He became better.** He became more informed, more adjusted, and more *suitable.* This is what happens when one is forced to rethink his strategy…he comes up with a better one.

Our quests for success are based on what we think will work at any given time. When we find out that there is more work that has to be done, it gives us a chance to stay up to date and on pace with, if not ahead of, the times. **This is called adaptation.** You have to be more than *willing* to adapt, you have to be *able.* Many people believe that they are *willing* to adapt, just to find out that they are not *able* to. This inability causes all forms of physical disease, depression, drug addiction, and suicide. These are referred to in Coaching/counseling as *coping mechanisms.*

Adaptation is a Must

The paradigm shift is a prerequisite to success, because if one is not able to adapt he will die. Simple. If the summer turns to winter and a person cannot wrap his head around it and change his wardrobe, he will freeze or at the very least have his *feelings hurt.* It is best to be *flexible and well adapted* to change, as we learned in the last chapter, we have to accept that previously held notions may be subject to change upon the encounter with overwhelming evidence of possible error.

Very few people succeed at what they set out to do, the way that they set out to do it. Most times it takes overhaul and revamping a number of times. Furthermore, people may find success at a different venture altogether, after learning that what they were trying to do initially was not going to bear fruit, or was a lost cause. Still some others may find that they have to change their trajectory (*aim*) because that which they sought out success in, was something that brought them absolutely no joy or sense of satisfaction whatsoever. Have you ever started something and then realized that you no longer wanted to do it….*at all.*

Change of Degree Plan

This is the case for many people who change their major in college. They initially think that they want to do something particular, get a degree in a specialized area, but once they begin to learn they find out that they are much better *suited* to do something else. The passion for the initial undertaking has waned in comparison, or maybe they found out that such and such a position pays 50 thousand dollars more per year, with the same amount of school time required. That would be a great example of a paradigm shift. One that I could say I had, it's like an *epiphany*.

The introduction of new knowledge is one thing that allows this to take place, because a person just does not know, what they do not know, until they know it. Does that make sense? This is why it is hard to give someone advice, or become heartbroken because they do not take advice. You can see someone going down the road to perdition and warn them against that direction, and recommend other courses, but that is all, because ultimately it is the prerequisite of *individual personal development* for people to learn things on their own. **This is called a process.**

The Difference Between Knowledge and Experience

You cannot give people the Paradigm Shift that you have had, it is an experience that is *unique unto you*. Experiences are for each individual to *have*, the same as knowledge is for each individual to *accept*. Just because you say something is so, does not mean that people are going to believe you. Sometimes even after you prove it to them, beyond the shadow of a doubt, they still lurk in the shadow. **This is why education, and the introduction of information, is the most powerful galvanizing tool that a person can wield.** It is in the *introduction* and *acceptance of* information that a person is able to have a Paradigm Shift, and accept what you tried to tell them all day long with no success.

Paradigm Shifts come from *understanding*, this cannot be transferred. **You can give a person knowledge, you can provide them with wisdom, and you can impart examples *from* your understanding.** However, you cannot give them *your* understanding. If you could, there would be a lot less accidents, premature deaths, and childhood mistakes, because parents would inject their children with *their* understanding from birth, and not leave them to '*find out for themselves.*'

Self Learning, Self Taught

People must find out for themselves, they must have their own experiences, develop their own understanding, and undergo their own Paradigm Shifts. It is not sufficient for most people to take someone else's word for it, **we are an investigative species.** Even when our mothers said, "*Wait to get in, the water's too hot now*", you didn't believe her until you stuck your big toe in the tub and could no longer feel it. Then you said, "*Oh, it's too hot.*" You did not understand until you tested it. That is because we are a scientific species. We need to *validate*.

It is through this process of validation that many things are invalidated, causing us to further refine our views and rewire our presentation. This is a fantastic situation. **Once a thing has been learned it cannot be unlearned, but it can be updated.** When people ask me, "Do I have any regrets?" I honestly reply in the negative. I have no regrets because anything I did in the past, I did based on the best information that I had at the time, and I stand before you changed, because the *quality* of the information that I had access to changed. I do not stand around like a lot of people do fantasizing that, "*If I knew then, what I know now*", because if you knew then what you know now, you'd make a whole different set of mistakes.

When the Student is Ready, The Teacher Appears

Everything has it's time, and it's place. This is one thing that we have to accept, the teacher will appear, when the student is ready. I could not write this book until I was deemed fundamentally ready to, until I had my arsenal of words and understanding fully loaded from experience and perspective. You could not read this book until it was time for you to read this book. I always feel sad for people who take credit for other's accomplishments, making statements devoid of understanding such as, "*if it were not for me, etc., etc.*" or, "*you should be thanking me, because without me, blah, blah, blah*". Rubbish.

The universe puts opportunities into place, and put specific people into place who can provide opportunities. So never feel indebted to a person for introducing you to a thing or *facilitating your introduction* to a thing, or managing your process through a thing. I am not saying to be ungrateful, no, just be grateful to the *true source* from which all things and opportunities are made available. If you've ever said this to someone else, which I have before I gained the right knowledge, **STOP!** Stop taking credit for something that was not yours to give. The blessing was given to you to give to others, and had it not been you, it would have been another, and the real question is; where would that leave you if you were not performing the duty called upon to do.

My response to such an arrogant person who just wants to take credit and throw things that they may have done for me in my face is, "*Honestly if it was not you, it would have been another. It was my time to receive this instruction, wisdom, blessing, etc. and if you were not here to give it to me, another person would have been, but I thank you anyway.*" This is understanding. When it is time for you to receive a thing there is not one who can take it away from you, and there is not one who give you something, until it is time for you to have it. This would be fruit out of season. It does not taste good.

The Importance of Due Season

I like to provide examples. Think of babies that were born out of term, or *premature.* The word premature indicates that they have not matured to the *point of completion.* Many times these infants have to be put into an incubator. An incubator is a man-made structure that has the purpose of mimicking the functions of the womb. They go through this artificial gestation period for the purpose of continuing the prenatal processes. Then when the proper term has been completed and they have matured, they can be born, or removed from the incubator and released from the hospital.

Think of those people who think that they are lucky to have won the lottery, or come into some money without having gone through the prerequisite courses to properly know *how to handle* such money. They are soon making foolish decisions that separate them from their winnings. **Some destroy themselves.** This is usually referred to as someone who has, '*fallen into*' some money. How does it usually go for them? Not well most of the time, would that be safe to say?

Imagine going to the hospital for a minor operation, and your doctor says to you, "*Guess what? I graduated the day after I enrolled into college!*" How proficient do you think he would be? Would you feel confident in their ability to perform the operation? They probably would not be proficient at taking your temperature, much less performing any kind of operation. What do you think? **Nothing succeeds like success, give yourself the proper time in which to flourish and grow.** This will give you strength and *staying power.*

The Importance of Due Process

Think of those who became successful without going through the proper channels, they usually use their successes as a way to injure other people. They may be malicious, vicious, and have a view of self that is without reproach, because they have not gone through the unit of humility in the failure prerequisite. This is a situation that will not do them any good, and the people they come into contact with will probably suffer as well.

This is for those who think that their *success is overdue*, some think that their success is way overdue. *They have a name for those who try to force success and money, out of season, into their lives.* **They are usually referred to as criminals.** Do not try to force it, let go and let it flow to you. Go through the proper channels. Why do you think a person has to learn to drive before being given a license and let loose on the highway? The morgue and funeral homes will bear me testimony as to this reality.

Think of how good food tastes when you follow the instructions and do not try to *speed up the process*. Imagine if you were to take a raw turkey out of the oven after cooking it for 13 minutes because you were hungry. What sense does that make? **Let it do what it is supposed to do.** The same thing can be said for your success, and both, out of season, may leave you with a *bloody mouth*. Think of wine and how it grows better with time. That is true with all things. Think of the difference between a person who has just arrived at training camp, and a *seasoned* veteran. Which one would you rather follow into battle?

Patience & Process

Hopefully this will provide you with a new way to view *patience*, and a new way of viewing *process*. The process of preparation. The art of patience must be exhibited within the scope of preparation, if you are not patient during the preparation process you may fail one of the prerequisites and *have to start over* in order to get the required learning. It is much better if you do it right the first time, try not to hurry the process, and do as good as you can. This way you can ensure that there are no more further delays, and that you **really can do what you say that you can do.**

Have you ever heard the saying, *"be careful of what you wish for?"* This is because if not properly vetted, or properly prepared, when you receive that which was the object of your desire, you may be rudely awakened. You may actually find out that it is not at all what you thought it was. Why do you think that lower level employees are *groomed* for management? **Everyone thinks they can do everything better than the person in the office above them, until they actually get there and realize it was more demanding than they previously thought.**

Once being given the job, getting a promotion, winning the lottery, getting pregnant, giving birth, getting in school, graduating from school, and in many different scenarios there is likely to be a very *humbling* Paradigm Shift. The Paradigm Shift may be accommodating, in other instances it may be more demanding to incorporate, in some instances you may want to, or have to turn back altogether. You will do much better in any situation if you have properly armed yourself with all the information possible. Then you will at least have a better chance at making what is referred to as an informed decision. At least for the moment, because as we have already confirmed, information's accuracy is subject to constant change.

The Fluidity of Facts

Information is always changing, as we exist in a constantly fluctuating world. Information has a very short pertinent shelf life, information changes almost instantly. We live in such an *information saturated society* that what became the new rule yesterday, has a likelihood of becoming extinct today. I grew up in New York City, and I can remember using tokens to get on the public transportation system. How quickly did that change? I can also remember the rapidly escalating price of a MetroCard. So if a person was to be acting on yesterday's information, and was to go to the train station with the exact amount of currency that was required to get to your destination yesterday, they may be surprised to find that they were *denied entry because they need more* money *today* for a MetroCard.

The same is true of today's doorways to success, the keys and security systems update daily. I have come to realize that in today's society an *Associate's degree is little more than a high school diploma*. At one point a High School Diploma was all you needed to be able to secure a living wage. Not so today. Today a *Bachelor's degree is like an Associate's degree* was ten years ago. Not so heavy. You will find today that many entry level positions require at least a Bachelor's degree just to pass through the security system, and gain entrance to the building. Now a *Master's degree* is what is sought after as the preferred pre-requisite of claiming higher education. **Now consider the cost.**

The cost of college has risen exponentially every single year to date. It costs much more to go to school today that it did *just 5 years ago*. The required amount of study has intensified as well, though there are some who say that more rigorous study was expected and required in years past. What does that mean? That means that the *cost* has *gone up* and some school's *quality* of education has *declined*. Still most would agree that the demands have risen. **This is a paradigm shift, either way, education affords the student a new world view.**

NEW WORLD VIEW

The need for a paradigm shift is so very crucial in today's world and time. If we do not have a paradigm shift, if we continue to do things the same way that we've always done things, we will continue to reap the same rewards that we have always gotten, and nothing will change. **If you are somewhere that does not provide you and your family with the things that you would rather have, if you are somewhere that does not provide you with a sense of security and fulfillment, you are in need of a paradigm shift.**

New Requirements Necessary

To experience a paradigm shift you must constantly provide your mind with new ideas and new information. Now the information that you receive may not be new in a fundamental sense, as long as it is *new to you*. This provides us with new views on life and aspects of life. A Paradigm Shift is the result of *study and present observation*. If you are not fully present, meaning *open and accepting*, then there may be things that you are witnessing that you are not privy to being what they actually are. **You may be seeing things that you are not really seeing.** Let me elaborate on this.

If you are closed minded, if you are not *receptive* to the information that you are receiving, it does not matter what you are presented with in life, it may do you no good. Let me provide an analogy. An analogy of this is two brothers who come from the same household. They eat the same food, sleep in the same house, yet one takes one path, and the other brother takes another path. One brother becomes a success story, *not rich monetarily per se*, just successful in the sense of fulfillment to himself, he lives an enriched life, and he is at peace. The other brother however listlessly drifts in life, from one problem to the next, never seeming to get his head on straight.

Did they have access to different information? Maybe so. What I see happen a lot though, is the *perception* of the same situations will take on a different light, or have a *different meaning*, to *different people*. What then, is the real difference? One *saw* things one way, and the other *saw* the same things in a different light, they took on a different meaning to the two, therefore having different results. **Different people, same circumstances, different perceptions, different results.**

One may go to college, one may choose to go to a trade school, or the military, or not go to school or the military, and perhaps one becomes depressed and sinks into alcoholism. *Don't we all know of this occurrence?* Two brothers who take two diametrically opposed paths? It happens all the time, one brother finds fulfillment in the simple accomplishments and does things slowly, and another cannot abstain from being anxious and wanting gratification immediately. It speaks to resolve, it speaks to *habituation*, and it speaks to paradigm.

Lost in Plain Day

This is true for those who cannot seem to find their path. They have no direction, they are right next to you in the same situation, yet if you ask them both how they view things, they will give you two answers that do not sound at all alike. It is important for you to have an open mind, to be *receptive to the signs* that you are given to be able to make an *accurate assessment* of your circumstances. As soon as the perception changes, the same can be said of the situation. It does not even matter what information you come into contact with, if it has not staying power, if it has no impact. **For those who have eyes, let him see, for those who have ears, let him hear.**

The Power of Perspective

A paradigm is a view. We can take two people in a dismal situation. One sees possibility, one sees hopelessness. The same *impetus* that becomes *fuel* for one, takes on the form of a *boundary* for the other. We know that this takes place, we just must decide which one we are going to be by the way we perceive things. **Therefore our paradigm, or worldview, is a result of our perception.**

How are we going to choose our perception? By enlisting alternatives. How do we learn of alternative viewpoints? Through the course of study, through *analysis*. I have been in situations that I could not see the way out of, until I learned of others who had the same circumstance, and I became *enlightened by the analysis* of how they handled it. This may not change our paradigm, but it gives us a possibility to do so. **Without knowledge there is no opportunity.** When we are informed. we can make an informed decision, we have informed *opportunity*.

Our paradigm is our responsibility, it is the result of the way that we *assess and internalize.* I have always been astounded by contrasting stories of those who share the same or similar upbringing and environment. What makes these people different? Their circumstances are similar, they are similar in age, they are similar in the information that they had access to. One saw things in one light, the other in another, and they end up taking too distinctly different paths in life. One is fulfilling, and the other is miserable, leaving much to be desired. I have always found this to be very interesting. **The difference was in the perception of the situation.**

How many times have you seen an *obstacle*, where another saw an *opportunity*, or maybe you are the one who perceives a *possibility*, where another sees nothing but *problems*. This is due to the difference in Paradigm. The importance of a Paradigm Shift cannot be understated. For many it is the difference between *life and death*, for some it is the difference between *poverty and prosperity*. We must inundate ourselves with information at all times, in order to open up the world of possibilities, for **one cannot act on knowledge that they do not have.**

Information = Opportunity

When you open your mind up to new information it provides us with a new world view. The world becomes a difference place according to the knowledge that one possesses. We have to continue in our pursuit of the information that will change our situation. It is this *information* that dictates the *opportunities* that we will have access to. You cannot have *access* to a thing that you do not know *exists*.

Sometimes it takes something terrible to happen before we can open our eyes, and shift our paradigm. Sometimes it is an illness that wakes us up to the knowledge that we have to do better by our state of health. Sometimes it is the death of a loved one that awakens us as to what's really important in life. This would be considered as success, would it not? I agree, a successful *breakthrough* in understanding. For some of us, the word success takes on a variety of meanings. Some would like to be successful in their marriage, some would like to be successful in the area of parenting, others look for financial success, still others familial relational success, and some just want to be successful at completing a book that they pick up.

Whichever variation of success is your focal point, a paradigm shift could be the remedy. **It has been said that foresight is blindness, and hindsight is 20/20.** Meaning that the awakening point can be long after the loss is suffered, after it is reflected upon. Charging ahead, so few really see what it is that they are doing, they are like the proverbial *bull in the china shop.* Yet after they have wrecked everything in their lives, marriage, or occupation, then they look back and have the **AHA! Moment.**

Natural Resources

This is when everything looks plain, and it is so easy to ascertain the understanding contained within the context. This is responsible for the saying, *"If I knew then, what I know now"* dilemma. **We don't, we never will, and we are not supposed to.** We grow as we go, and we cannot act on information that we do not know. This is why it is so important for us to *bathe ourselves in new information daily.* **The Paradigm Shift will come like an Earthquake, and when it is supposed to, like rain.** It is a natural occurrence, and you cannot afford someone else the benefit of your own. You can only advise, you cannot force someone to use the information that you impart to them. It is frustrating, but it is fact.

Once calamity befalls a person they tend to understand fully. This is why sometimes you have to leave Mad Scientists up to their own devices. You may know that the person in question is headed for a brick wall, you may advise, but you cannot grab *their* wheel. They must understand the gravity of the lesson that life is trying to teach them. A paradigm shift is what opens new doors for us to walk through. It provides the breakthrough. So to that effect, do not let what you are currently going through *break you*, instead let this be *your breakthrough.*

Sometimes we are so hard headed that we have to be side swiped just to get our eyes back in focus. How many times has your mother told you something that you ignored, only to have the penalties that she indicated were going to befall you, actually befall you, forcing you to realize that she was right the whole time? This happens very often, more in some communities than in others. Many times it is long after the person who told us has passed from this Earth, and we never get to tell them how right they were, and that we realize what they were trying to do for us. **This is why it is so important to stay open and present in the moment, because you may never have another.**

The Need for Continual Learning

Paradigm Shifts are so integral to our process, you will never discontinue to have them, as there is always a better way to do something. What you learn, if we are honest with ourselves, is *always how much more* we need to learn. We find out, with everything that we find out, how much more there is that we need to find out. The pursuit of knowledge is a never ending process. **Knowledge is to be sought from the cradle to the grave** to quote the Psalms.

Who is under the impression that they do not need a new world view? The same person who thinks that this world is perfect, and that they are at the pinnacle of perfection and cannot do any better for themselves. In other words, most *teenagers and fools.* Teenagers think that they have all the answers, and that no one can tell them anything because they have yet to fall upon the **knife of calamity**. They do not know what they do not know, but everyone finds out. Everyone gets an opportunity to see just how wrong they were, to give them a chance to straighten out and acquire a new world view. It never fails.

Think of it, have you ever known anyone who changed their life? A person who just became a part of something new, and they are reinvigorated for life? They have so much zeal, and enthusiasm for what they are involved in that you wish sometimes that they would just shut up already? **These are people who have had a revolution of evolution.**

They have had a paradigm shift, that altered their perception of reality, and they are never going to go back to their old ways of doing things. *This is what you need to succeed.*

Born Blank

As children we are blank sheets at birth, born blank. The story of our lives become that which we hear, see, smell, touch, etc. **The people that we become is based on our interpretation of the information that we possess.** This is why it is so important that as parents and custodians of our own lives that we *syphon off* that which is unproductive, that we shield ourselves from the unimportant and *potentially destructive.* Until a person is guided correctly and of age to fend for themselves, this is the parent's job. Once we leave home and become independent it becomes our job. This is why, when many people fail, it will be said that they were not ready to '*leave the nest*'. Think about that.

Observe Nature

In the animal world you will see parents feeding their young. They will have them off to a separate corner of the forest or up in a tree, way out on a limb for safety from predators, or in the case of the spider, in a web on their back, this is so as to guard them from the *wrong elements.* These seemingly unintelligent animal life forms should be watched for guidance by humans. They should be studied and their practices *incorporated* in our human way of life. **So many times we do not sufficiently protect our young.** We allow them to *eat anything, see anything, as well as listen to anything.* It is abnormal and completely unnatural, and we will be the harvesters of our ill judgement.

Everything that a person learns results in a shift of paradigm. Some much more powerfully than others. This is why it is of the utmost importance that we shield our children from outside intrusive factors. This is also why we, ourselves, have to be diligent in our protection of ourselves. What we *eat, drink, talk about, listen to,* and what we allow ourselves to *watch* should go through an **extreme vetting process**. If not we will be *shifted and forever changed* by the paradigms of others. How important is this and what impact, if any, does this have?

The Psychology of Sales

Salesmen are extreme manipulators, ask me how do I know? I know because I have always been one. I have always been able to sell anything to virtually anyone. I mean anything, a tape, a tape player (these refer to musical devices for the generation that may know not), a picture, a card and many other things. The point is this, **if a person can influence you from the outside they can control you on the inside**. I'm the guy who could sell the Wolf of Wall Street an entire pen company, along with barrels, and barrels of ink like oil. I would have no problem at all, because I believe in my product so much. What is my main product? **Me.**

I have the ability to galvanize, and so do all salesmen, well, all successful ones anyway. We believe in our product so much that you will too. You will want to believe in it enough to give it a try, even if you do not believe in it at first. It will grow on you. We are so excited, and so fired up that we will *transfer the emotion onto you* if you stick around long enough. This is why you have to watch what you allow yourself to indulge in; mentally, physically, emotionally, spiritually, and every other '*lly*', that there is. If not, **you will be performing the will of others without knowing it, because you have been shifted by *their* paradigm.**

If you find yourself shifted by their paradigm, you will find yourself benefitting or suffering as a result of someone else's situation that you had nothing to do with, in and of yourself. This is why mothers and fathers the world over try to shelter their children from the influences of others. They commonly say in defense of their children, that they did such and such *under the influence* of so and so, it was not *the influence* of so and so, it was *under the influence* of so and so's paradigm, and worldview, that they were shifted by.

I find it terribly disturbing when people are caught in a dead end situation because of someone else. I'm sure you have witnessed the bereaved parent saying that it could not be their child that has done a thing, because they know *their* child, and it is just impossible. Their child's world view however could easily have been shifted by the paradigm of another person. A paradigm shift is so motivational that the person who receives it is often powerless against it. You could know someone for a very long time, and then they go to a meeting, and it is as if you never knew them at all, that is how totally absorbent, and swift that a paradigm shift can be.

Mob Mentality

It is as if the curtains have been pulled back on a world that they never knew existed. I know I have not been using the best examples possible, but there was a reason for that, many times we learn the gravity of a matter through the *negative association*. I am sure every reader can relate to my analogies and symbolism, and everyone knows of someone, or a lot of people whose worldviews have been changed through association with others. I wanted to impress upon you the power of it, so you can see the importance of your conscious involvement with the process.

Do not allow yourself to be shifted by the paradigms of others. How do we control that? We control it through the filter with which we let information come into contact with us or with our loved ones. It is through this filtering process that we do not even give poisonous thoughts, or toxic possibilities the chance to take root. It is very dangerous to the mind of the child, and the immature, the following type. If you notice that a child is easily impressionable you have to be ultra proactive that they do not take on the worldviews of another.

Ideological Inheritances

Adults many times take on the worldviews of their parents, or their spouses, and end up bitterly regretting it in the years to follow. Example; imagine the young mother who is married as a teenager, quickly impregnated and then she engages in a twenty some odd year relationship. Only to be divorced abruptly soon thereafter. Many times they go through a wild phase where they then try to relive their youth. They may not act, dress, or talk their age because they are trying to make up for *lost time*. Did they lose time? No, they *lost themselves in someone else*, and that they can never make up for.

Think about the child who stays at home and does everything that the parent wants or recommends. They go to school, are in bed by a certain time, they go to college, with no breaks. They graduate, they take on the career that they parents advise them to, they marry the woman that their parents recommend them too. They are so out of touch with themselves that when the parent finally dies they have a break with reality. Their worldview has never been one of their own construct, so when the parents are gone the child is left to wonder who they really are. These children often have a midlife crisis.

The characteristics of this mid-life crisis are represented by breaking with convention. **They may get divorced, they may quit their jobs, and they may travel cross-country.** What they do will seem to be the *opposite of their personality*, it will completely contradict convention. They may shave their heads, or grow their hair wild. They will change the music they listen to, frequent places they have never been, start smoking, or stop, and find themselves with a member of the opposite sex that they did not even know they were attracted to. If questioned as to what they are doing, or why, they will often say that they are *"trying to find themselves"*. It is a sad thing to see, and an even sadder state of affairs to be in.

This is because they never developed their own world view. They have always adopted the paradigm, or inherited the ideology, of their parents, and now that their worldview writers are gone, they have to begin to write their own worldviews on the blank sheet of paper that is their lives. This is also true of the child of the restrictive parents, the kind who willfully force their paradigm on their child. The child cannot think for themselves, or act on their independent views, from fear of either reproach or bodily harm. **As soon as these children are outside of their parent's supervision they go absolutely bananas.**

They become reckless, and no one can understand why. This is often more intensive than the child of the restrictive parents, as they often engage in actions that are *potentially negative, and of a risky and dangerous nature.* **Their actions often bring them very harmful and painful consequences.** Hopefully they can survive the phase in order to be blessed by a paradigm shift and have their worldview shaped by the consequences they suffer as a result of their frantic search for an identity of their own, with no fear, as children are always given to the thought of immortality. This is their immature worldview, they are most in need of a new worldview. They are the most at risk in this situation and in dire need of a paradigm shift.

BACK IN THE GAME

very time that we open our eyes is a new year, a new you, a new world, a new chance, a new birth, and a new possibility. How much more so when we *open our minds?* I don't know what it is that's got you out. The death of a loved one? Little to no money? Job loss? Divorce? Illness? Whatever it may be, the moment that you open your mind to the new stimulus, the new reality, you have a chance to get back in the game.

You Were Born Victorious

Life may have fouled you out. You were born to parents who are alcoholics, parents who were abusive, parents who were children, parents who had no money, no education and little to no chance. You could have been born with a heart murmur, a handicap, a drug addiction (*this is very serious*), you could have been born blind, homeless, in a woman's prison, *these things happen*. You could have been born to many of these things, or more than one of these things. Many times people miss the most important part. If you were born under any of these circumstances, the most important part is that *you were born.*

You were given life, you fought, and you won the race. **You're already a winner.** You already have the championship belt *of life*. It was a fight to breathe air, to go from the *umbilical cord of liquid and blood*

151

to hydrogen and oxygen. It was a fight to open your eyes for the first time, it was a fight as far as the formation of your DNA. Albeit, it was a fight that you were unconscious of, still it was a fight, and by your mere presence on this Earth, and in this life…you won. You didn't quit. You didn't complain. You went through pain.

You Were Born a Success Story

You were born successful. You were successful to begin with, failures don't wake up, and **the successful sleep on a treadmill.** When the winning is done, then you can rest. When you have seen all there is to see in this life, when your hands have touched all that there is to touch in this life, and you left some for your babies, that's when you can leave. *Are you hearing me?* You don't have permission to leave this class (LIFE) until you are finished with the lesson.

You're in pain, good, that's a part of it. You're hurting, great, that's a part of it. You feel like life isn't fair? Now you're getting somewhere. It's hard. Are you just realizing that? Your baby, wife, son, brother, sister, mother, father, auntie, uncle died? You're going to get a lot of that. *Get over it.* Go give their bodies the respect it deserves for doing what it did for you when it was animate (*alive*) and get over it, get on with your life. Sounds cold? You know why? *We're all on the same road.* We're all going to get there, that's also a part of it.

Specific Prescription

Everything you are going through, you are going through for a reason. I can't tell you exactly why it is that you are going through what you are going through specifically. What I can tell you is it is prescribed for you. The universe, God, Allah, Buddha, Jesus, whatever name you call that Force by, has *a medicine that is prescribed and designed for your DNA.*

It is prescribed for *you and you alone.* It is prescribed for you to grow, to get well, to get better, and to get beyond. Some people have similar concoctions, a little of this, a 3rd of that, two teaspoons of misery, etc., etc. but no one has a duplicate of your exact medicine.

That's why it seems like some don't care, and the rest do not understand, it is because they do not. The ones who care for you can just hold you and support you, tell you how great you are and cry with you, saying it will get better. How do they know? Don't they know how you feel? Don't they know it isn't fair? Yes, they do, they have not had your exact batch of medicine, but *they have had their own,* everyone you know has. This pain and misery you're experiencing is a *rite of passage.*

Everyone on Earth gets some hurt, everyone on Earth gets their dose of unfair, everyone gets their spilling over glass of "*Why me?*" Everyone fails, some more than others, because they did not earn a passing grade, so they have to repeat the semester, some much more than others. It may take someone four years to do what you do in a week, these classes of learning are *DNA specific.* Everyone has a different gift, a different talent. To realize that talent it is going to take a specific kind of blinding white pain to realize, it's going to require a certain amount of frustration and '*it isn't fair*' to come to fruition.

Don't ask me why, I can't tell you what your dream is, what gift you were brought here with, how you are going to be used to contribute one of the universe's blessings upon Earth. Only you know that, and you may not even know it yet, you may not even realize it. Somebody *put something* in your luggage, somebody saw your bag, while it was going through customs and *slipped something* in it. I don't know what it is. I don't know *what* it is that is in *your bag,* but you'd better find it. **You'd better find what's in your bag,** before life hurts you...*bad.*

What is Your Prescription Description?

You have a job to do, you were not born to sleep. You were not born to go to and from work and back home, to go to sleep over and over, and over and over. Hamsters do that, a *species was designed to do just that*, and that isn't you. You were born with reason, you were born with intellect, you were *born for* a reason, and you were born to *interject*. You were born for a higher calling than you are now realizing. *"How do you know Shawn?"* **I know simply because you are reading this now**. This is a part of your *prescription*. The universe works miracles for people, the beauty in it is that it comes *to people from people*.

You are reading these words because these words are a part of your process, they are vital to your ticket, I'll get to your ticket some more after a while. **What we go through in life, prepares us for who were are to become in life.** Every hardship in life prepares us to become who we are meant to be, we are formed, we are strengthened by the unfair, and we are *forged by the fire*. You were molested, *so what,* I know a lot of people who were. I'm not being evil or not caring, I am very caring, and I just care about the '*how*'. Bad things happen to good people all the time. It seems to make no sense. Your spouse was murdered, *"I'm sorry, but so what?"* I know a lot of those people too. **This is your prescription.**

The prescription specifically finds the illness, it finds what it has to *eliminate*. It finds what it has to *accommodate*, what it has to *assimilate*, and it finds what it has to *accentuate*. **It finds what it is that is going to produce the person that you were meant to be.** I'm sorry but if you were meant for greatness, you are going to suffer greatly. If you're not really going to make much a difference, if you're not going to be too significant, if you're not going to be noticed, you may have a pain free existence, but *if you're hurting right now*, if your eyes are sore from crying, and your mind is sore from your weeks of searching for the reason why something unfair happened to you, welcome to the party. *This is part of your ticket.*

If someone has wronged you, if your circumstances make absolutely no sense whatsoever, if you cannot see the reason for the life of you, *trust me you will.* It may be an hour a week, a month, it may be a year, or a couple of them. **Sometimes medicine has a delayed effect and period of inactivity.** Then at the right moment it will make all of the difference. At the determined moment in time this will all make sense to you and become the *mechanism*, become the *reason*, become the *ability*, become what *enables you to reach the highest heights.*

Worlds Within Worlds

This prerequisite is so important, they all are so important in their own right and so are the units within each, they are like *worlds within worlds,* like *pain within pain.* You know what I'm talking about. There is hurt, and then there is hurt *within that hurt.* Take the common toothache for example, you've got a toothache, that is painful, I know. Within this toothache though there exists a *numbness*, there also exists a *coldness*, this coldness which will make you shiver, and cause your nerves to tremble. Then there is the *stabbing* pain, when you bite down onto something, and the root of the tooth stabs into your upper or lower jawbone. Then there is the *throbbing, pulsating* pain accompanied by a taste of metal, it is a *seven fold kind of pain.* A hurt within a hurt, a world within a world, **life teaches you lessons within lessons.**

Micro & Macro

There is a macro and a micro purpose, a duality of reason, a surface and a more *internal* reality. On the surface you may have lost your job, and cannot find another for quite some time. On the internal, life may be *teaching* you about *appreciation, delayed gratification, patience and how to deal with frustration.* These are priceless prerequisites to success, but it takes a deeper understanding to see the internal possibilities of purpose. Most of us are fixated on the visible, what we see, as opposed to what we think. **Many times we do not consider at all.**

Boxing & Life

Perhaps this is the reason, have you ever had bad things seem to meet you over and over again. Does it seem like life has mercilessly pummeled you, and you can't raise your arms to defend yourself? See, the profession of boxing states that there must be a referee present, and when a fighter gets knocked down the referee has to stop the opponent from hitting you while you are on the ground. Well, the ring of life has no such rules, *the ring of life has no referee.* This is why it will seem, and it will actually be, that life is hitting you while you are down.

The universe has no emotion, there is no right or wrong, it just does what it is designed to do...*make you.* It has no concern whether or not you fell, it does not pull punches, it does not care, it was *set in motion one time and will never have to be set again,* and there is a reason for this. The fight in your life is not supposed to be won on the cards, there is no score sheet, you are either going to be a *champ or a chump*, there is *no runner up.* The ref is not going to stop the fight. He is not going to enter the fight, the referee in this fight does not exist, as he is a figment of your imagination, a participant in a different sport.

You are going to have to fight your way back up. This is the purpose, life is not going to relent, it is not going to give you a chance, and it will not pick you up. It is designed to test your mettle, to qualify you, or you will qualify yourself as deserving of greatness by not giving up, by fighting from your back after being knocked down to your knees, and then **fighting your way back up** to your feet from your knees, and then becoming victorious by knocking the hardships of life out of the ring. By knocking it senseless, unconscious, incapacitated, by rendering it harmless, then all the naysayers will appear.

Then your ring (*life*) will be full of those who said you could never do it, those who thought you'd never *rise to the occasion, those who did not believe in you.* There will be some supporters but not many. There will be the sharks who bet against you, and there will be the laughing hyenas. There will be those who come and thrust your arm up in victory, hug you, and smile in your face even though deep down they hate the lungs that you use to breathe, and they hate the heart that gives you your life. **These are the shady promoters in the boxing ring of life, oh yes, there are many parallels between the squared circle and the circle of life.**

You have to fight your way back from obscurity, you have to make yourself known. Life is not going to search you out, you have to *earn your position* in it, and you have to earn your *validity*, earn your *title*. Whether you want to be known as the heavyweight champion, the CEO, the CFO, the creator of anything that you create, there is a process, a *vetting process.* You are going to be examined by life, you will be given to a rigorous exam that only you can pass. No one will be able to fight the fight for you, no one will be able to take your test for you. **Pass or fail it will depend upon you, your hand, your will, your power, your initiative.**

No one can come to your aid as much as they may like to. No one can *take the blows* of life for you. It is hard to see someone you love get hurt, fail, go through trials, but there are your own to take, and there will be trials for those whom you love, who choose to go down the road that they choose to go down, and you will *not be able* to get in the ring *for them.* You will have to sit by the sidelines and let them make their own decisions. I will give you an example.

Who Cares for the Caterpillar?

There once was a caterpillar. The caterpillar was in a tank, the tank was owned by a boy who glorified at the marvel of nature. He had read all there was to read about the caterpillar, and the *metamorphosis* that takes place in the life of a caterpillar, and he thought that he was ready to see that. **We are never prepared for the pain that our loved ones must endure.** The caterpillar used to crawl up the arm of the boy, and the boy loved to feel all of the caterpillars' legs on his arm as the caterpillar slowly crawled from his wrist to his elbow, and from his elbow to his shoulder, every morning they would do this.

One morning the boy woke up and looked into the cage for his caterpillar and it was nowhere to be found, in its place there was a *cocoon of what used to be the caterpillar* hanging from a small tree limb that the boy had placed into the cage. The boy looked sadly at this husk for days, then for a week, then two weeks. Somewhere in the third week the boy saw the cocoon begin to wiggle. The boy thought to himself, "*Oh great, there is my friend.*" He left for school and came back expecting to see the butterfly. He returned from school later, *no butterfly.*

Instead he saw the cocoon slightly open at the bottom, and he watched all evening as the caterpillar struggled against the cocoon making no real substantial process. The boy felt *obligated to* the caterpillar but did not want to *intervene on the process.* The caterpillars' process was painful for the boy to watch. Here was his friend, struggling, and he could just rip the cocoon open at any time and facilitate his friend's exit from what seemed like a casket of eternal pain. However, the boy did come home from school the next day to see progress, the head of the butterfly, now jutted out of the bottom of the cocoon, it still could not get out, but *he was working.*

He was struggling, he was working and the boy swore he could see pain on the expression of the caterpillar, now a butterfly, who had grown some long antennae that the boy was not used to seeing. The boy was very eager to see the rest of his friend and he wanted his friend not to suffer anymore. He began to think it unfair and quite cruel of him to sit by *idly* while his friend suffered when he could *so easily help him.* The boy had finally had enough, he *could not sit and watch any more.*

So the boy went into his crayon box, and got some safety scissors so as not to hurt his friend while he helped him. The boy reached into the cage with the scissors in his hand and he gently cut the cocoon a little bit, reached in the cage and carefully tore the cocoon open enough for his friend to squirm out and fly. Instead, what happened was this slimy blob jutted out of the cocoon and oozed down onto the floor of the cage, he had a bloated lower body. Half of his body was wet and bloated. He did not have wings, he did not fly, he rolled over on his back and he kept rolling, going nowhere. *The boy could not understand.*

It is the squirming painful process that shoots the blood of the caterpillar into the wings giving life to the wings, and this is what separates the wings from the body of the caterpillar. It is this process that causes the wings to open up, and in his haste to be of assistance that the boy *actually stunted the growth of his friend.* The caterpillar was supposed to be able to continue the process of molting, and complete the formation of the rest of his body. He was never *allowed* to do so. He squirmed around on the floor a couple of days, he did not eat, and soon thereafter he died. *He had never flown, and he had never become the butterfly that he was destined to become.*

Painful Truth

In your process you may wonder why no one comes to your aid. Why doesn't someone help me? You may ask. Why doesn't someone come to my assistance? You may plead. You may want help, but the wise amongst you know all that they can do is talk to you. They cannot just *write you a check*, they cannot just pick you up, as you were meant to be able to walk on your own. They will stunt your growth, they will *arrest your development*, and they will leave you malformed, as in the case of the undeveloped caterpillar, unable to fly.

They will kill you, and you will kill others if you try to be of too much assistance to them in their painful trails. Your trials are your own *destined to transform* you, their trials are their own *destined to transform* them. You should not intercede in this process you should not hurt and disable people by trying to help them. No matter how much it hurts to see a loved one in distress you cannot be so selfish as to rid yourself of the pain of watching, and inadvertently leave them scarred for life, by your act of giving.

The best thing that you can do is to be there for them, and that is only up to a point. There are going to be times in your process when no one can be there for you, and you are going to be in pain. Tremendous amounts of pain that you did not think was humanly possible. You are going to experience this, you are going to have to watch, and endure the pain of your loved ones going through these rites of passage. That is their process, and they have to *grow* through it. These are stages of maturation, these are all parts of *their ticket*.

They will not survive, they may live *but they will not fully live, they will not thrive, if you do this for them.* If you do this for them, they will not successfully *develop their wings*. They will not possess all of their inherent faculties of ability if you stunt their process. **It will be painful, it will be hard, and it will be worth it.** Think of how great the feeling, when they earn their own validity. Think of how great you felt when you overcame a seemingly impossible hurdle in life. It is supposed to appear unclimbable, you are supposed to feel fear, you are supposed to feel terror, you are supposed to feel like giving up, and you are supposed to feel like dying. That is part of the process. You are not supposed to see how you are ever going to make it. It is intended to be this way. No one can live for another. **Two bodies of mass cannot exist in the same exact place, at the same exact time.**

Nature's Correlation

Look at nature for this miracle peek into life. Let us take the example of a deer giving birth. The mother deer gives birth *standing up*. The fawn falls to the floor, unable to stand. The mother nudges the fawn with its nozzle, prompting the fawn to stand, the fawn struggles and falls down, it may roll over onto its back. It does not want to stand, it is painful, the fawn is clumsy, it just wants to lay there as it did in the womb, and it is *unaware* that it has been born.

Still the mother, more urgently now, pushes and pokes at the fawn, as if to say, "*Stand up, little fool, do what you are supposed to do.*" Still the fawn stumbles around. You see, if the fawn does not stand up quickly it will become easy prey for the predators, it must stand, it must walk, because in order to survive in the environment it will soon *have to run*. After poking and prodding the fawn some more, the fawn goes from it belly to its knees and from its knees to its hooves and it begins to walk, slowly at first and then it begins to run. It likes to run, it was *born to run*. This is a beautiful sight and a most telling instrument, for those who have eyes to look and a mind to see.

You were born to run, you were born to fly, born to soar, and born to win. You were not born to cry, to lay around, to be lazy, and to complain. You were not born to live life *on your back,* or you would not have been given legs with which to stand. You were born to stand up, man or woman, you were born to stand erect, back straight, legs firmly planted under you, and you were born to peer ahead, *chin up.* No one can do this for you. You may have to be retaught, and trained to do this again, if you lose this ability at some point from an unforeseen accident, but initially you cannot be taught *how* to walk, you must teach *yourself.*

You can be supported but no one can take the steps, required of you to take on your own, for you. **This is part of your ticket.**

This is Your Ticket

This is part of your ticket, this is your life. **These are things that are components of your prerequisite course, if you are ever to be successful in this thing we call life.** No one can breathe for you, no matter how much they may want to, the universe will forbid it. You must endure the pain, you must live the *experience of uncertainty,* as this is your lot in life. There will be challenge after challenge, rite of passage after rite of passage, you may get dizzy, and you will fall down. That is a given, your reward, however, will be based on how well you are at getting up.

These are your components of a ticket. **It is a ticket that will gain you entry into the arena.** It is your entry ticket, your stamp, and your qualification *to compete.* This is not a guarantee that you will be successful overall, because there are *qualifying stages to success.* There are prerequisites that you must pass. They are the **threshold for success,** and you won't graduate to the next level if you do not pass through these chambers, so do not *resent it, or run from it, embrace it, embrace your process.* That will not necessarily make it easier, it will, however, make it easier to accept. These parts of your ticket comprise your ability to get **back in the game.**

CHAPTER 5

Belief

"You have to believe that things will get better, because if you don't they won't."
Shaan Rais

HOPE

ope is a very powerful tool, if used correctly, it will have a tremendous amount of impact on your outcome. Hope brings virtue, hope is a motivator, hope is a stimulator, and hope is an innovator. The power of hope is underestimated at best. Where there is no hope, there truly is no hope. No help comes to a person who has not put in a request. Have you ever heard the axiom that *'A closed mouth doesn't get fed?'* This is so true. **How much more so the mind?**

A Closed Mind Doesn't Get Fed

If the mind does not have hope, if it is making no requests, it has no expectation. The *expectation is what gives life* to hope. You have to expect that things will get better. Your expectation is your driving force, it is what galvanizes the effort. Without hope there is no cause, thus there can be no call to action. Hope is what makes you move, expectation is the *intensity* behind the movement. The expectation is what brings about the result. Imagine if we lived in a world with no hope.

The lack of hope is what will allow people to become crippled by circumstance. We all have circumstances that we would change if we could. Hope is what assures us that we can, that things can get better, expectation goes further than this. **Expectation is what gives us the**

ability to comprehend that they *will* get better. This is the emotion that the universe responds to, your *active consistent request.* It is what removes the question of; *if,* and replaces it with the question of; *when.* Things will get better if you have hope, and are actively engaged in the expectation. **Expectation adds heat.**

Expectation is the *activation* of the internal component of hope. People can actively hope but be *inactive* in terms of their *engagement* in expectation, at the same time. Hope without activation is like an empty request. It is like you saying you want something, but not defining what it is that you want. Expectation is *definitive,* expectation is *particular.* You can hope things get better, but then you must engage in the expectation, expressing that a certain thing is that which you expect to receive, to **facilitate the response.**

What if Your Predecessors Were Just Like You..

Imagine if your ancestors had no hope. Imagine if the earliest forms of human life had no hope. Hope is what allowed them to press on in life, with the expectation that better things were around the corner. **If you have no hope then there is no reason to continue to try.** Hopelessness is the *death of a dream.* Every successful person you know defied denial and failure, with the power of hope. This is why they were not deterred by the presence of momentary setback. This is why they were, instead, inspired by the state of things as opposed to being crushed by the weight of the current circumstances that they encountered.

Hope is like unto a fire that lights one's way in darkness. Hope gives you the presence of intention to be persistent, it is defined as '*a feeling of expectation and desire for a certain thing to happen*[1].' Without it we are doomed. You have to further distinguish your hope. You can hope for things to get better, and it may turn out to be a sunny day instead of a rainy one, but still the gas bill will not be paid, for example.

You have to further distinguish, or *add definition to your hope by adding the expectation* of the arrival of enough currency to pay your gas bill. Does that make sense?

Hope is what the forefathers had when there was no electricity, it was what allowed people to learn that whale blubber actually lit a lamp. How would people have endeavored to even test it out to see if it worked, if there was no hope that they would *ever escape darkness?* No. Initially the prerequisite had to be hope. The same is true of us today, in the present world. If you do not believe that you can overcome the adversity you are presently faced with, you will cease to have hope and you will not have a prayer in the world. These small axioms and hints thereof have significant meaning.

Where There is Life There is Hope

Where there is hope there is life, and where there is life there is hope. As long as you can still breathe, *therein* lies the possibility. After hope and *significant expectancy*, there must follow *work*. We must work for what we want. There are different levels of work, some say, "*Work smart, not hard*", some are of the mind-state that nothing can be accomplished without hard work. Whichever stance you take, you are correct. First, it does not determine how much work you do *if* the work is subpar. Also, it defies reason to believe that anything can be accomplished without the element of work, and what comes easy to one, another would see as being hard work. Regardless of personal contexts **all accomplishments require work.**

Industrial Motivation

No work will come where there is no hope. This is why it is of the utmost import that an employer has *incentives* for his workforce to strive *towards*. **If an employee has the component of hope, that is expectancy.** By that I mean, if they expect to receive a promotion or more money for a better work performance they will be *inclined* to work harder, or *smarter in pursuit* of the goal. *However, if there is no goal and no hope for advance, there is a great chance that your business will suffer from complacency.*

Where there exists no desire, there exists no fire. If a person has no desire to advance, do not even hire him, unless you hire him with the full intention of inspiring him. Most companies do not have the time to inspire people, so they wish to find people with the inherent *desire* for more. They **hire will, and train skill.** Those who *expect, excel.* Therefore, they provide an excellent service. With a workforce that is comprised of this *internal resolve*, there is hope for your business.

Places of business that do not provide this feeling of expectancy for their employees will suffer greatly, they will suffer from poor performance, they will suffer from internal power struggles, and they will suffer from intentional sabotage. **Places of business seek to acquire people with a business-owner mentality.** They want people who believe in the vision of the company, and those who exhibit complete buy-in to the *ideology* of the company. This is the result of giving your team hope. **A corporation that provides this kind of compensation will enjoy lifelong employees.** Companies that do not provide this feeling of hope will have lackluster performances and a high rate of turnover.

In order to obtain success, hope is a most important pre-requisite. Both for you, and for your team. If you are leveraging the efforts of others to reach your goals, these others have to be hopeful of their rewards. If there is no hope of ever obtaining any form of *acknowledgement or recognition,* why should they do tasks that they do not have to? Why would they ever go the extra mile, or do work that is not required of them? **They will only do this if you have a company culture that provides them with the enrichment of hope.** This hope cannot be empty.

If you are skilled in the art of *supplying* hope to your people, you must also be skilled in the art of *fulfilling* this hope. There has to exist a concrete solid answer to their hopes and aspirations, a form of reward. This does not have to be in the form of money, it can be recognition. Some employees you are going to have to provide monetary incentives for, while others are just looking for a pat on the pack, someone to peek into the office and say, *"You're doing a heck of a job"*, or an employee of the month plaque on the wall.

After hoping for these results for so long they are going to have to be realized or you are going to lose an employee. As a manager or the head of a company, this is counterproductive. **It is counterproductive to keep having to hire new people, because at some point no one is going to be around long enough to really know what they are doing, and your company is going to be known as a dead end job, wherein lies no hope.** No one will want a job like that, unless they need it, and under these circumstances they will not *perform well either way.*

Psychology of Sales

As a salesman/woman, if you can provide your prospect with hope, if you are able to *capitalize on their hopes*, and then *demonstrate how* your product is able to follow through on their expected results, you will be successful. Simple enough, right? This is why you have to get to *know* your prospect, you must ask *probing questions*, designed to get at their *motivations*, their *hope*. What do they hope will happen? What do they expect to receive? What do they hope to accomplish? **What is their internal motivating factors?** And so forth.

Think about yourself, if you do not hope to lose weight, there will be no *motivation to purchase* any weight loss supplement. If you do not believe that you can do it, or that you need to do it, why will you even put forth the effort or the money? Chances are you won't, is that easy enough to assume? However, if you are *made to believe* that you can do it, and you hope that a specific product will help you to do it, and if it meets or exceeds your expectency, you will become a **loyal customer and refer the product to others** with the same aspirations.

The Process of Reconnecting

This is the same in the aspects of your own personal development. You have to believe that you can do something, no matter what that thing may be, perhaps it's a situation of love. After you believe that you can love again, this becomes true for you. Let's say someone has hurt you. You've been through an *abusive and tumultuous* relationship. At first you do not think that you can be successful in a relationship. You tried with all of your heart, you gave it everything you had and still it failed. You do not know what else you could have given.

Then at some point after the heart has had time to heal, you begin to believe that you can do it again, it is at this point that *there is hope* for you. So you begin to date, you get back in the game. You are hopeful that you can win, you have hope that you can be successful. If you go into a relationship with the confidence of a loser, it will be picked up on, and it will trigger the same emotion in your intended counterpart. **If you do not believe in yourself, no one else will believe in you either.** But if you have enough hope to try, then someone else will have enough hope to try with you, and you will both be hopeful. This will enable the relationship to be full of hope.

What's Next?

After the hope comes the work. If you believe in something and you are hopeful of its success, it will enable you to work towards to success of it. *This is empowerment.* You will have an opportunity of success because you believe in your ability to make it work. Now the odds are in your favor. Let me restate something that I said earlier in this book. **It is true, the person who believes that they can accomplish something, and the person who does not are both correct.** Now of course, the variable is the work, the thing that is going to enable the success is the work, but it is the hope and the belief that enable the work. It is the hope and the belief that will enable the work.

Where there is life there is hope. You may be broken, something may have hurt you, and we have all experienced that. However, if you are able to hope then you are *able to win*. Your hope has to be huge, your belief has to be huge, and you cannot be successful at anything with less than huge belief. This hope and belief has to defy odds. Things are going to happen, a storm will strike your hut, to test your resolve. If you can stand firm, if you can *weather the storm*, then your success is ensured. Success in anything is always a work in progress.

Success is fluctuating, *success is fluid,* and it is not stagnant. No one becomes successful, and stays successful without the appropriate work. It takes an effort, in the matter of love it takes an equal effort on both people's part. You cannot be hopeful and believe that you can be successful in a relationship, and actually be successful, if the other person is desperate to prove you wrong. You may be successful at doing your part, but the relationship will still not work, because a successful relationship is determined by the efforts of two people, not just one.

Two people must possess and dedicate a combined effort toward the desired result. This is why it is said that there is *'strength in numbers'*, and that everyone should be on the *'same page'*. It is true in a relationship, in marriage, and it is true within a company. It is also true within your internal composition, this is why it is said to be of *'one mind'*, and to stay focused, and not to allow for distractions to take you off of your path. **Hope is the first intentional component of success.**

Brief Recap

For the purpose of providing a brief summarization of what we've learned so far; hard times are going to happen, and you are going to fail; a lot, which is how it's designed to happen to strengthen your *experiential muscles.* You have to accept what takes place in your life, and you want to continue to learn, to introduce your mind to new information consistently, it is from this act, internal and external that you allow yourself the benefit of a paradigm shift. Then comes belief, which is strengthened by hope. Hope is a choice, it is caused by your perception, and with it you add power to your belief that things can get better, *before* they actually do.

Active Engagement

Without hope no one will get very far. You will not see the purpose in continuing your quest for greatness, or success in anything, if you do not have that hope. There must exist hope, I cannot stress this enough. Hope is the choice, the first choice of success. These components are cross-referential, you will find them closely connected to each other. When you get to hope you must remember to *add the expectancy* to it. You must actively engage in the expectation that it *will* get better, not just that it *can* get better. There is a difference.

Without hope one will never push the envelope. The bodybuilder will not get under 315 pounds if he has not the fortitude of hope that he will lift it, if he does not believe that he can. You will not go to take that test that you have been putting off, if you have no hope that you can pass. The wife will not return home to her husband, if she has no hope that things will get better and that they can work it out. You can schedule the appointment, and do all the work entailed to get a job, but you will make it to the front door and then turn back around and leave, if you have no hope that you can be successful. Are we in agreement?

It is the hope that ensures the progress, which makes the progress possible, because without hope you will not even try. We may know someone who could be successful if they would only tweak a couple of things and put forth the effort. The problem with this is that they, in themselves, do not have hope. They do not believe it themselves, or in themselves. These people can only be shown examples of others, who like themselves, may have come from circumstances that were not conducive to their success, but still they made it.

The Power of Examples

If you can expose a person with no hope to success stories that correlate their own situation, you may be able to override their sense of hopelessness with examples of inspiration. They may be inspired to hope, they may become galvanized to believe, if they see enough proof that anyone can overcome anything set before them. They may see the rays of hope within the darkness of their current predicament. This is what you can do to revive the life of hope. Most people had hope until they were shown otherwise.

Hopelessness is taught, this is why it is so important that you do not give up. **Hopelessness is infectious.** People are always watching you; your children, your spouse, your employees, your business partners, and more. If you show them no hope, if you yourself do not believe in yourself, in your marriage, in your company, in your *mission statement,* then no one else will. It is like your life. It starts and it ends with you. You are the example for all who see you, and all who follow you. When you engage with other people you are stepping on the center stage. All of your actions will be monitored and scrutinized. Closely.

You must not give up, even when it gets tough. These are the times when hope is most pertinent and crucial, when things do not look good. It is easy to be hopeful and joyful, inspirational when the quarter looks good, and in the party atmosphere. It is when things go bad though that everyone looks towards you for motivation, for inspiration, and for a sense of direction, that you and you alone must be able to provide. This is your responsibility to the success that will be yours.

Goal Oriented Focus

Listen, it is not easy to be successful. If it was, everyone would do it. You have to choose, with intention, where you will be in the scheme of life, come 6 months, 1 year, and 5 – 10 years from now. Where you will be is, in part, determined, by that which you focus the power of your hope *toward*. It can be yours, no matter what it is. This is why it is so important to monitor that which we allow our minds to focus on, because as John Spence says, "*We become what we focus on.*" This is so true.

I cannot stress the importance of inundating yourself in the positive examples of those who came before you. Those who were in the same predicaments, or worse, as you now find yourselves. It is your responsibility to strengthen your **muscle of hope**, so that it becomes strong. You cannot allow it to weaken. Your hope is your vision, your *elevator* to get you to where you want to be. You have to see it first, you have to have a destination. This is the importance of setting goals. Let me provide an example.

If you were to get on an elevator in a building and you had no idea where you were headed, if you knew not where it was that you wanted to go, what button would you press? **This is your intention.** The elevator may get stuck, it may pause midway, and it may strain to reach the floor that you pressed, but if you have no hope you wouldn't even get on the elevator in the first place. So, you can rest assured that you would never make it to where it is that you would like to be, because you had no destination set. Does that make sense? Good.

Now that you have a destination, your *intention* allows you to see the direction. *"Well, I want to go to the financial division (example), the financial division is on the 14th floor."* Now you know what button to press. It is that easy, now you know where you want to be to reach your destination, to get your goals met. **Get your goals set, and then get your goals met.** You are no longer just walking in the building of life listlessly and aimlessly, you have what I like to call a *definitive purpose.* **In the realm of belief, first there is hope, and then there is purpose.**

PURPOSE

*I*t is the purpose that you have in life that determines the direction in which you will arrive. Without purpose there can be no fulfillment. Every turn that you take, every direction will be fruitless because you have no idea where you are headed. That just does not make sense. Why even be here? You will definitely not be successful without a purpose, you will not even know why it is that you are here. Who gets into a car without an intended destination? Not many people.

Who Knows Their Purpose

Purpose is defined as the reason for which something is done, or created, or for which something exists[3]. It is the *justification* for your life. You have a purpose, it is up to you what that purpose is. What is your purpose? Why were you born? Was it to devote every waking moment to a job? If you determine that this was the purpose for which you were given life, you'd better make sure that it is a job that provides you with satisfaction. If your *purpose does not justify* what you are currently engaged in, then *change your engagements.*

Your purpose becomes your driving force, the motivation of your direction. It is the reason why you do what you do. You should not do things just for the sake of doing them, which is an aimless existence. What you do should be done for a reason, it should be done *on* *purpose*. Your purpose is your focus, it is what you believe in. Think of missionaries, they have a purpose, they believe that God put them here to spread the gospel, that is why they are found in distant lands doing the work that they believe is their purpose. *What is yours?*

Why are you here? What were you put here to do? No one else can define this for you. *You alone* can determine your purpose. This is on the interior, you feel it, you know it is right, because you can taste it in your mouth, you feel it in your gut. There is such a sense of fulfillment that is derived from being purposeful in life. This is what does not allow for the outside world to distract you from your ambitions. Your purpose you may not know just yet, and this is fine. You just follow that which seems right to you at the time, and you will find your purpose.

Many people do not find their purpose for a very long time. You are going to be subject to many a situation in life, many things are going to happen, which will teach you along the way. On this course you will find your purpose. It is the strongest motivational force that there is. Once you find it you will know it, it will be seen as the reason why everything else happened. Good or bad. Purpose many times will dictate a person's movements through life, whether they are aware of it at the time or not. **When a person finds their purpose it justifies all that has happened.** There is no such thing as coincidence. The universe has a purpose, it has a purpose for you. Your purpose is not to be miserable, or a failure, no, these are signs that you have yet to find your purpose, though you may be well on your way. This is why it is very important for you to stay *sober and in a present state* of mind so that you do not miss the signs.

Purpose Driven

Have you ever known a truly purpose driven person? These people are much focused, they do not know detour, and they do not allow for distraction, they do not waste their time or other people's time. They are always in a state of action, they are following their purpose in life. You cannot tell them anything that will change their minds, *this is a successful state.* Success to you will be different than success for me. Unless we are both of the mind state that we have the same purpose. This has happened when you see people working together for one common cause, united and not divided, with a singular purpose, a relative aim.

This is how the best relationships are achieved, this causes for no disagreements and arguments, and this is how things get accomplished. Many times it is not the goal that brings the satisfaction, it is the pursuit of the purpose. Once the goal is attained and success has been achieved, you must find the next purpose, the next *reason.* I have undertaken the writing of this book for a very distinct purpose. I am doing it with a much focused reason, I believe that I was born to write this book, and many others, this is one of my purposes for existence. It completely justifies everything that I have been through. Bad or good, it was for the purpose of providing me with the information that I needed **in order to be able to adequately help others.**

Specialized Purpose

How could I advise people on that which I knew nothing about? How could I be in the capacity of a Coach/Consultant/Counselor, if I did not have experiences in the areas in which I Coach/Consult/Counsel? It would be pretty hard wouldn't it? Yes, as a matter of fact, it would be phony. I am not a consultant to nuclear physicists. I can consult them in the area in which I am trained, in *Leadership matters, matters of staff development, or enhancing the human efficiency, and performance.* When it comes to the scientific precepts regarding their work, not their performance at work, but the actual details of what it is that they do, I am no longer effective, and they must consult someone else. That is not my purpose for being there.

This is always beneficial, it is good to know your *specialized purpose.* Everyone is not meant, or equipped, to do everything. I know some very good people who would be extremely ineffective in the capacity of what I do, this is not their purpose. I would be completely ineffective on their job, or trying to do what they love to, and are trained to do, that is not my purpose. **When people are truly aware of, and in touch with their purpose, they tend to stay out of each other's way.** Do you like people who think they know every single thing, inside and out? Probably not so much. What if a person came on your job to fix the heating and a/c service, only to try and tell you to let them do your work in your office?

Stay in Your Lane

That probably would not work out too well would it? You know why? That is not the purpose for them being there, that is not their reason for being present. They would make a complete mess of everything that you do. That is the reason why *you* are there. You are not there to get into the a/c system, and start crawling through the ducts to fix the electrical wiring. That is not why you are there. That is not your area of knowledge, your specialized training does not entail that scope of practice. That is simply not your purpose.

You enjoy yourself when you are actively engaged in your calling, your purpose. You usually do not feel stressed at work, because you are compelled to follow your purpose, you are attracted to it. You generally love it, and *as much as others would be unsatisfied* doing it, you are content within the scope of your practice. There are people who would accept a tremendous pay cut to be allowed to do what they love to do, that which they see as being purposeful. People will stay on jobs that they do not like, stay in relationships that are not conducive, stay in situations that are not entirely safe to stay in even, to fulfil a required purpose that they believe that they are suited to do, that they were *born for.*

Become a Detective

You are here to find your purpose, you are here to find that which you love to do, that which brings you satisfaction. It may be the accumulation of wealth, although the accumulation of wealth is usually a byproduct of following your purpose, and not the other way around. It is generally engrossed in your purpose wherein you find success. **How many people quit a job that you would never leave, because they said that they did not like it?** No matter how much money they make. See, therein lies a priceless jewel of wisdom. *Money does not, by any means imply success.*

Finding Your Purpose is Serious Business

How many people do you know who you regarded as tremendously successful, by your understanding and estimates of success, *who felt empty?* Who felt worthless within the scope of what they did for a living, who felt *unfulfilled?* People who were successful and highly regarded, yet had not found their purpose...**for them.** People like Whitney Houston, Robin Williams, Amy Winehouse, Seymour Hoffman, people who you may've been willing to trade your life with, who were actually so unfulfilled in life that they **took their lives** through the use of drugs.

People use drugs when they are trying to escape their current situation, they drink to feel something that they do not feel in their life. They use drugs and stimulants to get a feeling of stimulation, because their lives do not cause them stimulation. They are not stimulated by their existence, which many others may envy. This is why so many people are surprised when they find out that people they thought were successful have committed suicide. The witnesses never in a thousand years, would have thought that a person was unfulfilled by that which causes outsiders to envy them. *This is very important to understand.*

This is why it is so important that you follow your own precepts, that you follow what *feels* right to you. That which you *know* is right for you. Others may not understand, they are not supposed to, they do not live in your skin. You are ultimately the one who is going to have to live with the decisions that you make. **I think you would be rightly advised to make the decisions that you make, *on purpose.***

Not because someone else told you to. Not because, "*my mother or father wants me to*", not because, "*my wife or husband wants me to*", but for *you*. For your own saving grace and peace of mind. You must do things that are satisfying to your soul, that make sense to you, that put you on the path that you want to be on, that provide progress in the direction in which you are trying to go. It is perfectly ok to make mistakes, to think you want to go right, and then finding out that this was not the way you wanted to go when you arrive, and it was not what you thought that it would be. That is fine, for some time.

The Strength of Purpose

I don't think you understand just how strong purpose is. Try to talk someone out of something. Try to tell someone to change their course in life, to change their *religion*, to change their diet. Try to tell a student that they should change their major, tell someone to quit their job, tell a person that they should get out of the *relationship* that they are in. Depending on their sense of purpose, three things may happen, in varying degrees. They may laugh at you, they may consider what you are telling them, or you may have to run, because they will outright attack you.

People who are driven by purpose, and on purpose, will not be detoured or discouraged by numbers, they can be all alone by themselves in their pursuit. This is their story and they are sticking to it, come rain, snow, sleet, hail or high water. They are resigned to their decision, it makes sense to them, and they have a purpose. A purpose is the rock, it is the foundation upon which you decide the action that has to follow, and it is also the anchor. Your purpose will be that which keeps you strong in the face of all opposing forces.

Your purpose will be the reason why you stay the way that is going to get you to your destination in life. Some people waste their time in frivolous acts of nonsense. You will not see someone with a strong purpose doing that. Some people party all the time, and associate with people who are not driven, *who have no purpose.* **You will not find people with a strong sense of purpose within that crowd.** People with a strong sense of purpose do not frequent places that are not conducive to their *mission.* It is from your purpose that you derive your mission statement in life. It is your mission statement that gives your focus a diamond edge.

Diamond Edge Focus

A diamond is the hardest surface on earth, it can cut through anything; rock, steel, metal, and any other hard surface. This is why I say that your mission statement in life, from the identification of your purpose will give you a *Diamond Edge.* This Diamond Edge of your mission statement in life will be that which allows nothing else to interfere with your plans. It is this *conviction* that will crucify all opposition. You will become one of those ultra-focused representatives of *concentrated purpose.* You will not accept no for an answer, or allow interference to distract you.

This is the kind of purpose we must have to be successful. Purposefulness does not allow for small talk, things that have no substance, and time off. **You do not take time off from your purpose, as your purpose becomes who you are.** It symbolizes what you stand for, it *becomes you.* Everyone around you knows it, and you could not hide it even if you wanted to. This is the kind of conviction and assuredness that is conducive to overall success. You will not achieve greatness by mistake, it will not happen by accident.

Success is the result arrived at from intense focus, planning, and strategic maneuvering. It does not come by default. You can inherit money, you can inherit a company, but you do not *inherit success.* Success comes as a direct result of the work you put forth, the idea that you had, the thought that you put into it. *It is your baby.* Imagine a mother and father with a baby on the way, they do not take chances. They have an intense concentrated focus, they are one, and they are united. The purpose of this analogy is for you to estimate the level of precaution and protection.

You Have to Nourish Your Purpose

Your success is your baby, the same way a woman does not give *birth upon conception,* do not think that your idea will come to fruition simply because you had it. How many children are stillborn? *How many dreams are buried with the people that had them?* This is the result of the work that was required, not being done efficiently. **The magnitude of your dream will determine the amount of work that is required.** This is, in the baby's case, the result of things not working right within the mother's womb. It is so much easier to conceptualize than to conceive.

It is demanding of relatively no effort to *speculate, daydream, and imagine.* Some people cannot even do this, but most of us have no problem with well-wishing, and thinking of things that could be successful. *It is the transference of that idea from our minds to our hands and feet that is the hard part.* People actually have to bring a dream from their mind's eye to their physical eye. They have to create it, they have to make it. If you can go from an idea to a state of activation, the odds are much greater that you will be successful. For those who cannot get off their rear ends to start, failure is a promise. So don't worry about it.

What about the male and female lion? How protective are they of their unborn children, their litter, and their pride. How defensive and protective is the male and the female lion when the female is pregnant? *Try to think on that and estimate the level.* This is how you must defend your unborn baby. You want to write a book, you want to go to college, you want to play ball? You'd better be good at defensive strategy, you better be good at warding off attackers, and this is because people dislike to see the dreams of others come true. **Miserable people are like the predators of the wild,** especially when it comes to the case of a dream with validity. Coming from someone that they know. *Whhhoooo boy!* You'd better call the Rangers.

They are going to come to assassinate your dreams with smiles and promises of loyalty. They are going to come to rent your dreams asunder, with huge teeth smiles and pledges of good intentions, they are going to pledge their support for your purpose and cause, while undermining every step toward progress that you make. There are some friends that hurt people so bad they make the person's enemies jealous. It is truly something to behold.

A Purpose is Measurable

A purpose is such a beautiful thing because it can be measured. How can one measure something that is formless? Good question. You can *measure the quality* of your purpose by the *actions that you engage in* on a daily basis. Do you smoke? Do you drink alcohol? Do you engage in other risky behavior? Do you sleep a lot? Waste time? Just stand around waiting for something to happen? If you answered yes to any of these questions then you can safely say that your purpose is not that important.

A person with a truly valuable purpose will not do anything that is counterproductive to their attainment of it. This is your *Why*

Factor. This is why you get up in the morning, this is why you go to sleep at night. This is why you surround yourself with the people that you do, in the places that you do, and this is why you engage in that which you engage in, to *fulfill your purpose*. **A person with no purpose, or a person who has not found their purpose in life is a very dangerous person, especially to those with a purpose.** Their actions cannot be accounted for.

People With no Purpose

These people, without a Why Factor, without a purpose, will do any and everything, at any given time, to anybody. They do not value their own lives, much let alone yours, because they have not found a purpose for their lives, so they do not understand what a purpose is. They will not respect your purpose, or what you are trying to accomplish, they will laugh at you and your dreams, in your face because they simply do not care. People with a purpose are like a *different species* to them, they cannot relate. You may as well be an alien to a person who has no purpose. They will view you as strange.

You will look, to the person with no purpose, like an alien, like an outsider, and like a fool to them. **They will not speak your language, they will not understand your intentions.** It is best to stay away from them as they have not yet *found themselves*. So if you follow them they will surely lead you astray, and off the path of your own purpose. For them it is not *on* purpose, *nothing is,* they just have no direction. They will not respect you or your purpose and they will destroy you, and your purpose with you, if you let them.

This is why it is so important to regulate those with whom you associate. I don't care how attractive this person may be, stay away from them at all costs. If you are trying to accomplish something, you are warned to *associate only with those who are also on the pursuit to accomplish something.* The accomplishments which you are in pursuit of may be different, but at least you will have something in common. They will be able to identify you, and you them. **Do not sacrifice your dreams and goals for the sake of association.** This is what you do when you associate with those who have no definitive purpose in life, they are the most dangerous of all people.

You see these people all day, in one form or another, they are the disgruntled employee, who does nothing but talk negatively about everyone else. *They are the people who hang out on the corners of life itself.* They have nothing to do. They know no bounds, they will engage in any and every form of risky behavior there is, for this brings them *momentary fulfillment.* They will hurt people, intentionally. They will engage in all forms of abuse and try to convince you to do it with them. They are the miserable, and their only pursuit is the company of others.

People with a purpose validate each other. Well, people with no purpose validate other people who have no purpose, this is why you will see two sorry souls in a relationship that is going nowhere quickly. They do not respect each other, they have no loyalty to one another, or anyone else for that matter. They will hurt each other, and engage in negative behavior, with and towards one another with no regard as to the risk it entails, or the harm that it causes. I implore you to *protect your purpose* from these people at all costs. The worst of them will not just be satisfied with the loss of your dreams, and the loss of your purpose, they will not be satisfied until you lose *your very life* as well.

Relation & Association

Herein lies the importance of association. **Your purpose should dictate your associations, and those who you allow into your circle of influence.** You only want people of *high moral character* within your circle, if you are to be truly successful in life. You want to seek out people who are on the same path as yourself. If you are a student in high school who is aspiring to attend college, hook up with those students who have the same aspirations. You can be supportive of them, and they can be mutually supportive of you.

If you are into working out and training, you cannot hang out and associate with a drunkard. They are not going to understand your eating schedule. They sleep a lot, and people who are into health and working out, are into being active a lot. Can you understand? You may be thinking '*it's been two hours, I have to eat again*', and they'll be thinking '*it's been two hours, I have to drink again*'. It just won't work. **They'll either end up at the gym, or you'll end up at the bar or the liquor store.** If your purpose is important enough to you, you will not gamble.

If you are aspiring to write a book, associate with authors or aspiring authors, engaging in active pursuit of their purpose of writing books. Get with those who are doing what it is that you want to do. *What if you don't know any authors?* Well if you're reading this, you know me, call me, or write me. Look us up, connect with people who are doing what you want to be doing through every form of social media that there is, come to book signings, get autographs, introduce yourself. Write. **Set goals, and devise a mission statement in life.** Disassociate with those who are unsupportive of you, or neutral. Align yourself with those who inspire and support you.

This is done to intensify the purpose, to give it heat, to provide a picture, and to solidify the purpose as your future. The closer you get to those who are doing it, the closer you are to *doing it yourself.* Ask questions, take notes, join a club, join a group, and get out of your comfort zone. Believe in it, pray for it, eat, sleep, drink and breathe it, and most of all do not ever forget to believe it. Your quality of belief will determine the quality of your follow through, and the pursuit of it. Whatever it maybe.

Proper Preparation

Maybe you want to be a doctor. This is not unable to do. Get in school, and *do well in school*. Study, volunteer, watch documentaries, go to hospitals. Just to walk through them. Play dress up, go there, and imagine yourself on the phone speaking to nurses, consulting with a patient. **Practice.** Practice on your purpose. There is no greater form of preparation. **Prepare.** See yourself there. Purchase your equipment, purchase the instruments and tools, and visualize. See yourself operating on someone and saving their life. Hear the family thanking God, and saying '*thank you*' to you for saving their son's, mother's, father's, or daughter's life. **You have no idea of the power that the mind and visualization has in determining the outcome.**

Do nothing else, allow no intruders, allow no down time, no play-play, everything is real. Life is serious and you've got *one time* to be here on this Earth, use it to accomplish your purpose. I do not know what your desired purpose is, but that does not matter. Whatever it is, if you do not do this, you will be very sorry that you did not. Do not give up, if you do you will be very sorry that you did. There are people graduating from Med School every day. *Is it easy?* No. *Is it worth it?* Yes. If this is not what you want to do, fine.

Find it, do research, find what it is that clarifies your purpose and let no stone go unturned in your pursuit of it. Go mercenary on it, let no thing, nor circumstance, nor person stand in your way. I heard Kevin Hart say one day while speaking to DJ Sway that he, "*Was just a guy who heard 'no' for 19 years.*[4]" Let no one tell you no, that you cannot do it. Know that they are going to come, know that the hard times are going to come, the failures, accept them, allow them to shift your paradigm, believe in it, be hopeful and expecting of it to take place…all of these factors, all of these experiences, all of your efforts will compile together, and they will comprehensively work together to create your…

WILL TO ACT

J ump on it. Seize it by the short hairs, and dig your teeth into it. *"You have to want it as bad as you want to breathe[5]"*, to quote Dr. Eric Thomas. Be relentless about it, rip the eyes out of circumstance, pull the tongue out of the mouth of rejection, and dig your nails into the feeling of despair until blood runs. You have to be *ferocious* in pursuit of your success, so become that way. Be a lion, you cannot beg your way into the history books. **No one remembers the names of squirrels.** Be relentless.

Enter a State of Action

No matter what happens in your life, you must have the will to act. The will to act is definitely a most important prerequisite to anything being accomplished in life. Things will not change in your life, your marriage won't get any better, you will not get that job, you will not create that company, and you will never write the book that's in your head, if you do not have the will to act. It is the will to act that takes your ideas from being just an idea, and brings the reality to fruition.

The idea that you have, once you have it, it is your responsibility to bring it to life. The will to act is what will allow you to do it. Think of people who have something to do. You know that they have to do this certain thing. Have you ever known a procrastinator? A person who had something to do, something that would change their life, and they do not act on it. Think about a college age student, who has graduated high school, they have to apply to college to actually get in college. They can have everything lined up, a great GPA, everything is in place, if they have not the will to act, they will never attend.

It is this will to act that compromises the *physical part of success.* The physical part is the actual work on the idea. This component and nothing else will give it life. It will come to pass due the physical acts associated with it. We all know that nothing comes out of thin air. Well-wishing will not do it, hope alone will not do it, acceptance alone will not do it. We must do the work. To do the work, one's belief has to be sufficient enough as a motivating force to initiate the doing of the work.

Don't Bury Your Idea

These prerequisites have units within them, units that are of the most importance, and the will to act is definitely one of them. *How many people get buried along with their great idea?* How many people have beautiful ideas? A great spirit, so much that they could offer this world, and themselves if they only had the will to act? I am going to expand on this topic exponentially due to severity of it. Imagine a child, at the time that it should be beginning and trying to learn to walk, imagine if it did not have the will to act. Imagine the fawn we spoke about earlier, if it did not have the will to act, it's mother at some point would have to *leave it behind* because it would be easy prey, and also make it's mother easy prey, if she was more preoccupied with it than survival.

This is why some families separate. Things may be getting bad, as far as the bills or the communication. If the partner that is not carrying their own weight fails to act, the dominant partner will have to leave the other behind to find a more *suitable* mate. A partner who has the will to act. We all know when the proverbial ship is sinking, we are all aware of doom, when it starts to encroach upon us, it is like an eviction notice. At the point that you get an eviction notice, if you have ever gotten one, you know that money must be obtained to remain within the home. If there is no will to act, at some point in the not too distant future the family will have to move. **Someone has to possess the will to act.**

If you lack the will to act, you lack the will to be successful, it's that simple. A mushroom is never successful at being more than a mushroom. As we spoke about the caterpillar before, a caterpillar who has not the will to act, will never be more than a caterpillar. It will never develop wings, it will never fly, and the same will happen to your dreams and aspirations if you have not the will to act. If you believe strongly enough it will move you to the point of action, so you have to believe. You have to believe. Think of the Sun. **Where would we be if the Sun lost the will to act?**

If the Sun lost the will to act we would immediately freeze to death. It would be over for us. **You are the Sun and your dream is your Earth.** If you lose the will to act, your dreams and your ambitions will spin out of orbit, and all life, all chances at life will cease to exist. It is absolutely vital that you act. Think of your lungs, or your heart. What if they lost the will to act? What if they never had the will to act in the first place? These examples are to let you know just how important your will to act is. The idea is the byproduct of the information you feed your mind, and the blessing that God gives to you. The success is the byproduct of the consistent effort that you put behind it.

No Progess, No Work

Without work there can be no progress, without the will to act there is no work. Without belief there is no will to act. Do you see the correlation? These elements, these prerequisites go hand in hand, for one to work the others have to be present. They have to present and they have to be strengthened. We see the things that we see, and are privy to others experiences, to *galvanize* in us, the will to act. When I began to *study* various author's backgrounds, it gave me the will to act.

The Power of Reference

The experiences of others allowed me to look at my own experiences in a new light. *I was able to see the possibilities.* This is also true of when I returned to school and focused my sights on a Master's Degree. It was the examples of others that I was able to reference, and then instill the belief in myself. I've overcome so many obstacles, how could this undertaking be something that I was unable to do? It was my belief that I could be successful, and my hope that I could get accepted into college, that *propelled me forward.*

I had many people that were worried for me. Many people, people that loved me, with good intentions, warned me against taking the prerequisite steps. Had I allowed those words of well-intentioned advice paralyze me with fear, I would have never acted. Ultimately, I would never have found how suited I am to higher education, and I never would have learned all the information that I have learned, and it is safe to say that this book may well have never been written. *At least by my hand.* This is how important it is that you foster, for yourself, the will to act. **Having references with which to refer will strengthen that will.**

People & Their Opinions

As long as *you* believe, that is **sufficient grounds** for action. Many people are not going to believe in you. *They are going to judge you by yesterday's work, but they don't know you today.* They are going to base their precepts by what you were involved in the last time that they saw you. They are going to remember this and remember that about you, that was less than honorable, and that is the lens through which they are going to view you. This, however, does not have to be your reality.

You do not have to accept the limits placed on you by others. People will not want to see you advance. Some will want to see you advance, just *not so much*. Still others will want to see you advance, they just will not be able to *see your vision* as a possibility, so they will try to talk the will to act *out of you*. They will be scared for you, they will not want you to feel disappointment, yet they do not *understand the prerequisites* to success. You have to go through hard times, you have to experience failure, pain, and the emotional hurt and doubt that comes with that. That is what you have to overcome, and you can, if you just do not ever lose the will to act, it can be yours.

Trust the Universe

You will never complete a marathon, if you do not begin. I was speaking to someone recently, and I told them, "*You have to have faith.*" You have to have the faith to take the first step. *Even if you see no floor ahead of you*, and you don't know what's ahead of you, you have to be willing to act, to the point that you take the first step. **That is when the floor materializes in front of you,** it is a form of magic. You have no idea how the universe will come together to make you successful, as long as you have the belief to take the first step. If you do not, if you do not trust, then you will be deemed as untrustworthy, and the power, the accomplishment, and the success will not be entrusted unto you.

You must earn the universe's trust, the way you do that is by trusting the universe. It is mutual, and it is a *cooperative effort* that will lead you to the waterfall of success. How many times have you heard the phrase, "*things just started falling in place?*" That is how it happens. No one can tell the future, you can *dictate* the future though, by the steps that you take today. I can tell your future for you right now, without having to look at your palm. Just read these next words to hear what your future will be. **If you do not find the will to act, your circumstances will not get better.** You will stay where you are in life, things will progressively get worse, and as the planet Earth continues to move forward you will be left behind.

Take the Lead

That is your promised, guaranteed, and absolute future if you refuse to find the will to act. However, if you find the will to act, I have no idea what your future will entail. I can tell you that it will require of you, the travelling through the pre-requisites mentioned within this book. But where it will take you, I am not aware. You see, the moment that you act on the will to act, you become the *narrator of your own story.* You take your life and your future into your own hands, and the power becomes your own to say where you are headed. And you will know where it is that you are headed, because it is you who take the steps in that direction.

You become the playwright in your story when you activate. It is the principle of activation that allows you to *expand and grow* into your intended direction. *Without motion there is no life.* When you begin to understand motion you will see, that if you are not in motion opportunity will be withheld from you. It is with this understanding that you are able to change your circumstances, you must move in the desired direction to make progress towards your destination. There is a season for all activity, just because you plant some seeds today, does not mean that you will be able to harvest and eat tomorrow.

Seeds must germinate, they must grow. So too, will your dreams begin to germinate, the moment you take *decisive action* with them. As soon as you transfer the seeds of your success **from your hand into the soil of the universe**, a change will take place. The energy of your success will go from potential to kinetic based on your *application of activation.* This is another gravely important body of subject matter; the *application of your activation.* **Remember, just because you're doing much, that does not mean that you are getting much done.**

The Meaning Behind Movement

You must give *meaning to your movement,* you must add meaning to your movement. It is not enough to just have the will to act alone. You must have the will to act, but you must act in a manner that is *conducive to the birth* of your success. I hear people all the time, in Coaching/ Consultation complain that they, '*are doing so much*', that they, '*are so busy*'. Does that mean that they are moving in the right direction? Not exactly. It is good that you go from inactivity to activity. **Now you must learn through experience how to act.**

You must learn focus, and you must learn direction. There will be signs of this, to be found within the realm of your activity. You will be able to distinguish, once you begin to move, whether those movements are going to be *effective* or not. Think of the **Wrong Way**, or the **Dead End** signs that you see when you are driving and you have made a wrong turn. This is the same way that life will respond to your movements in the scope of everyday life. We all have an *internal* **GPS**. It is this internal GPS that will trigger an alarm of sorts in your heart, in your body, and in your mind, when you have ventured down the wrong path. **It is so important to listen to this alarm.**

You are more powerful than you know. You have no idea just how really powerful and inherently intelligent that you are. You possess all the answers to all the questions that you have ever asked, you just have to be *willing to mine these resources*, and you have to be willing to go down deep, to *excavate* these keys to your **hidden potentiality.** Once you have found these keys that does not mean that you are not going to make mistakes. No, that is the beginning of the mistake making. You are moving now, you will learn to make adjustments as you go. Do you know that the bald eagle actually gets *kicked* out of the nest?

I think it would be safe to say that the bald eagle either finds its wings on the way down, or it dies. Its mother may come and save it from imminent death on a few occasions, but at some point it becomes the responsibility of the baby to *apply the activation* to its own body before it goes **splat.** This is done through the will to act. Once you begin to drive for instance, you will be driving soon as if you have always known how to drive. There will be no fear, no hesitation and you will be hitting the highway, and able to make all kinds of maneuverings. Yet it all began with the will to act.

Mental Fitness

You already possess this will. It is fear that holds you back. It is fear of the unknown, it is fear of the possibilities, the possible successes and the possible failures, which restricts our movements initially. Let me tell you this, **the most difficult step to take is the very first one.** The first step that you take out of the shadows into the light are the most scary, hideous steps that you can take. It always gets easier once you begin. It is like the first few days of a diet, or a workout regimen. You have to be willing to begin, and then what does the body do? The body becomes *acclimated to the demands* that you are putting upon it. The muscles become stronger in proportion to the stress being put on them. The same goes for the *most powerful muscle of all,* and I'm speaking about the brain.

If you do not take your mind to the gym, it will deteriorate. If you are not introducing new information to the mind, you are not taking your brain to the gym. In this state it is suffering from atrophy. Atrophy is defined as when; *"(of body tissue or an organ) waste away, typically due to the degeneration of cells, or become vestigial during evolution*[6]*"*. Another definition is: "*gradually decline in effectiveness or vigor due to underuse or neglect*[6a]". If your brain does this, it is from the underuse or *lack of stimulation*. This is going to have a tremendous impact on the possibility of realizing your success. This is why '**leaders are readers**'. This is why you have got to read, and read things that are complicated to understand. When you do this you are subjecting the brain to *heavy lifting*.

I used to read until I fell asleep. Have you ever done that too? You ever wonder why that happens. It happens because when you read, *your brain is doing gymnastics*. It is *looking, seeing, reading, digesting, thinking, and learning* all at once. Lightning speed processing is taking place, this is why it is such a highly recommended habit for developmental purposes. You will learn, you will travel, and you will consider. You can learn if you have the will to act on the premise of picking a book up and reading it. Your mental muscles will grow big and strong, and subject matters that used to be heavy will get light, and the new strengths will facilitate the lifting of heavier subject matter. **This is motion.**

Again, to the component of motion, or movement, we must *add meaning*. The things that you read have to be something that is going to take you in the direction where you want to go. Back to the driving example, have you ever been driving and something caught your attention? *Something you saw*? Did you notice how your car drifted in the direction of that which you were looking at? This is the same way that the mind brings us **closer to that which we focus on**. When you take your mind's eye off of the target, the bullet (*intention*) follows the direction of your minds focus.

Very seldom, do I read for the purpose of pleasure. I do not read things that are meaningless, I do not watch things that are meaningless. I understand the impact and results of what you feed yourself. It is very important to your *mental development* that you put your mind on a *restrictive diet that is in alignment with your goals and your values*. You can say that you are about one thing, but if your movement is in the glorification of something else, those around you will tell you otherwise. Those around you will *let you know* what you are about, and more times than not, they will tell you that you are about that which you focus the majority of your mental energy toward.

Goal Setting & Attainment

This is the reason for goal setting. **Just to acquire the will to act is not enough**. Have you ever ridden in bumper cars? If you have, you have the understanding of what movement with no *preset destination* will result in. It will result in confusion, and literally a waste of time. You will have gotten nowhere, and you will hit others, and be hit by others, all to wind up, pretty much in the same place that you started, just a little bit more banged up than when you started.

So just as important as the will to act, is the act of goal setting. I am a proponent of the **SMART Goals** model. This is the *Specific, Measurable, Attainable, Realistic, and Timed model of goals setting*:

Specific - You have to be decisive about what it is that you wish to accomplish. You have to be of one mind, and you have to focus your energy upon the target of your specification. You cannot simply say, "*I want to become successful*", it is more than that. You want to say, "*I want to be successful at A, B, and C.*"

Measurable - You have to be able to say, "*Well if I do D, E, and F, it will get me to the point where I need to be, in order to get A, B, and C.*" You also want to be able to Measure your progress objectively. Knowing when you've accomplished D, and when it is time to move on the E component of your goal is key. If not you will get stuck in one area and not move forward.

Attainable - You want to set a goal that you can achieve, you do not want to say, "*I want to fly*", and then go jump off the tallest building you can find. I think we all have examples of people who have done this, and

I think it is safe to say we all know how that turned out for them. Your goal must be concrete, it has to be something that you can **quantify**, or identify. Don't make it too hard to achieve, you want to break it down. You may want to compete in a 5K race. A good start, and an attainable goal would be to set the goal of walking for one mile a day, then two miles, then three, and then picking up your pace a little, incrementally. That is attainable *depending* on your current state of health. Before you know it, you'll be ready for that five.

Realistic – you want to set goals that are realistic so as not to discourage yourself. Each goal you reach is a motivational factor, and a reason to continue to aspire to reach even loftier goals. You do not want to say, *"I want to turn into a ball of fire"*, for instance. You can say, *"I want to learn how to control my breathing in order to regulate my temperature."* This may be possible, dependent upon how much you are willing to learn, study and practice.

Timed – Next, you want to able to time yourself. To set an end goal time sequence. Let's say you want to stop smoking by using harm reduction, so you set goals of 10 cigarettes a day, then 8, then 5, then 3, then 2, and then 1 all done within 5 day increments. If this is executed properly you can say that you are going to stop smoking completely in 30 days. *This would be advised to all readers of this book,* for the sake of enjoying your success after you attain it, because you cannot take it with you, and smoking cigarettes will surely shorten your time here with us.

You can apply the steps of this **SMART Goals** model to anything you wish to accomplish in life, and it will supplement your *movement with meaning.* It will give much *wealth* to your *will* to act. It will add another dimension to your development, this will put things into perspective for you. It will strengthen your resolve if done correctly, because every couple of days or weeks, your course will be edified by the completion of one of your goals. Another way to explain this is through the use of the *M & M Goal* model.

M & M Goals Model

The *M & M Goal Model* is one of my own design standing for Micro and Macro goals. Micro means small and Macro means large, so Micro means less significant or beginning goals, and Macro stands for most significant or end goals. In the same example we used before, a Micro goal can be to learn more information about the damage that cigarettes do your body, and then begin to implement harm reduction techniques. Then the Macro goals can be to get down to one cigarette a day, do this for a week, and then quit. With these models of *goal setting*, it presents a course or a path through which to obtain the main goal of that which success mean to you.

Remember, as good as all of this sounds, and regardless to the inherent validity of the concepts, it is all just theory if you do not make it applicable. You can attest to the truth you are reading about, however, if you do not breathe life into it by taking it off the page and applying it to your life, it will remain inanimate and be of no use to you. Again, you must possess and utilize the will to act. Many a time a person will be looking for what they call '*the perfect time*' to do something. What those of us who stay moving forward know, however, is that there is not a more *perfect time than the present*. Your situation changes by your will to act. Your situation will not change to *thereby facilitate* your will to act, the universe just does not work that way. **If it did everyone would be successful.**

In Sum

You must decide for yourself, what part you are going to play in this lifetime. Will you be subjected to the will of others, or will others be subject to your will? Will you be gracious and giving, or will you be disdainful and withholding? Will you be successful, or will you lead a life that is lacking fulfillment? Will you be a part of a successful marriage, or will you *die alone?* These are questions that no one can answer but yourself, and the answers are dictated by your willingness to act, and then further determined by the meaning within your movement.

This brings me to the close of the chapter on belief. Can you see just how pertinent the prerequisite of belief is to your success? You will never set goals that you can accomplish without the prerequisite of belief. No one does anything for the sake of nothing. Why waste time? I agree. You have to possess the belief that you can and will be successful, first. This will *compel action,* and a main prerequisite of this action is that you have to have ***Faith.***

CHAPTER 6

Faith

Complete trust or confidence in someone or something[1].

PERSISTENCE

Faith provides for persistence. Faith is so powerful, this will *almost ensure* your success at any endeavor that you are actively working towards. This is due the terms of faith noted above. The terms of faith are '*the complete trust or confidence in someone or something*[1a]'. Key word being complete; meaning 360 degrees, no lack thereof, and no possibility of denial. Faith many times contradicts reality, and this is perfectly fine. We do not *see* air, do we? Yet we know it is present, don't we? Of course it is, because without it we would be dead.

Faith Without Works is Dead

So is it with the success of whatever it is that we are engaged in. If we have complete trust in the fact that it will be accomplished and become successful thereafter, there is no possible detours are there? No, there is not. It is your faith in your ability, which will make your ability *sufficient*. There will be no denying you, and you will compel others to have faith in you, because faith is infectious. If it were not, then there would not be those who are known as *converts*. Faith catches on, it infects people, and *galvanizes* others to lend support to one common cause or person.

In order for others to have faith in you, most of the time it is a prerequisite that you have faith in yourself. The kind of faith that does not waiver, the kind of faith that grabs a hold and never lets go, never gets weak, and does not doubts. We are in need of *faith,* it is akin to belief, **but faith is much stronger.** It has been stated that faith is the *belief in things unseen.* So you may not have the success yet, but that does not stop you from persevering. You may be drenched in bad times now, but that does not cause you to pause, and many may have failed before you, but that does not cause you to stray. **This is faith.**

If you are at all doubtful of the powers of faith, I would urge you to step foot in any religious house of worship. I am not one to poke holes or state what is right or wrong about any particular faith or religious precept. That is not the purpose of this book. **What is the purpose of this part of the book is to convey to the reader a sense of how faith is a prerequisite to your success.** Faith is a prerequisite to your success in anything. If you fish you go to the lake, or to the fishing-hole that you go to, faithful that you will *enjoy* yourself, even if you do not catch a twelve footer, correct? If you did not have that faith would you still go? I know the answer to that.

When you have faith you have a reason to be persistent. You do not care how many times you are told no, because you have the components of faith, and it is this *faith that propels* one forward. One cannot lose when they have faith. When you shoot for the moon and land on a star, are you still successful? Of course you are, and now you are on a star, so the next time that you leap, you are more than half the way there already. This is the power of faith. Some people have no belief in themselves as far as their being able to accomplish anything. Yet if they still have faith, *they will move forward.*

People will move forward from the platform of faith, and faith alone. The success stories where people say that they had no evidence of anything, but they still had the faith required to move forward, and then they received that thing that captures the meaning of success for them, is manifold. Very plentiful are the resources of stories about successes based purely on the premise of faith. **Faith is what will keep us moving forward in the face of all adversity.** No matter what happens in our lives if our component of faith is sufficient, there will be no pause or distraction.

Faith is the Vehicle

Faith is satisfying in and of itself. A lot of times the faithful will find that it is not *only the vehicle*, but the *destination* within itself. Faith is nourishing, faith is fulfilling, and it gives *poise* to your purpose. It also gives you comfort in the face of calamity, a calm throughout the storm, so to say. Faith gives you a sense of peace, or inner composition and it is so essential to the biology of a Leader. A Leader needs to be strong in the face of opposition. His exterior must not crack, for the benefit of those following his lead. **Faith and an unwavering sense of resolve make us durable, which in effect, makes us reliable.**

Faith is an *inner constitution*, one that does not allow the outside world to ruffle the feathers of the one who has it. The person with faith will do things that are conducive or permissible by their choice of faith and not do actions that are not permissible, or conducive, according to their degree of faith. Faith compels the people who have it to action. It will cause people to write checks, but a check cannot be written for it. Faith cannot be purchased, it is something that the possessor, or seeker, must find within themselves. Again, I cannot stress enough the value of acquiring knowledge, as the **accumulation of your knowledge base will add validity to having faith.**

Faith is what allows us to try. Think of a baby, yet again, and *how faithful he is* that he will walk. They are so faithful that they will not stop *come busted lip, or sprained hip.* It does not matter how many times they fall, how many times they injure themselves, or how many times they cry. They are completely faithful that they will get it done, so they do not stop trying until they have accomplished the task. Then upon the accomplishment of walking *the dream expands* to include running, jumping, and so forth. So **never allow yourself to underestimate the power of faith.**

Study Faith

Study religion, study the proponents of religions, and see how much they were able to accomplish, under the harsh pretenses of the most arduous of situations. They may have faltered, yet they did not fail, and they base their successes in their faith. They contribute the glory to the head of their faith and desire no accolades, in most instances, of course. Others *use faith* to galvanize others, and make *themselves* rich. How many people can you think of that have done such a thing. They were a proponent of a certain faith and then got caught doing something that, so adamantly contradicted their faith that people realized they must have just been a scam artist. This is almost always following the acquisition of countless millions of dollars.

They will come back from the shamed situation that they put themselves in, and their flock will be waiting for them *regardless of evidence to the contrary*. It is a matter of faith. Faith does not know desertion, **faith knows only a fierce loyalty** that one is willing to fight to the death to preserve. Many people have been taken advantage of on so many levels due to the powerful presence of faith. **Imagine if you were that devoted to your dream.** Imagine if you applied the kind of faith to the acquisition of success that a devoutly religious person applied to the practice of their religion. **What if you could learn how to apply that kind of single-mindedness to your success?**

Faith Multiplies Effort

What do you think you could accomplish? How long do you think it would take? What would your odds of being successful become? **Success**

has to be a religion for you. You can have a religion, but success has to take on the same kind of *meaning* for you, for you to truly devote the kind of time and focus to it, that is required to reap the rewards of your desire and dedication. Faith knows no boundaries, it is not contingent on, '*What if?*' There is no '*if*' in faith. Faith allows for no ifs, ands, buts, or maybes. **Faith is convinced beyond all shadow of a doubt.**

I'm sure you are aware of all of the terrible things that take place in one's quest for success sometimes. These are instances in which one must have the adequate amount of faith. **Faith adds character to your credence,** it does not allow for others to be trampled upon, because it is faithful that success will come to its owner without having to hurt anyone else. Faith is patient, it is waiting, and it is calculating. *Faith does not need recognition,* it is not out for glorification, as these are not the aims of faith. Faith is fine, in and of itself. It is at peace, *it submits totally to the process of becoming.*

The Virtues of Faith

True Faith does not allow for cheating, stealing, or hiding records in the name of success. Faith's true possessors have no need to lie or conjure up schemes to convince others. Faith stands solely on its *merit* alone, it is *transparent and obvious* for all to behold. Faith brings about a work ethic that is otherwise unknown. Faith brings about a state of happy work. People are happy to do the work that they are faithful in. You never see clergy arguing about the cleaning of the church, or the position they may hold in relation to the work that has to be done. There should exist no power struggle for position. Now, we know that these situations exist, but they only exist where a *lack of faith* also exists.

You are not going to convince someone *out of* their faith. See faith makes you so strong, you are going to be able to weather any storm in which faith is present with you. **It is a most trusted, valuable soldier**

within the scope of your endeavors and pursuits. Faith makes any opposition that you find yourself against wither in comparison to the objective. Faith makes anything *doable*, any height that you are reaching for *attainable*, any success that you are aspiring for *acquirable*. There has been no partner of the human being that has enabled him in the way that the partnership of faith has, ever. **Nor will there ever be.**

When you have faith, the kind of faith that knows no limits, then will you be made to act in a way of confirmation. When you act in the way of confirmation, this confirms it for others. They begin to have faith *in you*, they begin to have faith *in your ability to do what you say you are going to do*, accomplish what you have set out to accomplish, and they will be *compelled to contribute* to your efforts. The faith you have in your quest, they will begin to replicate and produce on their own, and you will have the most fruitful of alliances if you understand this concept.

Faith Negates Doubt

You must never question if something will get done or not. You can question as to *when*, or *how*, or *why it's taking so long*, and *what else must be done*, but never question as to if it *will happen* or not. **It is done, it is accomplished in your mind and so, it is already so, and you're just giving the universe the time to catch on, and catch up.** This is the acquisition of success. Use your faith to guide you to the watering hole, just let go of all supposition, and be guided to the gold by your faith. It is a very good guide, you will know whether you are engaged in the correct situations if you just *get quiet and listen* to your faith.

Faith will empower people to put down the things that they never thought they would put down, faith empowers people to pick up things they never thought that they would pick up, and faith allows people to acquire things that they never thought that they would be able to acquire. Faith allows you to do things in weeks that take others months to do, and accomplish in years, what it takes others decades to scratch the surface of. It affords us a deeper understanding and a *sweeter satisfaction* than those who do not have it. Faith is a most valuable prerequisites to have. If you do well in the class of faith, you can put the vehicle on cruise control.

I say that you can put the car on cruise control, because nothing too disastrous is going to take place, and whatever does take place you will be built to handle. People with faith do not become as *easily, or as deeply, shaken* as those who do not have faith. You will be able to tell who has faith by seeing how they handle bad news. You can tell two people of a terrible tragedy. Both may cry, both may feel sorrow, but the one with faith will grieve *less, and less intensely* than the one with no faith. **Faith amplifies our aptitude to accept.**

We will not *struggle in life as if we are lost,* because faith provides us with a keen sense of direction. We will not become depressed, as faith gives us *pleasure and conviction* that we are on the right road that we are supposed to be on, no matter how scary things may look. Faith gives us a *cool.* It is like a fresh glass of cold lemonade, while everyone around us is *on fire.* Faith will empower you to make the right decisions, and it will afford you an undeniable respect.

This is one of the main reasons why faith is a prerequisite to success, because people will respect you. I'm not saying that they will emptily respect the fact that you may be a deacon. No, it is not that easy. You need not wear your faith on your forehead, as a matter of fact people who try to do that, often have the opposite take place and they lose respect. I'm talking about people who have *internal faith.* The external house of their faith need not be identified, because they are internally *fortified* from it, so no matter what the name of it is, or where it may come from, is neither here nor there.

Symbols of Faith

The tell-tale symbols of faith are very similar. *Discipline, chastity, virtue, calm, sincerity, consideration, single-mindedness, concentration, generosity, and more.* There are many variables of each of these symbols, but I believe that you get the point. What I am saying is that faithfulness need not be defined as one particular faith, or another, when it comes to **respect.** Just having a root of faith that keeps you grounded will be sufficient enough for most to be respectful of you, and they will be able to see the connection with faith that you have. This will help others to identify with you, and make you more successful in *relationship building.*

Have you ever heard that strength detects strength? This is also true of faith. **Faith is a form of strength,** and it is not hard to discern another like unto yourself. No matter where you are, you just have a common bond, and it is easily recognizable by those who have it. Birds of a feather flock together, and the old adage of, *'show me who you're with, and I'll show you who you are'* holds true on this affirmation. So be full of faith, and **it will be very conducive of your dreams turning into success.**

The beautiful thing about faith is it makes you successful *by default.* I have known many people who did not reach the pinnacle for which they were aspiring. Yet they were able to make some very good distance between themselves presently, and where they started from. I will give you an example. A person wants to become a millionaire. That is their initial definition for success, they want to have a million dollars in the bank. That is their definition of success. So they strive.

They meet a spouse who wants the same thing. They get married, they share the same aspirations. They go to college, they join a body of worship, and they do this together. They grow *out of impoverishment together, as one.* The woman gets pregnant, and they have a beautiful baby girl. All the while they are climbing the ladder to success. They graduate from college, now they both get decent jobs, with titles, and offices in the respective sectors of their education. They continue to grow, as does their child.

They grow older together, with focus, both growing and reaching. They teach their child *morals and values,* and they are widely respected by friends and community. Time goes by, the daughter leaves to college, and they are now mid to late forties. They have not made their million dollars...yet, but **would any of you assume that they have not been successful?** I would not, I would say that they have been very successful, and one needs just to pay attention to what they have gained as opposed to what they have not. Though, I would also assume that the people in this example would have no problem doing just that.

The 'Present' in the Process

True, lasting, substantial success is not found in the end goal, but it is *present within the process.* Within the striving, that is where people uncover valuables that they never knew were present. They learn things about this world, others and themselves, that they never would have known had they not embarked upon this journey, and it is satisfying. It is so satisfying, in fact, that some just stop where they are and say that, '*this is enough*'. This is enough for me. I set out to land on the moon, and I landed on a cloud. My friends are the stars and the sun, and that is enough for me. This is success, and I agree completely. **Success is a state**, it is not a possession, but you have to figure that out for yourself. This is why I always say, '*success...whatever that looks like to you*'.

Everyone has their own definition of success, and also of what is positive and negative. Everyone has their own process of qualification and quantification. No one can decide for another, the way that they see something, nor should they. This would stunt their process of growth, and we are not here to do that. We are here to pass on wisdom, to *enhance* to lives of others. We are here to give other people the benefits of our experiences, wisdom, and faith, so that they may come to know that faith. The purpose of the inspiration, and motivation, the Coaching, the Consultation, the Mentoring, and the Counseling is to provide faith and personalized education to those who would otherwise not have it. We make the possibilities known to those who would otherwise know it not.

Touch & Transfer

Faith is transferrable, it is a learned habit. It is transferred through instruction, and example. When a child has a parent who is depressed, who sees no light at the end of the tunnel, who cries all day or refuses to leave the home, a great many of these ailments are passed down. They are *learned behaviors* that the child *must unlearn* in order to have a normal productive life. Such is the case with faith. If a child is raised in a home where there is faith, they learn how to respond to the event of life showing up, as it always does, with patience, constancy, fortitude, and faith. **They learn faith from observing it in practice.** This does not mean that they will have it for themselves, which is ultimately up to them. What it does do, is it increases the probability, and makes faith a possibility. This is what we do for each other.

Alas, I cannot reach in my pocket to give you a hundred dollar bill if I do not have it for myself. So in the same vein I cannot give someone that which I do not possess. I could not teach nuclear physics. I am not a Nuclear Physicist. I would be lost, I would give people the wrong instruction completely. In order for a person to instruct in matters of patience, faith and consistency, they must first have it for themselves. So if you understand the powers of faith and you want to make it available to others, your very own children and extended family, it is recommended that you possess it for yourself, so that you will not give the wrong instruction, or *contradict your message by your actions.*

A person cannot say that they have faith that things will get better, and then go commit suicide and leave a note that says, *"All is lost, and there is no hope"*. That will not come from a person who has faith. It may come from a person who has lost faith, but those who have faith are enduring, and they find a way through whatever calamity that has befallen them, hence the reason why it is a prerequisite of success. It is a proverbial must have. With faith, things will be easier, and success will be right at your grasp. Seize it. Hold it tight.

Faith is what will allow someone to go to bed *hungry with a smile,* and not set out to hurt someone else. Faith is what will allow someone to seemingly *lose everything,* and exhibit much internal fortitude, with the mind-state of *'everything happens for a reason'*. Faith does not allow for coincidence. Everything has a purpose, and it is a person's job to find out what that purpose is. **There is a Messenger of Misery, his name is Circumstance, and he has a twin brother named Calamity.** There is also a Message *in* Misery, and her name is *Wisdom and Understanding.* Allow the messenger to introduce you to the message. She is beautiful.

The Rich Fool

Faith does not allow for arrogance. That is one of the reasons why faith is a prerequisite of success. See, you can be successful by *mistake.* Just like there are administrative snafus, and someone makes a clerical error, which may result in a person graduating early. This is not due to any hard work or *brilliance* on the student's behalf, this is just an error. Well, if a small office can make a miscalculation, and allow someone to slip through the cracks, how much more a large universe?

So you will see success stories that make *no sense,* you have seen people who are nice and who are deserving of success, living check to check, or on the dole, and you have also seen unconscionable people who are downright evil, yet they obtain some modicum of success.

How many times have you come across a person who was *successful and arrogant?* Let me tell you that person, had not faith. If you have faith then you are aware that all of your blessings and successes generate from that **source** of your faith, so you do not get a big head. The Bible says a *fool and his riches are soon parted.* Well, I tell you that the same thing goes for an arrogant person and their success.

It seems just when a person begins to glorify themselves and lose appreciation for their gifts, their gifts are taken from them. As soon as people begin to think they are *self-made,* that they are this wonderful, all powerful, god-like figure, that's when all of their successes come crashing down on their heads. The reason for this is that they are entrusted with success, and they have to be humble or they will lose the success that they have been blessed to gain. This humility is quick to deny greatness. No, these people always can be heard saying, *"Glory be to...."*, and they fill the void with the **source** they have faith in, that created the path to success for them. **They do not take the credit**. For anything.

As soon as people begin to see themselves as the source of everything that they have, they lose their humility, they stop being thankful, and they stop being grateful. They lose their persistence. **Faith makes us persistent.** Faith makes us *consistent,* it makes us *constant,* and it makes us *transparent.* We have to be persistent, we have to be persistent in our pursuit of what we want, and we have to be **persistent in our thankfulness** for its attainment in order to keep it. We must also be persistent in *finding ways* to make our success of *benefit to others.* If not we may also lose it for that reason.

The Law of Increasing Returns

We have to persistently give out of that which we have been successful at attaining. If you don't have much, *give a little* from what you have, and you will be *trusted with more.* If you have no money, volunteer your time, if you have no time, give money. You see how that works? Everybody has something to give, it is within this realm of *persistent giving*, that we are *given persistently*. **So the use of faith will actually build your faith**. It works like this, if you can muster up enough faith to take two steps, and in return you are answered with 7 degrees of progress, wouldn't that enhance your faith? Well, try it out. Try it out and see what everybody's been talking about. See what's going on, and what all the fuss about faith is.

In Sum

You just have to be persistent, you cannot be faithful today and be *wishy-washy tomorrow*. This will result in lackluster results which, I'm sure, you do not think is going to provide you the success that you wish to obtain. Persistence is very key, it is one of your building blocks, and main components in your map building. It is an integral prerequisite to your success and it has to be *strengthened* by your faith. Lack of faith will allow us to stop, to slow down, to procrastinate, to freeze, to succumb to fear, and to lay down and die. Faith on the other hand will *invigorate* us, will provide us with fullness, strength, humility, and resolve. It will enable us to press forward, to overcome, and to outride any storm.

Faith provides the person who has it with staying ability. The person who has faith will not quit and give up as easily, as the person who does not have faith. That person will find it easy to throw the cards in and get up from the table. The person with faith is in his seat until the lights come on. *They did not come to lose…they came to win, and the game is not over until they have won, and won all that there is to win.* What faith says to them, is that they can do it, and no one can take it away from them. This is the key emotion behind persistence. Faith turns into A Knowing State.

A KNOWING STATE

There is a state of acceptance, there is a state of belief, there is a state of hope, and then there is a state of knowing. It is the state of knowing that is more powerful than all of the rest, though it depends on all of the rest to be full, to be able to exist. It is a culmination of all that we have spoken about within the context of pre-requisites that allow this state to come to fruition. A state of knowing, is what will allow success to *unfold*.

What State are You In?

This pertains to any topic that is the focus of your desire and commitment. This can mean *success in a relationship, job performance, your academic pursuits, and/or anything else that you wish to accomplish.* You must move from a state of want, and a state of dedication, to a state of knowing. It is the most resolute of all that came before it. **It is finality.** It is this state of knowing, that convince all who come into contact with the person that has it, that they already *are* it. Have you ever heard the saying, '*fake it till you make it?*' Well, this is not that. This is not faking it.

This is accepting the *reality* of that which has yet to become. It is a serene state of existence in which your dreams have already become true, though they may have yet to *materialize*. It is Zen, it is completeness, and it is done. We must still move forward, but it is akin to walking to a destination that is already set. The reality is waiting for you. It is like moving into a home that you have designed. A home that you have bought, and have had made according to your wishes. You have had consultations with the designer. This should be like that, and there should be a leather sofa here, and so forth. **This is a predetermined reality.** Predetermined by you.

This is the state that relies on you having made the vision board that we discussed in chapter 3. You have seen it so much, looked upon it so much, and visualized it so much, that it has become a concrete part of you. **This is a state of absolute peace, a state of heightened awareness.** All that you look at *resembles this reality* that you have etched permanently into the depths of your perception. This allows you to determine what roads to take, because there is but one direction, and that direction leads to the *fulfillment of your dreams.*

Waiting for the Check to Clear

This is a straight line. There is no distraction, nor detours able to turn you from your goals and dreams. This is wholeness, there are many pieces that have gone into this creation, and this is the sum of those parts. A state of knowing does not complain, it understands that all which is unfavorable, is a *temporary necessity* to obtaining the ultimate reality. **This is a state of having.** One of the best ways that I can describe this, is to use the example of a check that has been put into the bank. You have a dream, an aspiration. **You have deposited this dream, this curren(t)cy into the bank of the universe.** Now you are waiting for it to clear.

Everything is fine with the check that you have deposited. You are fully aware that the office that cut the check has more than enough funds to cover it, as the office is the source from which flows *all of abundance,* so there can be no worry. These checks come *certified,* and none have *ever* bounced. **All you have to do is wait for the check to clear.** This is a great analogy of the knowing state. The same way you know checks will cash, this is the same way that you must know that you *dreams will come to fruition.* That your aspirations for success will come to be. Think of the calm.

Think of the *calm* when you consider this check. There may be collection calls taking place and the bills may be due, but you are not worried, because you know that you have gone through *all of the steps.* You have gone through all of the prerequisite steps, you have consulted with the bank's director, you have signed the check, and everything that *can be done has been done.* Now all you have to do is wait. That does not mean that work stops.

No, while that check is in the clearing process, you are working for the next check. For the check, or success, that are soon to follow. It is like going to work for next week's check, while you wait for the check from last week to clear. Though this may be the check that will *cover a year, or a decade,* determined by the size of your dreams, and the work that you have put in. There is no doubt. The check is not in the mail, the check is in the bank, and now you're just waiting for the funds to be made available unto you. *Can you see the differences in perception?*

This is the *mental reality* that we must take on as our world view. Some checks take longer to cash than others. You may be able to just cash a check for $500. However, a check for $500,000,000 may easily take a bit longer for the funds to be made available to you. This is akin to the cashing in of your dreams. It is a reality, you dotted all the i's, and you have crossed all the t's. There is no more to be done, and you are now hard at work on the $800,000,000 check. It is your work on the $800,000,000 dollar check that will ensure the funds being made available for the $500,000,000 check.

Writing the Future

This is a much more *intense state* than just mere faith, this is not face value, and this is what is known as a **knowing state.** Therein lies no doubt whatsoever, there is not an '*if*' emotion, there is only a '*when*' *motion*. This is akin to when Jim Carrey wrote himself a check for $10,000,000 dollars for services rendered before he even knew what he would be doing to earn the money. As the story goes he wrote this check, continued to work for the next one, and got the call that would pay him the 10M. *This is the power of a knowing state.* You have to be *there.*

You have to be present in the cashing in of this dream at all times, you have to be *spiritually, or mentally calling the bank,* checking on the funds, in full awareness and expectancy that today will be the day they tell you to come to the bank and bring three duffel bags. Bring three duffel bags and three of your most trusted inner circle, because it has been made available. **You have to use the time in between to prepare.** This is why people will advise you to go do a walk-through of the house that you plan to purchase. Step foot on the lot, and test drive that monster that you plan to tame. Step foot in that jewelry store, have your wife's finger measured for her ring size, and let her try on that glacier that is akin to the 8th wonder of the world that she deserves. Do it, do it now, and don't wait. **It is already hers.**

This is practice, this is like mental gymnastics. This is preparing you for a state of abundance, but first you must make a swift departure *from the land of lack.* Call around, price the trips that you plan to take, get some estimates. I'm not saying to spend your money before it arrives, good sakes no, what I am saying is, to further will its arrival by making room for it. Think of this concept. I am reminded of Bob Proctor, and the 'You are Born Rich' series. Therein, he speaks on *making room.* Imagine you are having a guest arrive for the next two weeks, how would you prepare? What is there in the space that they are going to use? **Remove it.**

Make Room for Success

This is just how you must make room for your guest *success*. Hopefully it will not just be a *guest,* and it will become a *permanent member* of your home and of your family, for this to take place though, **there has to be reservations made.** Clean the doubt out of your mind, throw out all frivolousness, and do away with bad habits, like those of procrastination and worry. Clear the space in which *abundance is predetermined to reside,* or it will come, and finding unsuitable hospitality and space, *it will leave.*

Think of those who become successful for a season, *the one hit wonders*, and the millionaires for a day, who soon thereafter are forced to file for bankruptcy, because when success dropped in they were unprepared. This is such a serious prerequisite, **you must conduct a constant audit of yourself.** Are you ready? If your $500,000,000 check cleared today, what would you have ready to go? *Do it now, do not wait for it to come!* This is not the way to attain it. The way to attain it is to *clear a room, clear your mind, clear your body, and clear your soul* for the encroaching success. Make sure you have enough provisions, make sure to rid your home of all offensive materials that would incline success to leave you. **Be the person you are to become.**

Become Your 'Best' Self

See it, and then be it. It is that simple. If you were to paint the most sophisticated professional in your mind, what would they look like? **Become them.** What would they talk like, do they sound *like you?* If not, *fix that.* If you could not see yourself as a millionaire, yet a million dollars is what you are aspiring to reach for, *remove all that is not conducive* to its arrival. Are you going to put it in the safe? Is your safe full of baseball cards? Find another place for those. **You cannot be a CEO with the mind of a janitor.** You cannot be married with the mind of a playboy extraordinaire. You cannot be a millionaire with the mind of a bum. It just will not work. See, anyone can get money, it is not that hard to get. The hardest thing you will find out about money if you've never had it, is that it is *not so easy to keep.*

You have to be a gracious host. You must inspire the money that you do come by, to stick around, and to want to work for you. **This is the secret of prosperity.** You must exert mental control over the curren(t) cy. You must will it to stay, by clearing a place for it, and you must will it to go to work, by putting the mechanisms in place. If you are not ready, then it will be '*here today, gone tomorrow*'. You know what they say, 'Easy come, and easy go', trust me, you do not want to be *them*. You want to be the one that '*never looked back*'. In order to '*never look back*', you must never look back now. **There is no better time than the present to begin.**

Proper Stewardship

Imagine the check cleared today, what would be your first move? What would be your initial investment? How much would you give to charity? What charity? How much would you put into savings? For who? Where would you travel? With who? Whose lives would change? Why? How? To what degree would they change? These are very important questions, to which you may want to invest the answers, because the answers to the questions may very well *qualify or disqualify the funds being made available.* Practice makes perfect, it is very practical to have these answers and mechanisms in place for the universe to deem you trustworthy for the *stewardship of abundance.*

Imagine yourself in the magnitude of host. Would I want to allow my *son or daughter* to come stay with you? Would I fear for their safety, would I deem you responsible? This is the same way people are vetted for success. Are you lying to yourself? Would I send them, and then have to come and get them, because they are not being properly taken care of? Would I have to relieve you of the trust, I once had for you? These are questions that only you know the answer to at first, but then soon all are made aware, due to your state of affairs.

Life will tell on you. No one can hide homelessness, not for long anyway. No one can hide the fact that they have no money, after having plenty. That is obvious to anyone who is familiar with what embarrassment looks like; *poverty and want.* It is not hard at all to tell the person who has done wrong with what was entrusted to him, up until the point that it was taken. These are the people who look like life snuck up from behind and hit them behind the ear with a blackjack. They have a *glazed look of surprise,* like they cannot believe what has happened.

They also have a guilty look, because they are fully aware that they, and they alone are the cause of their predicament. They have had success, and they have lost it, they may have had plenty of money too, they have lost that as well. Now they just stumble to and fro, begging for a meal here, borrowing money for transportation purposes to get them back there, they have no shelter from themselves. They are not too fond of themselves and curse their misfortune. They do not look very happy. They look surprised, as they were not prepared. They are like the grasshopper when the winter descended, they were oblivious. **They had no idea.**

Reality Check

Everything is real. Life is real, life can be very hard, but it does not have to be so. Life can be a beautiful blessing, again, it does not have to be so. Money, success, and life is like unto beauty. It is determined by the beholder. Many times we'll here of someone saying, *"Next time, I'll know what to do with it"*, or *"Just this one more time"*. Many times the window of opportunity will have closed on these people, and they will desperately search for the universe to open itself once more to them. **I bid them good luck with that.**

Allow me to provide an analogy, are you ready? **The power that you hold in your mind is like unto the power of the universe.** Look at the beautiful plants that the universe has created. Then, by contrast look at the devastating potentiality of a black hole. The power that you wield with your life is similar, you can create, and you can use your life for the purpose of destruction. Either result can be determined by the use of your mind; your *thoughts*.

Thoughts Become Things

Another analogy is that of a gun. When you purchase a gun, it comes with directions, *use with caution. Danger, handle with care.* It can be used to protect and keep, or it can be used to destroy, and to kill. This is like the power of the tongue, with it you can take life, or make life more abundant. It can be used to whatever purpose the one who wields it determines. Do not take your own life, do not destroy your own success. **It is relatively easy to do both.**

Once it has been used to either end, it cannot be taken back. You cannot bring someone back to life after you have taken it from them. Do not be careless. You may be able to misfire once, you may be able to undo havoc done to your life, once or twice, or not at all. *Do not gamble.* How seriously do you take your own life? How seriously do you take your own success? You must develop a knowing state, and an enhanced state of awareness. You must prepare for that which you say that you want. Another saying to add emphasis to this effect is to, *"Be careful what you wish for, for you just may get it."*

Do not focus on things that are above your pay grade, or above your level of understanding. *Do not ask for things that you are not prepared to receive,* be humble, and be honest. Think of how many women get pregnant, only to wish that they had not, because they are not ready to be a responsible guardian of life, they are not ready to be parents. Many times they are the reason that their children go down the wrong path or get hurt, because of their level of responsibility or lack thereof. You may be able to convince others of an untruth, however, you cannot lie unto yourself. You will know whether or not you did all that you could, and *you will be judged accordingly.*

Take Your Time

You must possess a state of knowing *before* you take responsibility for something. You must know beyond a shadow of a doubt that you are in a *prepared state.* This is why there exists a qualification process, before you are determined fit for certain positions, this is why there is training. So what I am saying is **prepare yourself for success.** A specialist in any area is one who is properly trained to handle situations within their context of training. They are ready. They are so ready that actions that have to be done are like second nature to them. They call it a reflex. They have it so ingrained that there is no question as to how they will react under pressure, because they have been tested. *Test yourself.* They have so and so many hours of training. *Train yourself.*

Teach yourself the fundamentals of success, the pre-requisites, and if you are reading this book, *congratulations*, you are training your mind to know what is required of you to be successful. What you will be faced with, what to expect, and how to respond. This is so important. **You will be the first responder to your state of success.** You will perform many acts to procure your success. Much will be required of you to enhance your state of success, to keep it, and to amplify it. How well you respond will be based on the proficiency of your training. Your state of knowing.

First Responders

First responders are called first responders *based on their training.* Their quality and quantity of training allows them to be the first responders to an emergency. What emergencies and situations are *you qualified to be a first responder to?* How do you handle calamity? How adept are you at handling loss? The loss of others? When everyone else seems to be going insane, will you be able to gather and utilize your wits? Will it be natural, or forced? Will you know what to do, or guess? This is why success is not sudden. **Success is a process,** a process that takes time.

You must possess a state of awareness, a state of knowing, you must not slack, and you must not make the same mistake over and over. Of course you are allowed to make a mistake here, and there, as we covered in the failure prerequisite. But you are not supposed to make the same mistake, the same way, twice. *These people are relieved of their post immediately for incompetence.* You do not wish for the universe to deem you as incompetent because that will be the end of your blessings, and that will be the end of your trust.

It is much better to have thing, and not need it, than to need a thing, and not have it. Many times this is used to speak to the effect of things that may not be the most positive. But let's look at this statement. A person may not exactly need economic education, but how important would this education be, if they were suddenly entrusted by the universe with a large inheritance. It would be pretty useful at this point, would it not? Of course it would, as a matter of fact it could be deemed a matter of life and death. *Prosperity or poverty.*

Continued Education

This is why *continued specialized training and education* is so important. We must seek knowledge from the cradle to the grave, and all forms of knowledge. We will not know that which is going to come our way, and that is why we must have faith. We must, after faith, possess a state of knowing, that we are prepared to handle anything that comes our way, be it positive or negative. This will ensure our success in anything we encounter. Everything in life is not going to be positive, everything in life is not going to be negative.

This is why we must **diversify our portfolios.** I know this is often used in reference to one's investment, and it is no different here. Though in this instance I am speaking on the *curren(t)cy of one's energy and attention.* We must have diversified intellectual investments. I know many a time in school, we would ask ourselves, why do I have to learn this, when will I ever use it? Well, the answer is, that you may never use it, but how much *better is it to possess a thing, and need not use it, than to need a thing, and not possess it?*

Diversify your portfolio, search out knowledge, high and low. Search out knowledge that does not make that much sense to you now, you may be in the *preparation stages* for something you are unaware of at the present moment. **When opportunity comes to you, seize it.** Do not let it pass you by, nothing is of coincidence, things come to us in their own good time, and always on purpose, though you may not know what that purpose is. **When the student is ready, the teacher will appear.**

When Duty Calls

So you get called to do a certain thing which you may have no interest in. You are surprised with the opportunity to enter a field or forum, for which you did not apply, or take the initiative to pursue, that does not mean that it is by mistake. **The universe's grand design does not allow for mistake.** It vibrates on such a *high frequency the meaning may not resonate* with you, it may be a part of something that is so far above your head that you cannot, for the life of you, *determine the reasoning.* That does not mean to let it escape your grasp. That does not mean that it is not meant for you. That may just mean that you have yet to rise to that level of comprehension.

Know this, know that there is a pertinent reason behind all that is questionable in your life at this point. It is fine, do not second-guess it, and just let it flow. Water always finds its level. It will find its level throughout the course of your life. Things that seemed to make no sense, at a prior state in time, were made revealed to you at a later time. Is this not so? I know it is. It has always been this way, and it always will be this way. Rise unto a knowing state. Too much speculation, leads to hesitation, which ends as procrastination. **You are being groomed towards conviction.**

CONVICTION

A *knowing state gives rise to an attitude.* A state of certainty, a certain *taste in your mouth.* Conviction, you can feel it in your bones, in your blood, and in the very essence that is you. Conviction means, a "*firmly held belief or opinion*[3]". The key word here being *firmly.* When you are convicted of a thing, there is permanence, there is an *intensity of purpose.* Conviction means no doubt whatsoever, as to the evidence of. You must be convicted in the realm of your success. You must be **evangelical** in the pursuit of your success, you must be a beast about it. Not meaning you have to be a savage beast, but you must give all that you have for it, as denial will not suffice.

Business/Success is War

You cannot be asking all cutely for success, a closed mouth does not get fed, and he who possesses the loudest roar will obtain the most food. You have to be ferocious, and an animal about it. You have to *sleep and dream* your success, you have to awake to and consume a bowl of your desire. Your desire must be something that you are willing to sacrifice all else for, it must be the object of your firm, unwavering conviction. It must be something that you can see, touch, taste, hear, and smell. It must be present within your five senses at all times.

You cannot beg success, nor can success be borrowed. Success is like the love of a highly sought after female companion, it is like her heart. It must be fought for, on many levels, and it must be won. There is a competition taking place that you may not be aware of, do not become lax in your duties, and do not become complacent. The moment you do, there are *wolves at the door*. There is no sleeping on this job. No, there is only reaping on this job. Success is akin to food, without it, on some level, you will cease to exist. What are you willing to do? **If success looks like a mountain, become a mountain lion.**

Learn to Earn

No one is going to give you success, know this, and know it well. People are given money, they lose it, they misappropriate the funds, make foolish investments and they lose it all. They do this all of the time. This is because they were *given* the money, they did not *earn* it. Earning something, as opposed to having something given to you, incurs a feeling of success, of satisfaction. **There is a very distinctive difference.** One is the result of a handout, the other is the result of hard work. Which one do you think is the most cherished? I agree.

Some people misunderstand this principle, and they are always in a state of want. They always want more to be given them, these are the same people who blame all of their losses on external forces. It was never they, who did the wrong thing. It was those lawyers, instead of themselves for hiring those lawyers. It was those financial consultants who messed up, as opposed to the blame being on them for having never invested in the study of finances themselves, and effectively *making themselves prey*. **People who do not earn what they have are easily relieved of their possessions.**

You must become a grizzly bear in the pursuits of whatever success looks like to you. You must mount an *aggressive offensive strategy*. A deadly defensive strategy that no man nor force would ever dare to stand in opposition to, and you must follow through. A lion will not attack an injured animal, *why?* It is out there to eat, it is on the hunt to secure food for its family. So why will it not attack an injured animal? The lion is such a *beast,* and so convicted about its imminent success and survival that it will wait until it finds a prey worthy of its attention to *hunt.* **It is the hunt that does it for the lion, they do not hunt for pheasants.** They hunt for big game. You must become a lion.

How Big is Your Goal?

You must become a lion about your success, or you will be hunting small gain and you will have the equivalent of *pheasant success.* You may acquire just enough, but never too much. You will never procure that which you want, you will only have that which you need for the moment. You will never have '*Me*' time, you will only have '*need time*'. The '*need*' to do this, and the '*need*' to do that. You will never have spare time, or enjoy the '*need*' to relax. You will not know what a vacation means, you will never do things simply because you want to. This is why it is of the utmost import that you '*do what you need to today, in order to be able to do what you want to tomorrow*'. **You need big game.**

You need to set your sights on the big game, **the big goals**, and the big successes. Question: *Where do you exist in the food chain?* You are going to want to be on the top of the hill, on the top of the food chain. You are going to have to position yourself there. It is going to take conviction to set out to get there, it is going to take conviction to get there, and it is going to take conviction to remain there. **Conviction is a prerequisite to your success.**

There are bramble bushes in the way, there are thorns that will tear you apart, and there are wolves that will **eat you alive** on your way. *Will you become a victim, or become victorious?* That is wholly up to you. It is contingent upon your thinking, your belief, and your paradigm. These will determine your subsequent positioning in life. There is nothing inherently wrong with *being a janitor,* this world sure needs them, but it your choice, you determinations that will determine whether you are one of them, or whether you own the company that employs them. Choose wisely.

4th Qtr. Living

Again, your success is defined by you, and you alone. Be honest with yourself, do not decide something that you will later deem of insignificant value. **There is nothing as depressing as an unfulfilled life.** There is nothing as painful as knowing that you *should* have done more, that you *could* have done more. I want you to be as comfortable on your deathbed, as I want to be comfortable on mine. There is much that I have yet to do, but I am getting there. Can you state the same? If not, *get busy.*

If not, *get busy (no misprint).* You will be *convicted by* your choices, so you may as well be *convicted in* the choosing of them. Only you will know whether you could have done more or not. This is not for others to determine, they may think that you could have done more, only you have the choice to prove them right or wrong. **Do not wait until the 4th qtr.** to determine that the only reason you lost is because of yourself, and your own lack of conviction. You will not be pleased with yourself under those circumstances. There are going to be many uphill battles, but you were born for them. *Live your life in the 4th Qtr.*

Quantify Yourself

If you so choose, you can overcome and learn from, any obstacle that is in your way. *You have the power to change the weather.* Not exactly alter the weather, but you can be warm where others are cold. You can use situations to *propel you* forward, or to *stop you cold*. You see all the evidence in this when you study the lives of others. There are some people who were born into deplorable conditions who **overcame their adversities,** and now they are in the process of helping others to overcome their own. Then there are people who were born with the proverbial silver spoon in the mouth, who could never measure up to sustain it.

What is your conviction? What do you believe in with every fiber of your being? What do you know to be the absolute truth? This is not a question of what you are willing to die for, as much as it is a question of **what are you willing to live for?** What makes you come alive? What is it that raises the hair on the back of your neck? *What motivates you*, what will you absolutely refuse to be told no, in reference to? What makes you whole? Again, this is completely determined by you.

Conviction is a state of being, it is **a fluid state** it is always taking into account the changing of circumstance, and it is *contracting or expanding* in response to these conditions. It is of no matter though, as the *conviction overpowers both circumstance and condition.* These things are of little effect on the big picture. **Circumstance is slaughtered by conviction.** Truth and falsehood. Which one is real?

Most people would say that truth is real, yet many people are *frozen by falsehood*. The belief that they cannot do something. The voices of unsupportive parents, and peers, cloud the judgement of those who find themselves unable to accomplish a task. They just lack the prerequisite conviction. **Maybe they were never introduced to this form of learning.** This is why I must acquaint you with it. The only thing that can stop you from accomplishing anything in life is a *limiting belief.* You decide whether you hold ownership of this limiting belief or let it go.

You cannot determine how you begin life, it is not your decision as to who your parents are, what skin you are born in, your state of health, economics, or the state of the world at the time that you are born into it. **What happens from that point on though, is up to you.** The state in which you leave here, whether you have enhanced the state of life for your future generations, or the world on a whole, is most definitely within the realm of your control. This is up to you. You can act on the principles of wisdom or folly, no one but you can control this.

Conviction Compels

People have done some pretty amazing things due to their conviction. Many times conviction comes from a root of love, a root of responsibility, or the root of the fear of not trying, yet the results have widely been the same. The results have been the accomplishment, success, and acquisition of that which they set their sights upon. Truly unworldly feats have been accomplished by those who would be deemed unable to produce these results. *Think of the mother who lifts the car off of her child, so that the child is not crushed under the car's weight.* Have you ever heard of such a thing? I have. I know it to be true. These results are reproducible. If the conviction can be replicated so can the act.

Hold on. The results are reproducible? If the conviction can be replicated, so can the act? *What does this mean?* **This means that you can do anything that anyone else has done, if you can only replicate the conviction.** The firmly held belief that enabled the person to accomplish the seemingly undoable. This is the reason that I implore the *study of others successes*. Because if you can become acquainted with the successes of others, perhaps you can become *acquainted with your own ability* to overcome your own obstacles, thereby allowing for conviction to take root.

Bare Your Fangs

It is your exposure to the knowledge that something can be done that allows you to begin to entertain the notion that it can be done, **by you.**

If someone else has succeeded at something, and they were born with the same faculties that you were, then there is sufficient reason to believe that you too can accomplish the feat, **in the same or greater capacity.** This exposure must be magnified, it must be enhanced, and it must be enlarged into a worldwide portrait. It must transform from the realm of possibility to conviction. *This will be where you get your fangs.*

A person without conviction is like a wolf without fangs, or a lion without teeth. *They will not be able to eat sufficiently, they will not be able to procure that which is for them to procure, and they will be living the life of a vegetarian.* I am not saying that there is anything *inherently* wrong with a vegetarian. This is not what I am saying. I am saying in the realm of success, a person without conviction will only be able to meagerly survive, like unto a *vegetarian lion.* This is an abnormality, it goes against nature. It simply should not be. *The whole concept it is a contradiction.* Where are your fangs? Where is your conviction?

Are you eating grass, when you should be eating meat? What could you be doing, that you are not doing? Why are you short changing yourself? Why are you settling for less, when you were born to be great? What is it that you need? *Find it.* What is it that you need to see to be inspired? *Look for it.* **Human beings are an accumulation of their thoughts.** All that we are is the total sum of what our minds have produced. All that we have is the return on our mental investments. Look at it as income tax. You cannot be in possession of that which you have not produced, *so get to the producing of that which you want to have.*

Audit Your Books

If you have less than you want, perform an internal audit. Audit your thoughts, see what goes on in that department, and make some adjustments. If you have employed limiting beliefs, *fire them on the spot,* as you only have one life, and acts of sabotage cannot be tolerated. Have bad habits and lazy procrastination escorted out of your mind, by force if need be. Pass out a memo, that all thoughts must be of one accord, all who remain must work toward the attainment of said target, or suffer expulsion. **Period. Get some guts, get some internal fortitude.** Practice at this, build up your protective wall against *negative self-talk, escort unsupportive people off of the premises* of your circle of influence, and do not allow the naysayers to be of any undue influence. **Set a fire around yourself** to keep out the intruders. Relight said fire every day, and make sure it **stays lit** throughout the night. You have to be resolute in the defense of your dreams and aspirations, because ultimately it is your success that is at stake, no one else's. Therefore, it is also your responsibility alone to bring them to life, and no one else's. *Do not expect assistance.*

You Are in a Fight

There is no National Guard, there is no Navy *coming to rescue you* from the deep waters that are sure to come your way. You must be built to weather the storm. You, and you alone must set the pace and keep it, in the pursuit of your dreams. Where will you be three years from now? How about seven years from now? **It is up to you?** No one is going to substitute themselves for you, and pass tests for you. That is called cheating, you will be suspended, and in life you will also be hit with a fine. You will have a price to pay, the weight of which will be contingent upon the severity of your negligence in respect to the rules. You must earn your own successes in life.

You have to be a bruiser, you have to get your legs under you, but firmly. You have to be willing to do what the competition is not to get to the top. When they are asleep you have to be awake, when they are awake you have to be awake. Imagine the conditioning and training of a world class boxer. **Your core repetitions must be clockwork,** there is no *room for error* when you step on the performing ground. You have to perform, or you will get knocked unconscious simple and plain. You have to sharpen your talons, you have to make ready your claws, because you're going to have to *dig deep*. You're going to have to dig deeper than the competition, and you're going to have to dig even deeper to remain on the top.

You think it takes a lot to obtain success, or to get to the top? Think of how much harder it must be to *maintain that first position*. This is what you are being prepared for, unless you want to be one of the many forgotten one hit wonders. Victory takes a vicious vision, a furious foresight, and a cruel concentration. It is always **you vs. you** on the battlefield of life and you can never be easy on yourself. The moment you try to put your defenses down, and the moment your arms get tired, the left hook is coming to take off your head.

The best defense is a strong offense. Bruce Lee said that he is not worried about the fighter who has practiced 10,000 kicks, he said that he is scared of the martial artist who has thrown 1 kick *10,000 times*[4]. Become a master of your craft. Practice relentlessly, until it feels like your leg is going to fall off, and start practicing from there. *It doesn't begin until it hurts.* You have not even begun, if you feel no pain. Train this way and you will **never lose…anything…ever.**

Conviction will give you your fangs. It will provide you with the persistence required to *burn the midnight oil* in the pursuits of perfecting your craft. It will allow for the ease of mind that comes with knowing that there is no more that you could have possibly done in the way of preparation, this gives us a **zone.** We are in the zone when we know that we are fully prepared, and ever ready for that which is coming our way. This has a lot to do with **association.** Let me ask you, *when was the last time you saw a pack of wolves walking with a herd of sheep?*

Eagles do not fly with pigeons, let us be clear on this. You have to be convicted as to who you are. Then you will be convicted as to where it is, that you belong. Then you will become convicted as to whom you allow around you. Some people are good for you, they have strong energy. **Others are food for you,** they have weak energy. Show me who you're with and I'll show you who you are. This is crucial. You will be judged by the company that you keep, so the same way that you choose your travels and your goals, let others do the same. You cannot choose for them, or be negligent of respecting their choice. Winners cannot associate with losers, lest they become like unto them and lose all that they have fought so hard for.

You can love someone, and not be able to be in the company of them for many reasons. Perhaps they are weak, perhaps they are an energy vampire; they drain you, perhaps they are a criminal, and they will incriminate you. This does not means that you cannot love them, it just must be done from a safe distance so that none of their consequence become yours. *None of their habits can become yours, vain talk, wasting time, intoxication, this is not the fruit or the food for a wolf.*

Soldier of Fortune

Killer instinct, edge, loyalty, laser focus, these are the attributes of conviction. You always can tell a person who possesses conviction, because they do not become distracted or engaged in the mundane. Many people do not like a convicted one, because they exemplify all that the slackers wish that they were. When a convicted one walks onto the workplace, the co-workers feel dis-ease, because he is going to either make them raise their level of performance or he is going to surpass them, and usually the latter. If he has properly trained himself, then he operates at such a heightened level of awareness, and effortlessly he executes such a high level of proficiency people are intimidated by him, and they begin to hate him, from fear of their safety around him.

This is what happens when a soldier appears. Especially a soldier of fortune. **A soldier of fortune is one who is so intensely focused on the object of his success he sees nothing else.** Oh yes, he sees it, but he does not really acknowledge it because his focus is set on the greater goal that is to come. Many of these people have problems with their supervisors. Let me rephrase that, because these people do not really have problems with anyone, they just *do not afford them that much recognition.* Supervisors have a hard time with these people, because most times, they are of such high *merit and performance,* that they are usually more equipped to do the job of the supervisor, than the supervisor is. The problem is the supervisor is usually aware of this.

The Code

The convicted do not beg for acceptance, they do not bow, or curtsy. They growl and they will render ineffective, any who dares to stand in their way. **This is the way of the code.** There is a code of the successful, and I have given definition to many of these codes here. One of the most important codes is that of discipline and conviction. You will not be able to distract a convicted person. He may be skilled in the art of blending in, so as not to cause alarm, or to galvanize the focus of opposition. But *be ye not mislead,* he is not paying you any attention. He is only pretending to, so as not to put undue focus on him and his mission.

 This warrior, this samurai, is always on a mission. He is always *enlisted in active duty.* His duty is to his faith, himself, his family, his vision, usually in that order. He has come to *take* ownership, and not to *beg* your permission. He *strikes fear into the hearts* of the ordinary. The regular people feel a breeze of *ice down their necks* when he walks by. He is authority, he is the Boss, regardless to title or occupation. He is just waiting for the rest of the world to catch on, and to catch up. **He is the proponent of unyielding tenacity.**

CHAPTER 7

Tenacity

Sometimes it's going to feel as if you're climbing up a mountain, with a backpack full of boulders slung over your shoulder. It is made to feel this way because only the strongest, and most enduring make it. This is akin to Darwin's natural selection theory. The food chain is materialized in this manner, and it is through this process that we determine the pecking order. The pecking order is defined as: *a hierarchy of status seen among members of a group of people or animals*[1]. It is definitely obvious in the pursuits of man.

Tenacity is defined as the quality or fact of being able to grip something firmly; grip[2]. It is this *grip,* this tenacity that allows us to climb forward, onward and upward despite the rocky terrain, and regardless of what the elements may throw in front of us in the form of resistance. It is this resistance, that tenacity is a prerequisite of overcoming. Those without the strength to endure will be somewhere close to the bottom of the mountain, having thrown in the towel and resigning early on in the struggle.

These are the people that we *pass everyday* on the way to work. Hanging outside of the liquor stores waiting for them to open early in the morning, and coming home from partying all night, as we head out to catch our food in the mornings. These people are a destitute bunch, they try to beat the system in all manners, usually ending up worse than when they began, for their feeble attempts at getting something for nothing, or for very little. They are the bottom feeders. They are like unto shrimp. They lack the interior fortitude to continue. They give up in the first leg of the race, and they have very little tenacity.

CORE VALUES

Your tenacity will be determined by your core values. What do you rely upon? What do you believe in? Do you believe in yourself? Do you believe that you are unworthy? Do you value hard work? What is your work ethic? Do you believe that someone *owes you* for your being here? Do you believe that others are supposed to make your way easy for you? Do you believe in communal effort and things of this nature? Do you believe in a God? What do you think you owe **Him?**

Quality Indicators

A person will be able to easily discern your core values by how hard you go after your goals. The core values of a man are on display when you are aware of how he deals with adversity. You will see those who are *broken*, and those who are *record breaking*. You will be able to see the core values of a person. Such as what makes them tick when they are in a precarious predicament. Those given to weak core values are much more apt to give up, and walk, or run, away. Those with stringent core values never give up, they press on in the face of whatever opposing forces may be present.

This is how you quantify the composition of character. A person's character, the creed that that governs their existence, their *very* *breed* is exemplified by how they approach adversity. Many people are given to weakness, they flee, they turn their backs on others, they hurt other people to protect themselves, and they see everyone else as expendable. A person with a strong *moral fiber* can never do such things, they suffer for the group, they take responsibility for themselves and their team, and they will never turn their back on you. They are trustworthy. Who would you rather have on your side? *Which one are you?*

You must possess a high degree of tenacity to be successful in any undertaking. He who is in pursuit of much will be required to give much, which is *proper measure.* Those who understand the principles are fine with this requirement, and would have it no other way. This suits them just fine. **They have been prepared for the fire.** They will not burn up, they may sweat, that is normal, but they shall persevere. This is due to the core values at the core of their composition. This can be determined by the person in question, based upon the information that they possess, and their interpretation of this information. Someone may have read about great leaders all their lives, it is how they are moved by this information, their *interpretation* of this information that will determine who they become.

Tenacity is the measure of one's will. At what point do they call it quits? At what point do they stop? You can be broken, you can cry, and you can see no way to make it, and scream, "*Why me*"? That is a part of it, remember the chapter on the hard times prerequisite. That is not valid reason, however, to throw in the towel on your aspirations. This should be the *impetus* of your continuation. This should be the affirmation of your purpose, this should galvanize you to move forward. **Your core values will tell on you.**

Who Are You

What do you stand for? What comprises your being? To what point can someone count on you, and to what end can you count on yourself? Will the taste of your own blood in your mouth cause you to stop fighting, or dig deeper? Success needs deep diggers, those who can overcome the insurmountable odds against them and come out victorious. Remember the *'success is a woman'* analogy. Are you willing to go to college to support her? Of course you do not have to go *to college*, but if that is what you decide to do, will you follow through?

This brings me to the point in the book, wherein I am going to reference **10 Core Values** that will comprise the prerequisite of tenacity.

Honor

Do you have it? What does it mean to you? The definition of honor is **high respect; esteem**[3]. This is the definition of honor as a *noun*. I am more interested in the activation of honor, the *verb* form. The verb form of honor means fulfill (*an obligation*), or keep (*an agreement*).[3a] This is the form that is very important to us at this moment.

When you have a vision, when you become aware of an opportunity, from whence does it come? Whatever your answer is to that, I will leave that part up to you entirely, but I will ask you this following question. Do you honor the **source?** What honor do you give to the **source?** What does this **source** deserve from you in the ways of honor and obedience? Do you honor your obligations? Do you have people who are depending on you? Do you honor them?

Honor is a form of **self-respect.** What honor do you do unto yourself when you quit something that you have set out to do, simply because the going gets rough? All religions tell us to honor our parents. Those who gave us life. This is a major **source of strength** when people are hurting and struggling for some semblance of fortitude. It is the honor that they hold for their mother and their father that makes them refuse to submit until the war is won.

Honor lends staying power, it is a *sense of honor to duty and to service* that some of the most successful people in the world possess, and that the more unsuccessful people could use a bit more of in their quest to perform better. Do you honor your agreements, your partnerships, and your alliances? What does this mean to you? Do what is honorable and you will never have to second guess yourself. Do you want to know one of my measurements of honor? **It is how well I get along with my mirror.** I have a certain relationship with my mirror that has been cultivated over time. Remember you can lie to everyone else, but not to yourself. **Every night I have a self-assessment with my mirror.**

Did I do everything I could have done during the day that has past? Are there things that I could have done better, and if so, what are those things? I have to be able to look in my mirror without shame at the end of every night. Therefore I must put forth the best possible effort each and every single day, or my mirror and I are going to have some problems. This comes from the sense of honor and duty that I have unto myself.

I have a sense of honor and duty to those outside of myself, but I have a serious conviction of responsibility and duty to the only person that I have to *wake up in the skin of,* and that is me. I urge you to utilize your mirror to take a very good, deep and probing look at yourself. Can you respect yourself? Can you respect your efforts? What could you have done better, and when will you begin? These are the inquiries you want to make of yourself. I believe in pledges and oaths.

I'm old school, I believe **a person's word is their *bond*.** That speaks to the importance to pledges and oaths in my life. I am bound by them, and I do all that I can to honor them. This will increase your tenacity, this will enhance your motivational factor, and this will add intensity to your *Why Factor.* Where does your honor lie? Find out for yourself, every night in front of the mirror and emerge from this consultation a better person every morning. I lay down at night with thoughts of what I'll do better tomorrow. **I lay down with honor.**

Integrity

If I lay down with honor every night, every morning *I wake up with integrity*. Integrity is defined as the quality of being honest and having *strong moral principles; moral uprightness*[4]. I will not lie, I have had some problems with this in the past. That is fine, we all have dull points that are made sharper by our experiences and our consequences. Another definition of integrity is the state of being *whole and undivided*[4a]. This is the particular definition that I would like to speak to.

How much of your day was spent in the pursuit of that which is most valuable to you? What are you involved in that could potentially change your life for the better? If you are not devoting the meat and potatoes of your day to this end, you are doing yourself and your potential success a grave injustice. What do you hold as more important than your future, than your wholeness, than the wellbeing of yourself and loved ones? **A person's integrity will be defined by their daily activity.**

Are you divided, with no singleness of purpose? Are you easily distracted? Do you happen to go in whichever direction the wind blows, or are you firmly planted, rooted for your cause and that which you say that you stand for? Are you transparent or evasive, do people think more of you than you truly know that you are worthy of? **What is your nightlife like?** This is very pertinent to your success, because that which does not come out in the wash, will come out in the rinse. So you want to be **accountable** for your actions.

You will be judged, and thereby rendered of significant value or untrustworthy, based upon your degree of integrity. Do you have *habits, secrets, lusts,* that you hide from others? I think we all have imperfections, and every one is a work in progress. That is fine, as long as it is a work in progress, and not a **duality of character.**

Have you ever known someone who was one way around a certain group of people and a classic opposite when in the company of others? A complete contradiction? You do not want this to be you. No one will trust you under these circumstances, your integrity will have **no validity,** and you will easily not be considered of much value to anyone. Successful people, people who retain their success, are those who exemplify high levels of integrity. They are the dependable. **The resolute.**

You want a person to speak highly of you. You want a person to say, *"I have known (your name) since grade school, he has always been the same. He has tried to help people when he was able, he was always smart, and above all he is **genuine**"* You could not ask for a better reference. What will your reference sound like? If it is the complete opposite of this you may need to do some work in this area. You do not want to be a victim of circumstance, you want to make your circumstance bend to your will, and the best way to do this is to be a person of integrity. **Your integrity component will not allow you to fail in your tenacity.**

Discipline

How are you at being disciplined? Is this one of your core values? If not, **you better go and find some.** A person who is not disciplined cannot be trusted. A person who is not disciplined cannot hold money or valuables for others, as they find it hard to hold their word intact. A person with no discipline can have something to do, and *firmly intend* to get it done, and then become easily distracted by something and mess everything up, and let everyone down.

If you have no discipline it will be posted on your forehead, by the content of the discussions that you have, and the behavior that you display. The ability of discipline is to accomplish the task at hand, and delay gratification. A person who is not disciplined cannot trust *themselves.* So who would be foolish enough to trust a person who is not disciplined? Undisciplined people cannot stop themselves from overeating, how then can they be expected to be in control of a budget? **They can't, they will overspend.**

Do you have problems with discipline? If you answered yes, practice getting your *appetites* under control, because people will *discern* your lack of discipline, and they will not hire you, they will not like you, and they will not trust you. You can give all kinds of opportunity to a person who lacks discipline and they will squander each and every one. Practice putting limits on yourself. **Practice not speaking.** This is so powerful, people are not overly fond of the person who does all of the talking, all of the time. Know this about others, and do a *self-inventory*. Be honest with your findings and administer change as required. Discipline is definitely one of the pre-requisite core values that determine tenacity, because with it, you will not give up.

With discipline as your ally, you can weather any storm because it is nothing to experience some discomfort. **What are your daily regimens?** Do you meditate? Do you exercise? Do you attend religious gatherings? Every time you are supposed to, or sometimes do you *drink too heavily* to make it? This is an honest question, deserving of an honest answer, as I think we all have done things that we should not have done. This is for the experience of making us better. Allowing for us to determine *which the better version of us is.*

Think of war, because it is definitely a battle to strive for, obtain, and then maintain success. **Are you going to die if you do not eat for one day?** How about two? If you were not adequately composed to handle such a situation's occurrence, how trustworthy would you be under extreme pressure? Not so much, huh? Practice, deny yourself some creature comforts from time to time. This will make you a better person on a whole, allow you to enjoy the creature comforts that much more, and allow you to strengthen yourself in this most important area.

People who are disciplined view people who have not developed discipline as *children*. **They are immature and given to vice and folly.** They are not serious yet. It is extremely important that you work on developing your discipline as it will add credence to the next core value. That of…

Character

What is your character, and how important is it to you? If you were writing a script, and you were the star, **what would your attributes be?** Would you describe yourself as strong, enduring, a caring and compassionate soul, or a tyrant; *the fiend?* Would you be supportive, or greedy and self-indulgent? The **quality of your character** will determine who associates with you, which will have a large part to do with your success.

People do not generally associate with those whom they have nothing in common with, so what Leadership traits do you possess? What makes you destined for success? Real talk for a moment, if you were your character, what traits would you say that this character possesses that *predetermines his success* in life. What is **your merit, your grit?** What are you made of? What makes other attracted to you, or repulsed by the *very sight* of you?

As you choose these traits, make sure that you really possess them, and if you are doing an honest evaluation and find that you are lacking in this area, that is the point of this section. Ask yourself, if you were to change something about yourself that would add greatly to your efforts and dreams, what would that something be? **This is called introspection.** Locate it, and abandon it, find it and change it, you determine the overall quality of your character by your **behavior.** Are you shady, are you disloyal? If so, why are you this way? You see, this is where we delve *into the heart* of a person. What do you not like about yourself? A good way to come up with a list, is by writing a list of what you do not like about other people.

Now, what do you and these people on your list *have in common?* Many times we do not like a thing, because it reminds us of ourselves, but maybe we just are not that *good* at doing it. Like gossip, if you talk about people, don't you hate when you hear other people, talking about other people. I know that this is a funny analogy, **but it is also a true one.** Many times the people that you may choose to complain about another person to, are saying to themselves, that *you are the exact same way.*

This is called externalizing. You may externalize a thing that you do not like about yourself, by complaining about the same trait *in another.* Work on yourself, is the point. Work on your character, give it **definition.** Get rid of that which is not going to help you become successful. That which may effectively thwart your attempts at achieving your goals and aspirations. Work on your character. Read books written about great people. Pick an idol of yours, what are they like? Study them.

After you study them, compile a list of what it was about them that contributed to their successes? What did others say that it was about them? This is usually the most accurate depiction of a person; through the eyes of another. Fine tune your list and then begin to infuse those *character*istics into your person. There is no copyright infringement, this is **personal development.** A person suffering from a lack of character is usually suffering from a lack of self-esteem as well. So see what it is that you base your naughty behavior and attitude on.

Try to trace time back to where these **character defects** began to take e shape, what triggered them and what belief systems fostered them? What *peer groups* allowed them to flourish? Depart quickly from these people, as they most likely have the kind of personalities that encourage such detrimental attributes. **Successful people build their character.**

Love

There is such a tenacious capacity when speaking in the realm of love. Love is defined here as an intense feeling of deep affection[5]. I want you to focus on the key word, which here is *intense*. **Intensity is a key component of tenacity.** Very much in the same way that your core values will be on display when in the pursuit of your goals. So too will your love be *obvious* to those closest to you. If you have an intense love for someone, or something, you will quit at nothing to get it.

I think of women, and what men will do for them. The same of course goes for a woman who is deeply in love with a man. Think of your children (*if you have any*), or a sibling. What would you not do for them? Are you there for them when they need you? I remember listening to a closer (*sales*) on the phone one day. The closer was speaking to a prospect who was saying that he did not have the $300 dollars to join a company, that the prospect had stated that he was interested in, and that the closer was already a part of.

The prospect stated that he did not have the money available to join a company that he had already stated that he had understood would help him to reach a certain goal that he had. So the closer said, "*Ok let's say you have a child, and this child is in need of medication. However, the medication costs three hundred dollars, what would you do?*" The prospect said, "*Well if that was the case I'd find the money*", and the closer said, "*Well, then let's go find the money.*" Later that evening the prospect was no longer a prospect, he was in a company that has benefitted him tremendously ever since.

See, what the closer did was, he **tapped into the emotion.** He tapped into the emotion of love, and that was all that he needed to do. The prospect was able to tap into this same emotion of love, and **love moves mountains.** Love leaves no stone unturned. There is *nothing that can stand in the way* of true love. If you can transfer the love you have for someone, or something, and focus that level of intensity *onto your success*, you will surely have it.

The power of love is almost other worldly, the way in which it encapsulates those who have it in a bubble. **Young women leave their**

families, and young men leave their homes. People who were drunkards get sober, people go back to school, and some just turn their lives around completely when they have someone, or something important enough to them to love. People do not notice the insignificant daily drama when they are in love. **When you are in love, you feel it in your chest so strongly, there is no room for anything else.**

When you feel this way about your success, when love is one of your core values, there will be no stopping you from reaching your objective. Let the love of your wife, your husband, your life, your children, your parents, the poor, the disenfranchised, or the love of success in and of itself, propel you to heights heretofore unseen. Where there is love, there can be no doubt. Love is able to endure all, it never gives up. It is said that the creation of the universe itself was a labor of love. **Do you love yourself enough to be successful?** Can you stay up late, and wake up early, can you go for three days without sleep? If that was a prerequisite for you to see the love of your life again, you could do it. Of course you could, hands down, no questions asked.

So my question to you is, **what do you love?** *Transfer this emotion* onto the object of your desire, and hold on for the ride. Succeed for the sake of love. I *love* to work out, so no matter where I am in the world, no matter the situation, I will find a gym. I have found gyms all around the world, open all times of the night. It is a must have for me. *What is a must have for you?* See yourself and your loved ones benefit for the rest of your lives together from your success. **Let the power of love and passion fuel your tenacity.**

Honesty

When people know that they can trust you, you will be successful in aligning yourselves with them. They will go to bat with you, if they know that they can count on you. *You have got to be honest.* You may not have good news all the time, but that is fine, as long as you tell the truth. **Total transparency** is what we're speaking about. You have to be honest as to what it's going to take to be successful. If you do not lie to yourself, and you are honest about the hard work that is required to be successful, you will be prepared.

You cannot lie to yourself about what the cost is going to be. You are going to feel pain, you are going to feel loss, and you are going to be confused. **You are going to have some lean nights, and some even tighter mornings.** This is on the road to success, all who travel this way must meet up with these entities. You can save yourself a lot of pain by just being honest with yourself right now. Maybe you do not have what it takes, to reach as far as you think you want to go. *Study.* Learn what was required of those who came before you. Be honest. Maybe you do not want a thing as bad as you think you do. Maybe you are not willing to pay the cost to be the boss. That is fine, it is up to you. If you are honest with yourself you will be successful, in that you will not do something that does not make you happy. Honesty makes one prepare. If you value honesty, the first beneficiary of this honesty is you, yourself. You will not fool yourself as to what it takes.

Honesty goes two ways. **The same energy that you put forth will be your reward.** So do not try to deceive the universe, or others in it, *as if you are something that you are not,* because it will come back to get you. *Even people who do not like you will respect you if you are honest.* Earning someone's respect is a measurement of success within itself. Honesty is one of the most valuable core values to possess. **It gives you the power of fearlessness.** You will not do something that you cannot say that you did, because if called to question, you will tell the truth. **That is personal accountability.**

Personal accountability will give you a sense of desire, a passion to achieve your directives, and you will not tolerate those who hold you back, or hurt you, to be in your circumference. You will alleviate that possibility because you will be *honest with them.* You have no idea how many people cannot be honest with other people, and tell them that they are not headed in the same direction, and therefore would only waste each other's time. The people who do just that are seen as cold by some, and heartless to others, but that is simply not the case. **They are just brutally honest.**

Let me make one thing clear right now, and I'll do so in the form of a question. Would you rather someone tell you that they are in possession of something that belongs to you, and you can come over right now to get it, and then not have it? Or would you rather someone tell you that they lost whatever they were supposed to have for you, and do not want to waste your time, and *have you make a trip for nothing?* I'll let you answer that for yourself. People may wish you had not lost what you were supposed to have for them, but they will **appreciate and admire your honesty.**

Honesty is a core value. You must see it as being sacred, because it is. If you are honest, you will not make a fool of yourself or others. You will be honest about that which you want, and what it is going to take. You will have a reasonable estimate as to how long. This will ensure your tenacity. This will fortify your resolve, as you were aware of what the requirements were when you began. You were honest with yourself. This value makes for success.

Hard Work

How about hard work? How do you see it? Do you respect it? Do you believe that anything of value or quality would ever be free? Do you want a handout? Certain people value a hard day's work, and would not trade it for anything else. **It is satisfying to the soul** to perform their job requirements, whatever they may be. These people would not accept anything for less, they have too much *self-respect.* They are not looking for the easy road.

What is your work ethic? Do you show up late and leave early, or do you show up early and leave late. This will have a lot to do with the success you meet later in your life, as it will determine the amount of tenacity you are able to exercise. When a person works out regularly, they are prepared for a hard day at the gym. People who never worked out are not so prepared, and it will leave them sick and sore. What about yourself?

Are you able to go hard for your dreams, *to go all in for your success,* or are you hanging on the fences of life, **waiting for your lottery ticket** to fall into your lap? Good luck with that, by the way. Many times this core value can be related to what your parents or your guardians did for an honest day's wage. When I say hard work I do not mean, specifically with a jackhammer, or a welders uniform. I mean it's going to come with some requirements.

If you were not born successful, **which no one is, by the way,** you are going to have to grow successful. This growth is not easy. You are going to have to *shed conventional thoughts,* you are going to have to *exit your comfort zone,* more and more, as you get closer and closer. It is going to be required of you to sacrifice some things. You are going to have to make tough calls. **You may lose friends, and even loved ones, because they are not supportive of you or your vision.**

It is easy to read, for some it is not, and that is a given. However, it is not going to be easy, *when you realize the amount of reading you may have to do in order to be truly successful.* Truly successful people read a lot, and those that don't find themselves and their success soon parted, because if you do not read, you will be taken advantage of by those who *do read.* Knowledge is not power, in and of itself, it is inert. **Applied knowledge is power.** Just an example of hard work.

Staying grounded once you come into contact with success will be hard work, harder for some than for others. It is easy and natural to want to celebrate a minor success, but be careful *not to give up the good for the great.* **Implementing all of the lessons that you learn from this book is not going to be easy.** It may not be the hardest thing that you've ever had to do, but that is for you to determine. Understand; easy come, easy go. I do not want anything the easy way, because then *I will not value it.* I find that money in exchange for work is more worthy of respect, than a hand out. **People would not do the wasteful things that they find to do with money, if they actually had to work for it.**

If you hold hard work as one of your core values, *you are so close* to success already; because you are going to be built for the tenacity that is required, and you will not be surprised by the long hours. You will not be bitter from the amount of work that you have to put in. A **solid work ethic will be one of your best friends** on the journey to success. This is because they will not complain when they are called upon to perform, as a matter of fact they are counting on it, waiting for it, and that's *why they showed up* in the first place. They just cannot wait to roll up their sleeves and get to work. This is tenacity.

Pre-Summary

I want to take the time to tie the last three together and show you the *relativity* of them. If you are *honest* with yourself, you are going to choose to follow your *passion,* and involve yourself in something that is *meaningful* to you. You are going to be that much more apt to seek success in something that you truly **love.** A few questions that you can ask yourself to determine whether or not you are on the right path; do you *love* what you do? Does what you do provide you with a *sense of fulfillment?* If not, **change course.**

When you seek success in doing something that you love, it is not really an act of *seeking.* **It is a state of being.** If you do what you *love,* **success comes naturally.** Remember success cannot be measured by monetary gain, *success can be measured* however, by the way it makes you **feel.** Do you feel **content?** Are you **satisfied?** Do you feel that the service you provide **makes a difference** in the lives of others? Are you **of consequence?** Are you **valued** at work? *Do you* **make a difference?**

If you can answer **'Yes'** to the questions above, then the hard work, which is required to be successful will not feel like hard work at all. **This is the psychological component behind maximizing human efficiency.** Match people up with occupations and tasks that give them a *sense of satisfaction,* then they will be happy at whatever task they are involved in, and where another person cannot understand how they do what they do every day, they would not have it any other way. So be *honest* with yourself, and do something that you *love,* so you will never have to *work* a day in your life. **That is success.**

Responsibility

How do you think about responsibility? Think carefully before you answer this question. The next question is, what is yours? *What is your responsibility?* Who do you stand on *the shoulders of?* Who paved a way for you to be where you are today? What is your responsibility to the *next generation?* What about the people who are here now?

Big questions, right? These big questions need some *big answers.* The definition of responsibility is as follows: *the state or fact of having a duty to deal with something or of having control over someone*[6]. We, as Leaders, as adults, have not only a responsibility to ourselves, we also have the responsibility for those who look up to us for an example. This is why we watch our language, conduct ourselves as respectable professionals, and so forth.

What are we responsible to provide? Do we want our children to see others dictating our movements in life? I have to recall my mother's conversations at the dinner table, whenever we were afforded the ability to eat together, due to both of my parents having uncomplimentary work schedules. **My mother would always mention her boss at the dinner table.** I can't help but to have wondered how that had to make my *father feel.* It was as if her boss, was a member of our family. He most certainly *was not.* But to her, he was important enough for her son to know his name.

I don't know about how you feel about this, but I am not too keen on *my wife* talking about another man so much, that it becomes commonplace at the dinner table my children eat at, or *any other table* for that matter. I am aware that everyone in the world may not agree with me, and that is fine. **I am honest with myself, it is distasteful to me, and therefore I have a responsibility.**

I have more than just that responsibility. I also have a responsibility to afford my children the **very best in healthcare and nutritious food consumption.** Success does not equal money, but *money will afford me the ability to be successful in those areas of my responsibility.*

I also have a responsibility to the life I was given, I have a responsibility to live it to the fullest, and to help others to live fuller lives than they are right now, if I can be of any assistance. I believe I can, therefore I do my part. I see this as my responsibility to the planet on which I stand. What about you? What do you feel is your responsibility? **Who will benefit from your time here?**

What charities do you donate to? Where do you volunteer? Do you volunteer? Do you *have the time* to volunteer? These are questions that will conjure up some emotions hopefully, as that is their intention. This is to make you think of your responsibility to the things you want to do, the things you would like to facilitate progress in. What are you doing to fulfill your obligations for your life? Do you feel that you are obligated to do anything other than perform the 9 life functions? I feel I am, **therefore I must reach a certain level of success,** so I can be more effective than I was before, and exercise some form of *control over my life,* to enhance the lives of others.

Is there anyone whose *development* you are responsible for? Be *careful not to complain* in front of them. Speak in hindsight, or make past tense references about discomforts, so as not to draw any undue attention to yourself or the sources of your frustrations. Instead work to overcome your **present state of adversity by investing in your exit plan.** Devise an exit plan, so you can tell your child, and those whose development is entrusted to you about *'the time when…'* if it is still that important. I seriously doubt it will be though, as busy people, responsible people, are usually too **present minded to speak about what was disconcerting at an earlier time.** Your sense of obligation, duty and responsibility lend to your tenacity and fervor.

Respect

How much respect do you have for yourself? For your dream? For your purpose? How much respect do you have for circumstance? Do you respect circumstance more than yourself? These are vital questions when it comes to self-inventory. Do you wish to be respected? *Your body is an organization of cells, neurons, emotions, thoughts, and blood and bone.* **Are you running a respectable organization?**

Respect means a feeling of deep admiration for someone, or something elicited by their *abilities, qualities, or achievements.* Can you comprehend this definition, and still say that you have the same amount of respect for yourself as you did when you read the first paragraph? If so, what are your *abilities, qualities, or achievements* that elicit this feeling of deep admiration?

Let's remember to be **honest.** What *abilities* do you have, and are you the only one who knows about them? What *qualities* do you have, and are you the only one who knows about them? What *achievements* have you made? With the understanding that if you have made any, then *you are not the only one who knows* about them. If you are the only one who knows about your abilities, qualities, and achievements, **why is that?**

If you're a great painter, why doesn't the world know this? Why doesn't, at least, *someone* in the world know this? I know some people are private, and some people do things for their personal fulfillment, and that is completely fine. I'm speaking to those who are admitting that they would like to receive more out of life, and yet still, have *talents and abilities that the world does not know that they possess.* **Why?**

I personally respect my gifts, I know that they are blessings. I know that I was not born on a planet by myself. I did not materialize on an abandoned planet, so my gifts *must be* for the *express purpose* of giving to someone else, whatever they get from it. Some get entertainment, others get a message, some get a feeling, some get understanding, it is for this purpose that I make known my abilities. **It is for the benefit of those around me.**

I think someone like Mozart would have been greedy, were he not to share his gifts and blessings with the rest of the world, and I think that the world has been *enhanced* by his offering. My point is, that I believe that you, *yes you*, **the one reading this book**, have gifts, that *only you* possess which would *greatly enhance the lives* of those who came into contact with it. Have you ever heard that, '*in order to receive, first you must give?*' This is why the lives of the great contributors to this world were enhanced, as a form of reward and justice from the universe they so graciously served, they were successful.

This is done out of respect. It is my belief that when you put together something that is constructive for other people *it is out of respect, caring, and a genuine state.* When you give something back to the universe it is a *gesture of respect, a contribution, a donation, and an offering.* I think it only just, that the universe respond back in kind, according to the weight of your donation to the universe. I am not saying to do this *because* you seek something in return, I am saying that *you can expect to receive something in return* contingent upon you doing this.

Show respect. Show some respect for the universe, yourself, and for humankind. You were given life for a reason, respect it enough to find out what that reason is, *then express it, activate it.* Use it for people's benefit, so that you may benefit by default. Your respect for yourself, should not allow you to give up on yourself. If you are not enough reason, then think of your ancestor, your lineage, those who came before and will come after you. Achieve success out of respect for them. **Pay it forward.**

Legacy

A legacy is something transmitted by, or received, from an ancestor or predecessor, or from the past[7]. It is usually something of value, though it does not have to be, as in the case of, *"He left me with a legacy of debt!"* What will you be remembered for? Is money all that you are going to leave to your progeny? Will you *even be able to* leave money? How about goodwill, how about leaving a legacy *rich in examples,* of how to **respond to adversity and persevere in the face of calamity?**

You have to value your legacy, **your name will carry on due to what you do in the present.** We have great examples of this when we speak of those who are no longer here, who have done much in the form of progression. We speak of these people in reverence, will you be remembered in the same light? Will people remember your name, or will your *existence be of little consequence?* Will you saddle your children with jobs that you could have done while you were present? These are serious questions to ask your level of tenacity.

You will be remembered hopefully, by *someone, somewhere,* and you have the *power to influence the way* in which you will be remembered. **Did you lay down on the job, did you fight for something, and did you have a cause, a calling, and a purpose?** Did you live for a reason, did you help people, and were you kind, or unjust and selfish? People will talk about you when you're gone, **just like they do now,** so what do you leave them to talk about?

What about your children, what will be *their inheritance?* I'm not talking about money, will you leave a legacy of understanding, or *will they have to figure this world out for themselves?* Will you at least have left them a **point of reference** from which to begin? This should determine your tenacity. **You are building your legacy every single day, with every single step that you make**. What will your steps accumulate to accomplish? Are your steps *purposeful?*

I personally feel, I owe something to the generations that come behind me. I do not want them to have to clean up my mess, I have to make things easier for them. This is my responsibility. If you think anything you have read thus far, made *any sense* whatsoever to you at all, if it *propelled* you forward, or *gave you something* to think about then **I have been successful.** This is my aim. This is my area of concern. I wish to make this **a part of my legacy.** Many people only live for today. We have no consideration for the future.

Think of those who have passed away. What could the generations that came before us have *done* to make things easier for us in the present? That is a rhetorical question, the purpose of this question is to ask yourself this question, from a **futuristic point of view looking back.** What will the next generation need, or expect from *this generation* that you are not *active* in attempting to create for them now? This should drive your tenacity.

Think of people who leave work early, and leave something for you to do that is not your responsibility. They were here, they left, and this was their job. Now *you have to stay late, and extra work is required of you* to do something, that they *could have* and *should have done before they left.* **Think about this on a big scale.** What are you doing, what do you have within your power to do, that if you do not do, will be someone's job to do in the next generation? **Just get it done.**

If you are not going to be of that much help, at least do not become a burden and a hindrance.

I wish for your legacy to be great. I would like for everyone who is reading this to become *so successful that your children celebrate your praises* for the world to hear. I want them to rejoice in your name and say things like, *"If it was not for them, we would not have what we have, be what we are, or be able to do what we are able to do. He/She was a great person, worthy of the utmost respect. They never gave in or caved under pressure. Thank God for (your name)!"* This should be what the recitation of your legacy sounds like. Be tenacious in the determining of it. It really is all that you have to leave behind of **core value.**

These are some of the core values that will give strength to your tenacity. Your ability to operate from a *foundation of resolve.* Think about these things and evaluate your presence among them, or their *presence within you.* See how you measure up, and if you find yourself lacking in certain areas, **find a Coach**, and/or get consultation. Information is so abundant in these days and times, that there exists no excuse for a person not to work on their **personal development,** a lot of information is given freely these days. However, **Specialists come with a cost.** The information on what they specialize in, by and large, is of a higher quality than that which is free.

With these core values in place you will never waver, you will never turn back on your heels, and at some point, the resistance you have faced will have no option other than to relent, and grant you entry. **You will be successful** when you add these to your inventory, and the *material will follow.* Whatever your dreams of accomplishing are, these will be of immense value to your pursuits. Success, *whatever that looks like for you*, is yours already, *you just have to put on the formal attire,* so to say.

If you are prepared to earn it, and you earn it, then none can take it away from you but the **source** who gave it to you, so stay humble. No one likes arrogance, *it is like a dead carcass dipped in eucalyptus.* It may smell good for a moment, but it is *rotten* inside. You have a job to do, you were **born for a reason,** and it was no mistake. What the purpose is, I cannot tell you, only you can determine that for yourself. What I can tell you is this, the human male ejaculate is comprised of somewhere between *40 million and 1.2 billion sperm cells…*each single ejaculate, and **you are the one** who made the touchdown. The prerequisite of your success in *even being alive* was tenacity. **You had it then, and you have it now.**

CONDITIONING

onditioning is defined as the process of training to become *physically fit by a regimen of exercise, diet, and rest; also: the resulting state of physical fitness*[8]. Now I know you're probably thinking, what does this have to do with being successful? Remember, this is the tenacity chapter, and it is the **feather in your cap** in terms of success. We just spoke about the core values that are required of you to have, some of them at least. There are definitely many others, but if you can just monopolize on those 10 you will be successful beyond comparison.

Are You Ready

Conditioning involves training. It involves knowledge, but it is the *fluid form of knowledge.* It is not static or potential, it involves movement, so it is kinetic. Conditioning is preparation, this is why I used the definition on the top of the page, so you can have an example, or a template, from which to draw the correlation.

Tenacity requires *vigor,* it involves ability, and it involves training. Serious training, *no play-play stuff.* When things get hard, and life hits you on the chin, and kicks you between the legs while you're down, it will be your conditioning that determines whether or not you rise again. Think of all the people that you have seen give up on life, who have been through less than you have. They did not have the conditioning to remain in the game. **They did not train for it.**

Conditioning is preparation, it is *training for something, constantly.* Constant training is the only thing that is going to bring you into a certain condition, wherein you will be able to exercise tenacity *in relationship to the acquisition* of your hopes and dreams. It is this condition that will keep you on your feet when the wind is knocked out of you, it will allow you to keep control of your poker face, when you feel like screaming at the top of your lungs, and crying until your eyes run dry.

The Perfect Time is Now

We all have those moments, none of us are exempt from the human emotion. However, some of us, have made it our job to **condition ourselves** for whatever happens. Some of us are fighters in life, and *some are the ring girls,* just holding up the number of the next round after someone else's performance. **Which one are you?** That is the question that you have to ask yourself. The position that you play in the game of life is going to be largely dependent upon your conditioning.

Do the right thing, all the time. Never look for the '*perfect time*' to do something right, it just will never come, and you will never do anything right if you're waiting for the perfect time. The great people in life make the right time. The great people in life do not wait for opportunity, they make opportunity. They *create, shape, fashion, and mold opportunity* out of regular everyday circumstances. So if you are waiting for the perfect time to create your vision, if you are waiting for the perfect time to take the right step to begin something, get comfortable.

Conditioning consists of work...before the work begins. Conditioning consists of *countless hours of practice* in preparation for the event. Key words being '*in preparation for*', this insinuates the time before the time. Before it is time to show up, *then is the time to show* *up*…to put the work in, that will earn you victory whenever the work begins. Does that make sense? Your answer will tell on your level of understanding.

People who are conditioned, physically by working out, and testing themselves, and mentally, by constant reading, learning about new things, and challenging themselves, these people have *less heart disease and high blood pressure,* because they are comfortable in their skin. They are not afraid of what might happen, because they are in a state of preparedness for whatever does happen. This is the **side effect of training,** it boosts your confidence, raises your self-esteem, affords you more respect for yourself, and lowers stress.

Why does conditioning result in lower stress levels? The reason is because people stress *what they do not know.* Will they be able to pay the bills? Well, if they are in a state of **economic conditioning,** they will be able to pay their bills. If they have a test coming up, they may stress whether or not they will pass it. However, if they are **academically conditioned** for the test, they are confident that they will be successful, and that lowers stress. If they are conditioned to be successful they will not *magnify the small stuff.*

Comprehensive Training

Conditioning is the state of your training. Warriors, marines, and army rangers are trained to be in a state of conditioning that allow them to *meet and defeat any mortal adversary* on any terrain. How confident do you think that they feel, when things go wrong? They feel a supreme sense of calm because they are trained, they have no questions, and they only have *variables of response.* Multiple solutions, the mind of a conditioned person says, *"Well if this happens, I'll do this, and if A happens, I'll respond with B. However if A, and B comes together then I'll perform a triple H and that'll be just fine."* This is the thinking of conditioning.

The regular person, the layman, does not afford himself the *luxury of training*. He would rather **save the couple dollars a month** to train, and then spend it on things that are stress and escape related, like *cigarettes, booze, vacations, more clothes, and things of a frivolous nature*. People who are conditioned are **peaceful in themselves,** they do not need stimulants, or external validation, nor sceneries to *edify* themselves. They are content. They are *masters of, and within, themselves.*

Mental Conditioning

Conditioning, will afford you ease in other's times of trial. You will be well put together, cognizant, and mentally present while the people around you are falling apart, and seemingly *losing their minds*. I don't know about you, but *I enjoy being grounded*. I enjoy having an idea of what to do, if something goes wrong. No one can be prepared for any and everything. **Remember this is tenacity.** In order to be able to implement and wield tenacity upon your pursuits of success, you must be conditioned for it. You cannot be the kind of person who is going to lament over the breaking of a nail. It just won't work.

Think of someone who is given to a profession of service, or one of the helping fields. They tell counselors to have a counselor. They also tell therapists to have therapist. This is so that they stay in good condition. Soldiers are *routinely trained daily* as a part of their regimen, police officers the same. **What are you in training for?** What are you training yourself for? What are you training yourself to do? What are you prepared for? What are your qualifications? If we were to test your conditioning, would you measure up?

Would you be able to read for an hour straight without falling to sleep, how about 2? Could you pass a college exam…*in statistical analytics?* What about an IQ test, how would you do on that one? **If you think you have spare time, you're incorrect.** You *have a duty* to do. Your mission to be successful in this life will have a prerequisite of tenacity attached to it, and tenacity will require you to be in top conditioning. **Mentally, physically, spiritually, and emotionally.**

Mentally you have to be conditioned to deal with loss, to deal with hurt, to deal with failure. You are going to need mental toughness, mental aptitude to rise to the occasion in life, and get serious about the things that you say that you want. Success does not happen by accident. **It happens by design.** It happens by *mental design,* and before anything takes place physically, it must first take shape mentally.

To get back up over and over again, after life just seems to pummel you, takes a **mental resolve** of tenacity. **Your focus has to be laser hot, your attention span has to be diamond, your stillness granite, and your will ultra-determined.** These are decided on a mental playing field. These are mental elements, habits, and traits that you must fuse into your being, if you want to be able to wield tenacity. If you wish to *tame life,* and make it eat out of your hand, if you truly want to be successful, you are first going to have to be tenacious-**mentally**-about it.

If you cannot be *mentally strong,* then you are not going to be of any use to anyone *physically.* It takes a certain degree of mental toughness to even show up on the court of physical conditioning. **True strength is a mental thing**. For all the weights that a person may lift, and all the working out that a person may do, if they are not strong mentally, then they are just **big-for-nothing.** Their physical strength can, and will, be easily turned against them. They are not the strong, they are the big, and *there is a big difference.*

The game of success is high stakes. This is not for the immature, or the weak of mind. You must have a mental fitness to sit down at this table, and think that you are going to be able to leave without being *forever changed.* The things that we have gone over in this book will change a person, thousand-fold. Think of how many people did not possess the mental strength to overcome their initial challenge of hard times.

Then think how many people you know that had great aspirations. They made an attempt and failed, and they could never recover from it.

Think of the examples of people who were not mentally strong enough to *accept* situations, and things that were out of their control. We call this the X Factor. This is that which is not factored in. You may have everything planned out, but those of us with experience know that, '*Man plans, and God laughs!*' This is because no matter how well you plan, you just cannot account for every single possible variable. Now, when one of these *sneak-thieves* comes into your life, and takes something, when you cannot believe something that just happened, when that which you never thought could've happened, does happen, you are going have to be able to *accept* it.

Please recall those who were not able to utilize acceptance. They regret, they hold resentment, they wish things did not happen, they are traumatized by, and/or depressed from the experience, and they can never *get over it*. These people cannot deal with the present reality in which they exist, because they are literally stuck in the past. These people will never be successful, because they cannot accept their prior failings, and so they give power to the negative emotion. These people need **Coaching/Counseling** to move on in their lives, make peace with their pasts, accept it and just let it go. Mental conditioning will enable this.

Mental toughness will defy the body's limits. When the body thinks that it is done, that it has had enough, and that it can go no further, that's when the *mental conditioning kicks in,* and takes a seat at the controls. The mental conditioning will take over where the physical conditioning has left the building. Were you ever called upon to do something? Something that you thought you could not do? You truly just had no confidence in yourself to accomplish what was asked of you, and you just showed up as a sign of willingness, and you ended up successful. It was the mental conditioning that allowed you to show up, and be willing to try.

This is so important to the pursuit of your success. If you do not possess this mental endurance, this mental conditioning, then nothing else will matter, ever, because you will be unable to keep the pace, or stay on course. Mental conditioning is what allow us to draw the proverbial '*line in the sand*'. It allows us to make a mental decision and then stand by it, **to be about something.** Let's say that you can now see the importance of mental conditioning.

How do we begin to condition ourselves mentally? Good question. This is the reason for my definition lending to the reader's understanding of the *template*. A template is an exemplary *outline, a structure* of sorts. Another word for it would be *framework*. OK, so you see the meaning. Let us read the definition again. Conditioning - *as the process of training to become physically fit by a regimen of exercise, diet, and rest; also: the resulting state of physical fitness.* **Now let us replace the word physically and physical, with mentally and mental.**

So now we have; **Conditioning** – *as the process of training to become mentally fit by a regimen of exercise, diet, and rest; also: the resulting state of mental fitness.* The next natural question would be, "*What would the regimen of exercise and diet, for the purpose of becoming mentally fit, consist of?*" I am so glad that you asked. The first step would be to *detoxify* the body, or in this case the mind. When you detox the body it usually consists of fasting, which simply said is '*the act of restricting intake of anything, besides sometimes water*'. So for the mental fitness I would recommend the same. Go through a detoxification process, or a decompression period. **Initiate a mental *fast.***

This simply means to stop the mind from being barraged with information of a questionable source, and for a questionable purpose. Do not read, listen to, or look at, and try not to think about anything that is *not going to be beneficial* to your mind on the quest to your success. After this down time slowly begin to pick up weights, or in this case **pick up books.** In determining which books to read, let me tell you how important this is. Weights come in metal or steel, sand or concrete, and water. *Your body will develop differently according to which kind of weight you pick up, and how you lift it.*

Your mind and your mental fitness will rely, in contrast, on the concepts and topics of these books, and the way in which you apply them. Buying books and not reading them, is like having a *gym membership that you never use.* Reading books and not applying the material therein, is like *sitting in the gym without picking up any weight.* Does that make sense? I had hoped that it would. In either scenario, do you think that you will be able to bring about any significant change or gain? It's probably safe to say none at all.

So you must begin by consuming quality information. *This is the diet part.* The diet of the body is for the purpose of only allowing nutritious goods in the body. The *diet of the mind* is for the purpose of only allowing *quality, beneficial information* in the mind. The exercise is to read, the diet is *what* you read. Then you have to subject yourself to a battery of tests. Take mental challenges. Write reports, go to an opera, or somewhere wherein something is going to make you think. Hard. Start doing puzzles, Sudoku, write with the *opposite hand* than you normally do. This is building mental conditioning, so this is building your component of conditioning.

Subject yourself to rigorous tests and exams, meant solely for the purpose of frustrating you. Practice on your memory, and *recall,* these will help you on your journey to success, in that, when the going becomes arduous you will be able to easily **recall the reason why you started** in the first place. All of this is key to your tenacity, this will keep you moving forward without relent, without surrender. I love the movie The Walk, and how the character exemplifies tenacity when everything seems to be going wrong. He refuses to be detoured and he accomplishes what he set out to accomplish. **This is tenacity at its finest.**

This mental conditioning is what allows a person to push against all forms of resistance. If you have gone to college, and graduated, then you understand this component. If you began college, and then began to drop classes, you probably do not know what I'm talking about. **It is the will to see the job complete.** Mental conditioning is what will allow you to comprehensively take the first, and the last step, *purpose driven.*

The first step, many say that it is the hardest to take, and it is not easy to begin, but then again, it is very easy to begin. **It depends on what angle you're looking at the process from.** Failures in life had no problem beginning, they began, and the reason that they are failures is because they had not *the will* to follow through. See college is easy until the 4th or 5th semester. Then you begin looking at it like…hold up! I've got *5-15 more semesters to go* (depending on the degree you're after), and it is at this point that people **mentally pull out.**

They may remain in college for a few more classes, but they have *already resigned* in their minds. They're thinking of alternatives, how they're going to let down their folks, and they're coming up with a party line for the neighborhood, who watched them go to college. They've got the whole, *"I'm going to take some time off, and get a job"* speech already lined up. They know who they are going to see, and who they do not want to see. These people become drifters, they have amassed a great healthy amount of *first steps,* yet they have no completed situations. It is nothing for them to be given an opportunity, and get a foot in the door, they are good at this, and they are also good for **crashing and burning in the first 6 months.**

These people are the reason why I may have to disagree that the first step is the hardest to take. Taking the first step does take *some edge*, but having the ability to stay the course, and to see the thing completed, that is the *true test of your mental condition and fortitude.* This is not for everybody, most people will tell you that they tried such and such, and it just didn't work out. They thought they were good for the position and so they took the job, only to find out that they did not know what they signed up for, and so then they got *out of there.* They will tell you they enrolled in school, and it was during that course that they realized that school was *not for them.* **In most cases success is not for these people either.**

Success is not for them because it requires tenacity, it requires a mental conditioning that quitters, and some-timey people just do not have. They cannot call on their powers of endurance when the going gets rough, because they do not possess it. They usually have a lot of failed relationships, they may not have a good relationship with their children, they are always *running away* from their reality, only to see it pop up again *somewhere down the line*, wherever they have run to. Most of the time, they have yet to realize that it was not where they were that was the problem, and **that the problem was inside of them the whole time.**

It makes no difference where they go, it makes no difference what they try to do, and it makes no difference who they are with, *their reality* will continue to be the same. No luck, no success, and no good fortune comes to them, because they lack the mental conditioning required to make the sacrifices necessary to see the job through to the end. These people are not dependable, and if you try to rely on them, they will only let you down, time after time. **I Coach these parties from a priority perspective.**

They do not have the prerequisites required to make it in this world with their current operating system, they will always exist off another's charity, because they have no tenacity. They are severely lacking in the *department of willpower.* They do not have enough respect for themselves to make others respect them, they do not believe in themselves enough for others to believe in them. They just do not have what it takes, they are missing the *unrelenting fervor.*

UNRELENTING FERVOR

U nrelenting means simply not yielding in strength, severity, or determination[9]. Fervor means intense and passionate feeling, or intense heat[9a]. **Intense heat comes from motion, and motion comes from life.** So the life you feel, or the feeling of being alive that comes from that which you are passionate about leaves you determined. *Correct?* **Unrelenting fervor means not taking no for an answer in reference to something that you have reverence for.**

The Purge

Remember when we were speaking about the fire of purification, the intense heat. This intense heat will *cleanse you.* It will be within the context of you pursuing your dreams and success, that all *bad habits and character defects* that you may have will be *purged in this process* of intense heat. **Somethings just cannot exist in the same place.** For instance hate and love. You will either hate something, or someone, or you will love them. There is no room for both of these emotions in one individual, pertaining to one thing. It will be one or the other.

I say this to drive home the point that you *cannot be of two minds* when it comes to your success. You cannot have *hope and doubt.* You cannot be *unrelenting and lazy.* You cannot be *lackadaisical and serious,* not at the same time, in regards to the same thing. So when it comes to your accomplishments, you have to be one way, or of one mind. When it comes to your success, the same is true. You have to be proactive, as inactivity will earn you nothing but bedsores.

Objective Perception

You have to be so passionate about that which you are in pursuit of, that it does not matter what else is going on, you will not stray from your path. Regardless to whom and regardless to what, you have to keep your *focus on your objective* and nothing else can be primary until you succeed. **You have to take a look at the people who have the kind of success that you would like to experience.** Are they married? Do they have a home life? Children? Do they stay on the road most of the time? Do they have down time? What does their downtime consist of? Do they waste time, or is all their time spent with direction and definitive aim?

Study your study. Look over your notes. *When you are not practicing, you should be reading,* when you are not reading, you should be doing, and when you are not able to do, read, or practice anymore, that is when you should sleep or eat, so that you can soon begin again. *People who are unacquainted with this behavior, will come among you and think that you are possessed.* This is why birds of a feather flock together, because people who are heavily concentrated in one area, rarely speak about anything else, they often have no opinion on other topics either.

This is not because they do not like you, or they are ignoring you, it is due to their unrelenting fervor. They have a **rapid boil of specialization,** they have but one interest, and nothing is going to distract them. They may seem to not pay you any attention while you are talking to them. They may be able to *fragment their focus,* to the point that they can recall what you said to them, but they were still not really paying you any attention. I actually have to practice not doing this, I have become so adept at it.

Regardless to whatever is going on in the room, I am having an *assessment/focus* conversation with myself. What did I not do today? What could I have done better? What will I be doing tomorrow? I'm meeting with such and such, at such and such a time, and we'll be going over.... *"Yes dear? Of course, I would love to go to Grisoldi's for dinner. They have an exquisite risotto, and the service there is pristine. You're wearing red? I'll make sure I put on my red tie."* Yes, when I get to this meeting we'll be discussing 3rd qtr. profits, and what he can do to improve them next quarter. *"What do you mean honey? I've been ready, just waiting on you."*

Not Personal ... Business

This is all day, every day. **It is not personal, it is due to an unrelenting fervor.** This is what allows certain people to become very successful, due to the fact that they *prioritize,* and will not allow themselves to be *distracted or imposed upon.* They keep their eyes on the ball at all times, and are always present...*even when they are not.* Remember tenacity implies grip, well, **unrelenting fervor applies the grip of a Grizzly Bear.**

Unrelenting means never stopping, this is why it falls under the tenacity prerequisite. This is the *final phase of your pursuit,* this is after the hard times and everything that follows, and this is following the paradigm shift. You've proven that you have both the belief and the faith. Now what do you do? **Now you seize the opportunity in your jaws like a pit bull and you shake.** You shake it with an unrelenting fervor, and do not let it go until it is no longer fighting you.

Success is Life & Death

This is when you can let it go, *slowly, and in increments to make sure that it's not just playing dead,* and the moment you let it go, it's going to jump up and run. As long as you succeed and it is a permanent success, this is when you get to relax a little bit, and enjoy yourself, outside of the context of your pursuits. **When the chase is on,** that is what you had better be about. Think about the cheetah and the gazelle. When the cheetah is after the gazelle, when they are sprinting, *one is running to not be eaten and to survive, and other is running to eat so that he can survive.*

You'd better decide which one you want to be, and it really doesn't matter in regards to my example because if *either one* of these two mortal enemies slips, stumbles, loses focus, and takes their eyes off the ball, death can be the next step. **Death from being consumed or death by starvation.** Failure is failure, there is no *'which one do you think is worse'*. I think coming home without success is deplorable. **There is no honor in poverty.**

There is no nobility in not being able to pay your bills, and evading bill collectors, that is not *anyone's idea of a good life.* No one said when they were growing up, "*Well, I think I'll try a lot of things, and I really hope I fail at all of them, so myself, and my family can struggle from check to check, week to week, and you know what? Someday, I hope it gets so bad that I can't even afford food. Yeah, that'll be a dream come true.*" No one says that. Yet, we all know people with these problems, or maybe they were once your problems.

If you can relate to these problems, if they are in your past, or it looks like these kind of days may be in your future, then you need to develop a **consistent pace.** You need to set a pace that does not allow for distraction. You'd better *proceed to the 3rd lane in life,* and produce the speed necessary to catch up. You'd better **develop an unrelenting fervor for success,** and not let it go, no matter what. This had better be your aim, or else you're going to be in trouble. I know a lot of people have this false assumption, saying it's, *'Never too late'.* However, there is such a thing as too late. I know they like to keep this truth away from you.

Too Late...

There is, definitely, such a thing as too late. Think of a spouse. You and your spouse are having an argument. They are saying hurtful things to you, and you are saying hurtful things in response, to them. Then they storm out. You hear the car start and your spouse pulls off. You are still hurt and bitter. You look at the phone to call them. You'd like to tell them that you love them, but they should not have said what they were saying to you, and so you decide to tell them tomorrow, and you go lay down.

The phone wakes you up. You realize its 3 am, and your phone stops ringing for a moment or two, before it starts all over again. You do not recognize the number, so you pick it up and say '*hello*'. It's the county morgue. They have some bad news to tell you, and they ask you if you would mind taking a trip to their offices downtown, so you can *identify a body*. There's been a terrible accident and your spouse, it seems, has lost their life. **Do you still think it's never too late?**

There is such a thing as too late, as this scenario proves, so my point is to *do everything you can do, here and now, to be successful.* Do not *lay down angry* with yourself, or your spouse. Do not *wait until tomorrow* to call your child and give them some advice, or just to listen to their voice, and tell them that you love them. **Do not put off stopping something that you know you should not be doing.** Also, never *wait until tomorrow* to do what you can do today, you have to have tenacity to get what you want out of life. What are you willing to put in?

You've Got to be Hungry

Unrelenting fervor knows no limits, remember, it is intense heat. When the going gets tough the **people with this characteristic feel right at home**. Nothing is going to lead them astray, or surprise them to the point of a stand-still. This component of tenacity is the *most recommended personality trait* that you look for when assembling your team. You will not know what it looks like if you do not possess it yourself. What does it resemble? **Hunger.** Key points: *Skill can be taught. Hunger cannot.* **Hire hunger. Train skill.**

When I look for a team member, when I look for an employee that I can trust, I need to see an unrelenting fervor. The person must convince me, that they are going to do all that they can to be successful, *short of trying to rob me.* If I can see that a person is hungry, *and teachable,* then you can almost be guaranteed that I am going to hire him. Why? They have all the earmarks of a hard worker, **they are a success story waiting to happen, and they probably remind me of myself.**

Hunger is one of the most vital possessions that someone vying for a position must have. *Success is a state too, it is a state of being,* it is not permanent, it is like unto an office, you have to hold your spot, and maintain your office. So it is this *hunger* that will guarantee ongoing success. You do not want the kind of success that *fizzles out* after a few bright lights. See the problem is people *think they have arrived and they become complacent, they become resigned, they get fat, and they lose hunger.* **A wolf without hunger is a dog, and a lion without hunger is a kitty cat.** Which one are you?

Hunger is supposed to be a state of being, it is like an unquenchable thirst. **I can't get done eating, and I'm already thinking about what's going to be on the next plate.** It is the same for me when it comes to *ink drying on paper.* Before the ink dries, I'm thinking about the next deal. **You've got to be hungry.** Your main thoughts should be '*who's next*'. What's next, where do I go next?

Success in Sales

In the art of salesmanship you are going to come across three things. When looking for success and asking for help, a loan, or an appointment, you're going to hear one of three responses. Now before I tell you what they are I want to tell you the key to winning. The key to winning is knowing *something*. Knowing what? The key to winning is knowing that it doesn't *matter what the three possible responses are,* because your initial response should be "**Great...next.**"

Let me tell you what these three responses are going to be. When you pitch, when you make a request, when you give a presentation, the response is either going to be, "*Yes, we're/I am interested*", "*No, we're/I am not interested*", or "*Maybe.*" The response you should have regardless of which response you get should be "**Great...next.**" I've had people pretty ruffled, but inspired by the strength of my **business GPA**. It doesn't make a difference what the people say at the meeting I am in, *I'm thinking about the next meeting.* It is anything but personal, it is nothing but business.

If they are interested, *great,* if they are not, *great,* and if they need to think about it some more, *great.* You should already have the next meeting set up, this is the definition of **hunger.** You cannot help but to notice someone who is hungry, determined, and so forth. They have this look of a predator, they have a, "*Don't get in my way, I'm hunting*" kind of look about them. They are all about business and they look it. **You feel it in your gut, especially if you are hungry too.** You can look at a complete stranger, if they are hungry, and you are hungry, your *frequencies will resonate,* and you can *tip your hat, or nod to them, and they will do the same back, as a sign of acknowledgement, and respect, not a word need be spoken.*

Work Ethic

A person can be more qualified, they can be brighter, more trained, and more talented than me, that is a definite possibility. What is not possible, unless I let it be, is that they **outwork me.** That is my decision, if I let them outwork me, it is my fault. A person may be older than me, or younger than me, they may have gotten started a *decade before me,* does that mean that they can outwork me? **No, the factor of work effort is in my control.** So if they outwork me I cannot blame their inheritance, their parents, or their neighborhood, none of that makes a difference. Only I have the ability to allow them to outwork me, and I'll tell you what. It'll never happen.

I'll never let a person outwork me, **I will be up earlier, and back to rest later,** or I may not even go to rest. I may shut my eyes for a brief *twenty,* and be back getting the work in. You only have one chance. You only have one opportunity, very few get multiple shots, but the beautiful thing is *time will keep you honest.* It's like a gun. Time is a present factor for everyone on Earth. They are going to age, and they are going to die. So we all have the same destination as everyone else. The only difference is **what we do before we go,** so let's not waste any time. If I recognize the lack of tenacity and hunger in a person, I realize that they just do not understand life. They are lazy, they are complacent, they make excuses and they think that tomorrow is promised to them. They have a lot to learn, and the lessons usually require pain.

Unrelenting fervor is the way to go. You are going to want to be able to count upon yourself, as well as be able to count of the person next to you. Gerbils usually do not get along with lions, and lions generally do not associate with rats. You are going to find your level in life, because people will attract *to* you, or get away *from* you due to your make up. Your interior composition will be a determinant factor in your exterior associations and relationships. **Show me who you're with, and I'll show you who you are.**

Your unrelenting fervor is that which will cement your success in anything that you endeavor to be a success in. It will be your driving force, your energy level, and your hunger, that will ultimately gain you victory. I know it is easy to say, but it is also easier to do once you know. You can build up your tenacity. Remember the definitive analogy to grip. How does one strengthen their grip? By exercising the muscles used when gripping something. This is elementary.

Let's Wrap It Up

If you are not going to give up, if you cannot fall short, if you do not know what it is to tap out, **you *will* win.** If it is not in your nature to relent, then you will be successful, hands down, no questions about it. **You just have to answer the call.** You have to answer the call, and be willing to make the sacrifice. You have to make the appropriate sacrifices in proportion to the magnitude of the success that you say you want. If you want grand success, the sacrifice required will not be minor, but it will be worth every bit of it.

If you want small successes, then you will be asked for small sacrifices. It doesn't take that much to get something small, but if you want to hang with the big boys, you're going to have to **dig deep** like the big boys do. You know yourself better than anyone else, you know what you're willing to give, and you know if you're the type that *taps out* or not. Be honest with yourself, because **your blood type will tell on you.** When the pressure comes down, and starts cooking people, we'll all be able to recognize those who melt, from those who are at home in the heat.

This unrelenting fervor is not executed without the use of **laser focus**. You must have a singleness of mind that is second to none, and you must have a **diamond edge** when it comes to *attention span*. A laser focus is just what it sounds like. You have to see your target with *thermal imaging*. Your target has to spring off the screen at you, and leave no room for distractions. **Remember intense heat…well, your focus has to be heat seeking.** There is no excuse for you to give less than 1000% of your effort in the pursuit of success, as a matter of fact this is tenacity, a prerequisite, without which you will never be able to see your dreams materialize.

Again, success is not by mistake, not at all. Great things happen on purpose, great people do not believe in coincidence, nor do they wait for things to take place, in and of themselves. Now, this is not to say that I do not believe in miracles, because **I do.** I just believe that miracles take place in the lives of those who are giving forth a *miraculous effort,* so as to be deserving of these miracles. I believe that results come from efforts put forth, and I do not believe that you can get something from nothing. So if you only have nothing to give, *get familiar with the feeling.*

I do not believe what people say when they say, "*It takes money to make money*" That may be so, in some instances. However, when you operate from a higher frequency, you understand that **energy is money,** and we explained that already as current(t)cy. When you use your full energy, your complete *tenacity capacity,* you are looking to receive a rich reward full of abundance. You just have to apply yourselves.

You have to be willing to experience the hard times, you have to go through failures, accept them, and yourselves. Feed your brain, set the stage for your paradigm shift, believe that great things will materialize before your eyes, and then have enough faith in them, to exercise tenacity in all that you do. **If you do this, whatever field, or level you are looking for success on, it will be yours.** Just do the due diligence and watch as it comes to you. Fully expect it to.

Build your dream board, meditate on it, see yourself in it, and call its name daily. The universe will follow your will, as long as you are true to it. This is not an empty mantra, or a machine like model. This is something that you have to be **emotional** about, you have to inject **passion, and a virile belief** into, and this is how you get it to work. You must take control of your future and hold it with a most tenacious grip. You get one shot at life. You will leave here, and you will not be back.

Since this is the case, don't you think it in your best interest that you get busy as soon as possible, *as seriously as possible,* and with a tenacity that is second to none? The younger you are reading this book the better, the earlier you can start. The older you are reading this book, the same applies, at least you have more mistakes and failures already experienced. **You can make this work for you immediately.** Young or old, it is best for you to be reading this book when you are, so you can apply this unrelenting fervor to your efforts in life, and utilize the power of tenacity to get the success you seek. *Right now!* The only thing that is standing in your way is your thought patterns, which govern behavior. Remove them with unrelenting fervor, and step into success. **It is already yours, it always has been.** *Welcome home.*

The 7 Prerequisites to Success
The Pathways to Paramount Performance

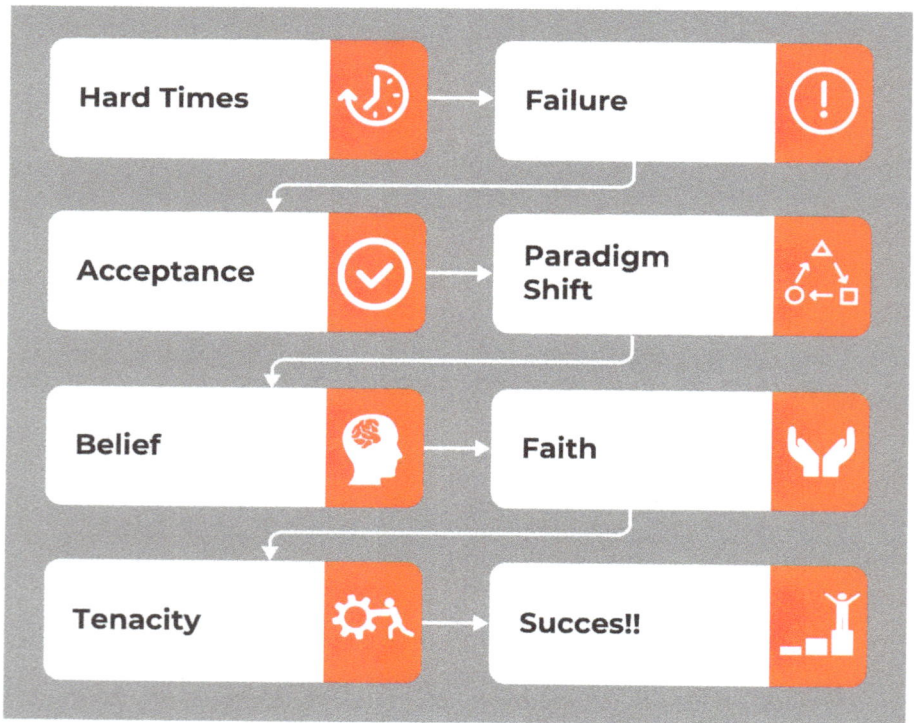

Hard Times	→	Failure
Acceptance	→	Paradigm Shift
Belief	→	Faith
Tenacity	→	Succes!!

7 Prerequisites to Success
Detailed Model

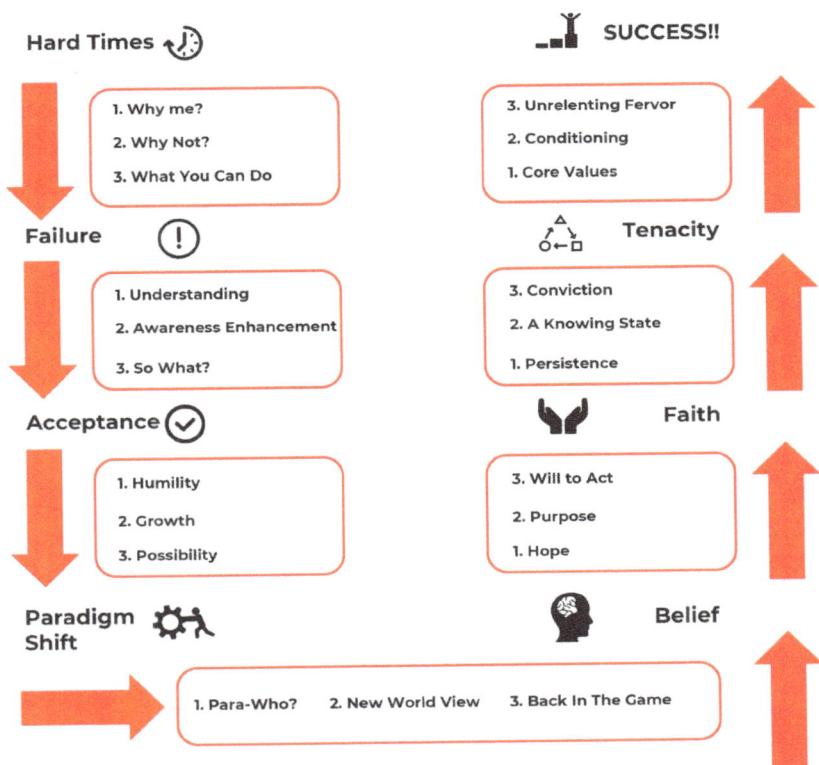

Hard Times 🕐

1. Why me?
2. Why Not?
3. What You Can Do

SUCCESS!!

3. Unrelenting Fervor
2. Conditioning
1. Core Values

Failure ⓘ

1. Understanding
2. Awareness Enhancement
3. So What?

Tenacity

3. Conviction
2. A Knowing State
1. Persistence

Acceptance ✓

1. Humility
2. Growth
3. Possibility

Faith

3. Will to Act
2. Purpose
1. Hope

Paradigm Shift ⚙

1. Para-Who?　　2. New World View　　3. Back In The Game

Belief

AFTERWORD

This book is a labor of hardship and love. You know, there is truth to the saying that man plans, and God laughs. I had such big plans when I moved from New York to a beautiful little town called Augusta, Georgia. *My* plans looked a little like get a job, work as much time as possible, stay in college, and have my children move down to Augusta with me. God's plan was for me to open multiple businesses, while he tests my reserve, build on my familial bonds, grow as a person, and write this book.

As stated, this was not my plan, and I resisted up until a point. It's as if all that I had gathered as far as data on success just made my cup overflow, and I could hold back no more. I wrote this book in 20 days. I set out to start with 10 pages a day, and at day 20 I had 295 pages, and I was completely to the end. I went through every pre-requisite within this text, a couple of times each, in my life, up to this point. I cannot tell you that I was prepared for what was going to come out, I just sat at my desk, let go of my fingers, and as each word was typed, the next ones were delivered.

I truly hope that this concept can be utilized by others as a curriculum, to help them find their current place, and to assist in navigating their way to success. If you are honest with yourself, you should be able to identify your place within the 7 prerequisites, and from there, know what you have to do to un-stick yourself, and move forward. For instance, if you find yourself accepting where you are in life, and you are humble and not arrogant, you have shown growth and maturation, and new possibilities are yours to claim.

The next step in your process is your Paradigm Shift, which is contingent upon you, and what you focus your attention on. If you are an avid reader, this would be best for you, as new information will enter your mind constantly, and it is only a matter of time before something clicks (AHA! Moment). Another example, if you have belief in something, the next step is to intensify your hope. Another word for this is expectation. If you can turn your hesitation into expectation, then your reward will be manifestation.

I learned all of this the hard way. Trial and error, pain, loss, and failure after failure. This is a tried and tested model as you can tell from the people who I've referenced throughout the body of the text. If you can learn from this, it will be much better than groping around in darkness trying to find your way. This is the purpose of the templates. If you can memorize these templates, and determine where you are at in the prerequisite courses, then you will know what class you have next.

This is just an introduction. I plan on following this up with a *7 Prerequisites to Success Series*, entailing success in marriage, business, Leadership, college, etc. I am a Board-Certified Coach, a Robbins-Madanes Certified Strategic Intervention Coach, I possess a Master's Degree in Industrial & Organizational Psychology with a specialization in Evidence-Based Coaching, I am a Certified Personal Fitness Trainer & Nutritional Specialist, as well as a National Recovery Coach, and Credentialed Alcohol and Substance Abuse Counselor, so there will be expansions into those areas as well. Most of all I am a Husband & a Father. **May God bless your every endeavor, and may all that you wish for, *of good,* become yours.** Thank you, from the bottom of my heart for your support.

- Shaan

Shaan Rais & Executive Team are always available for
Coaching, Consultation, and public speaking engagements.
Feel free to reach out to us for Questions or to Contact:
Shaan Rais
Coaching & Consultation
Omni Solutions Consultation LLC
(516) 962-0132

www.shaanrais.com

NOTES

Foreword

1   Definition of Tenacity – the quality or fact of being able to grip something firmly; grip. the quality or fact of being very determined; determination. the quality or fact of continuing to exist; persistence. tenacity. (n.d.). Dictionary.com Unabridged. Retrieved January 17, 2016 from Dictionary.com website http://dictionary.reference.com/browse/tenacity

2   See Above.

3   Bruce Muzik is the founder of Love At First Fight. He helps couples fix their troubled relationships and save their marriages. He's been featured on the BBC and TED and has built a reputation for being the guy couples therapists refer their toughest clients to. "The highest percentage of first marriage divorces happen here – around the 3 to 4 year mark." Muzik, B. (n.d.) THE 5 STAGES OF RELATIONSHIP: WHICH RELATIONSHIP STAGE IS YOURS AT? WHY DO SOME RELATIONSHIPS BREAK UP AND OTHERS LAST A LIFETIME? Retrieved January 17, 2016 from http://www.loveatfirstfight.com/relationship-advice/relationship-stages/

4   Definition of paradigm shift - a fundamental change in approach or underlying assumptions. A dramatic change in the paradigm of a scientific community, or a change from one scientific paradigm to another. Ah significant change in the paradigm of any discipline or group: paradigm-shift. (n.d.). *Dictionary.com Unabridged*. Retrieved January 17, 2016 from Dictionary.com website ghttp://dictionary.reference.com/browse/paradigm-shift

5   Tenacity – See note 1.

6   Les Brown – Messenger of Misery

Chapter 1 – Hard Times

1   "Every man thinks his burden is the heaviest." From the song Running Away. Marley, B. (1978) Running Away. Kaya. Bob Marley and the Wailers. Jamaica. Island Records.

2   Richard Branson throws head of bank out of his home - "I just pushed the bank manager out of my house and told him he wasn't welcome." Fass, A. (n.d.) 11 Inspiring Quotes From Sir Richard Branson. Retrieved on 1/18/16 from: http://www.inc.com/allison-fass/richard-branson-virgin-inspiration-leadership.html

3   gold processing. (2016). In Encyclopædia Britannica. Retrieved from http://www.britannica.com/technology/gold-processing

4   John Spence – The Most Important Thing: John Spence at TEDxUF. Published on Apr 17, 2012. Retrieved on 1/18/16 from: www.youtube.com/watch?v=SSFFGh4_hB0

5   Les Brown – "No Test, No Testimony!"

6   Emmitt Smith – Super Bowl 1993 interview. Baldwin, M. (1994, November 17). Adding Insult to Injury Emmitt's Time in Weight Room a Heavy Issue. Retrieved January 13, 2016, from http://newsok.com/article/2483991

7   Eric Thomas – "What if the slaves would have given up?" Secrets to Success Speech, given in MSU. Detroit, Mich. Published on Sep 16, 2013. Retrieved on 1/18/16 from: www.youtube.com/watch?v=sl_kv-6-I_s

8   Oprah Winfrey - Oprah Winfrey Biography. Entertainment Executive. Academy of Achievement. Retrieved on 1/18/16 from: http://www.achievement.org/autodoc/page/win0bio-1

9   JK Rowling: Scottish-arts-council. (n.d.). Retrieved January 14, 2016, from http://www.jkrowling.com/en_US/#/timeline/scottish-arts-council

10   Biography.com Editors (n/a) Sylvester Stallone Biography. The Biography.com website. A&E Television Networks. Retrieved on 1/18/16 from: http://www.biography.com/people/sylvester-stallone-9491745

11   Eric Thomas Story – Thomas, E. (2011). The Secrets to Success. Spirit Reign Publishing. Visit Eric Thomas at www.etthehiphoppreacher.com

12   Samuel L. Jackson - Biography.com Editors (n/a) Samuel L. Jacksoon. Biography. The Biography.com website. A&E Television Networks. Retrieved on 1/18/16 from: http://www.biography.com/people/samuel-l-jackson-9542182#famous-roles

13   Tony Robbins - OPRAH'S NEXT CHAPTER: Tony Robbins' Tough Childhood. Published on Feb 19, 2012. Retrieved from: http://www.oprah.com/own-oprahs-next-chapter/Tony-Robbins-Tough-Childhood-Video

14   Eric Thomas: See No. 7.

Chapter 2 – Failure

1   Allen, P. (2011) My Favorite Mistake: Paul Allen. Business. Retrieved from: http://www.newsweek.com/my-favorite-mistake-paul-allen-66489

2   Colonel Sanders – Life Story as found on http://www.colonelsanders.com/

3   Macy's Success Story – 2016. Success Magazine. Retrieved from: http://www.success.com/article/profiles-in-greatness-rowland-h-macy

4   The Henry Ford (2013) The Engineer. Retrieved from: https://www.thehenryford.org/exhibits/hf/The_Engineer.asp

5   O'Hara, K. J. (2011, March 1). Mark Cuban turns failure into success. Retrieved January 14, 2016, from http://www.sbnonline.com/article/mark-cuban-turns-failure-into-success/

6   Connors, R., & Smith, T. (2014). The Wisdom of Oz: Using Personal Accountability to Succeed in Everything You Do. Portfolio.

7   Kurtz, R. (2013) Richard Branson on Dealing with Setbacks. Entrepreneur.com Entrepreneurs. Retrieved from: http://www.entrepreneur.com/article/225536

8   See Note Above.

9   See Chapter 2 Note 7.

10 See Chapter 2 Note 7. "Congratulations, Branson. I predict that you will either go to prison or become a millionaire."

11 Success. (n.d.). Retrieved January 18, 2016, from http://www.merriam-webster.com/dictionary/success

12 colorblindness. (n.d.). *The American Heritage® New Dictionary of Cultural Literacy, Third Edition*. Retrieved January 18, 2016 from Dictionary.com website http://dictionary.reference.com/browse/colorblindness

Chapter 3 – Acceptance

1   acceptance. (n.d.). *Dictionary.com Unabridged*. Retrieved January 18, 2016 from Dictionary.com website http://dictionary.reference.com/browse/acceptance

2   Bob Proctor - The 11 Forgotten Laws: Law of Attraction & Vibration (Bob Proctor). Retrieved from: http://www.allaboutprosperity.com/11-forgotten-laws-law-of-attraction-vibration-bob-proctor/

3   Locus of Control - Lefcourt, H.M. (1966). Internal versus external control of reinforcement: A review. Psychological Bulletin, 65, 4, 206–20

4   Bob Proctor - The Best Law of Attraction Video Ever - Not Mentioned in The Secret - Must Watch. Published on Jun 10, 2015. Inspiration Zone. Retrieved from: www.youtube.com/watch?v=Dr9vBn9cKh0

5   Transcendental Meditation - Proven effective for stress and anxiety. Retrieved from: http://www.tm.org/reduced-stress-and-anxiety

6   humility. (n.d.). *Dictionary.com Unabridged*. Retrieved January 18, 2016 from Dictionary.com website http://dictionary.reference.com/browse/humility

7   alchemy. (n.d.). *Dictionary.com Unabridged*. Retrieved January 18, 2016 from Dictionary.com website http://dictionary.reference.com/browse/alchemy

8   See above note 7

9   – Bruce Lee Quotes – Largest collection of Bruce lee Quotes. Retrieved from: http://www.bruceleequotes.org/

10   See above note 9

11   See above note 9

12   See above note 9

13   See above note 9

14   Rick Pitino – Rick Pitino Quotes #17 - 247Sports with cbssports.com. Retrieved from: http://247sports.com/Coach/1458/Quotes/Humility-is-the-true-key-to-success-Successful-people-lose-their-36026640

15   Quincy Jones - Quincy Jones. (n.d.). BrainyQuote.com. Retrieved January 18, 2016, from BrainyQuote.com Website: http://www.brainyquote.com/quotes/quotes/q/quincyjone601577.html

16   Parkes, G. (2009, December 17). Jobs That No Longer Exist: 10 Industries Heading for Extinction. Retrieved January 15, 2016, from http://jobs.aol.com/articles/2009/12/17/10- industries-heading-for-extinction/

17   "You are upgrading your technology, and you've not upgraded yourself! You got the same operating system you had since 1995." Eric Thomas, TGIM - Thank God It's Monday!, TGIM! Be Obsessed! Retrieved from: http://www.etquotes.com/quotes/you-are-upgrading-your-technology-and-youve-not-upgraded-yourself/

18   Aesop, . (1867). "The Ant and the Grasshopper". *Aesop's Fables* (Lit2Go Edition). Retrieved January 21, 2016, from http://etc.usf.edu/lit2go/35/aesops-fables/366/-the-ant-and-the-grasshopper/

19   See Chapter 3 – Note 1.

Chapter 4 – Paradigm Shift

1   paradigm. (n.d.). *Dictionary.com Unabridged*. Retrieved January 21, 2016 from Dictionary.com website http://dictionary.reference.com/browse/paradigm

2   shift. (n.d.). *Dictionary.com Unabridged*. Retrieved January 21, 2016 from Dictionary.com website http://dictionary.reference.com/browse/shift

Chapter 5 – Belief

1   hope. (n.d.). *Dictionary.com Unabridged*. Retrieved January 21, 2016 from Dictionary.com website http://dictionary.reference.com/browse/hope

2   John Spence – "We become what we think about." (2012) 90 Quotes That Will Change The Way You Think. Achieving Business Excellence with John Spence. Retrieved from: http://blog.johnspence.com/2012/06/90-quotes-change/

3   purpose. (n.d.). *Dictionary.com Unabridged*. Retrieved January 21, 2016 from Dictionary.com website http://dictionary.reference.com/browse/purpose

4   Kevin Hart (2015) Kevin Hart tells Sway: I've heard 'no' for 19 years. Retrieved from: http://blog.siriusxm.com/2015/03/20/kevin-hart-tells-sway-ive-heard-no-for-19-years/

5   Eric Thomas – Want it as Bad as you Want to Breathe. Retrieved from: http://etinspires.com/

6   atrophy. (n.d.). *Dictionary.com Unabridged*. Retrieved January 21, 2016 from Dictionary.com website http://dictionary.reference.com/browse/atrophy

7   Doran, G. T. (1981). "There's a S.M.A.R.T. Way to Write Management's Goals and Objectives", Management Review, Vol. 70, Issue 11, pp. 35-36.

Chapter 6 – Faith

1   Persistence." *Merriam-Webster.com*. Merriam-Webster, n.d. Web. 21 Jan. 2016.

2   Bob Proctor (1984) You Were Born Rich. Speaks to the effect of making room for success. Retrieved from: http://www.proctorgallagherinstitute.com/you-were-born-rich-book

3   conviction. (n.d.). *Dictionary.com Unabridged*. Retrieved January 21, 2016 from Dictionary.com website http://dictionary.reference.com/browse/conviction

4   Bruce Lee – The man who studied one kick 10,000 times. See Ch. 3 – Note 9

Chapter 7 – Tenacity

1   pecking-order. (n.d.). *Dictionary.com Unabridged*. Retrieved January 21, 2016 from Dictionary.com website http://dictionary.reference.com/browse/pecking-order

2   tenacity. (n.d.). *Dictionary.com Unabridged*. Retrieved January 21, 2016 from Dictionary.com website http://dictionary.reference.com/browse/tenacity

3   honor. (n.d.). *Dictionary.com Unabridged*. Retrieved January 21, 2016 from Dictionary.com website http://dictionary.reference.com/browse/honor

3a. – See above.

4   integrity. (n.d.). *Dictionary.com Unabridged*. Retrieved January 21, 2016 from Dictionary.com website http://dictionary.reference.com/browse/integrity

5   "Love." *Merriam-Webster.com*. Merriam-Webster, n.d. Web. 21 Jan. 2016.

6   responsibility. (n.d.). *Dictionary.com Unabridged*. Retrieved January 21, 2016 from Dictionary.com website http://dictionary.reference.com/browse/responsibility

7   legacy. (n.d.). *Dictionary.com Unabridged*. Retrieved January 21, 2016 from Dictionary.com website http://dictionary.reference.com/browse/legacy

8   conditioning. (n.d.). *Dictionary.com Unabridged*. Retrieved January 21, 2016 from Dictionary.com website http://dictionary.reference.com/browse/conditioning

8a. See above note.